Issues in Ethics and Applied Ethics Series

Volume-V (Part - II)

Normative Ethics and Virtue Ethics

Issues in Ethics and Applied Ethics Series

Vol. 1 Ethics in Business, Applied and Environment
Vol. 2 Ethics in Feminism
Vol. 3 Socio-political Ethics
Vol. 4 Biomedical Ethics (Part I)
Biomedical Ethics (Part II)
Vol. 5 Metaethics (Part I)
Normative Ethics and Virtue Ethics (Part II)

Forthcoming Volumes

Vol. 6 Ethics of Business and Economics
Vol. 7 Ethics of Charvaka/Lokayata, Morality and Secularism (Part I)
Vol. 8 Ethics of the Jainism (Part I)
Vol. 9 Ethics of the Buddhism (Part I)
Vol. 10 Ethics of Values and Education

About the Editors

Sri Shiva Nath Prasad completed his M.A. in Philosophy from Patna University. After retirement from Government of Bihar, wherein he served in different capacities, started the publication of a bilingual journal of Philosophy, "Abhrant", as editor. Later, on, the persistent request of scholars of philosophy, he started two unilingual journals entitled 'Darshan Digdarshan' in Hindi and the journal of Bihar Philosophical Research, in English. He has authored a book entitled 'Carvaka/ Lokayata an Analytical and Hermeneutic Study' which was published from Janki Prakashan, Patna. Besides, he has edited an anthology entitled 'Phenomenology Methodological Introduction' with VT Sebestian, Panjab University, Chandigarh.

Debashis Guha, University Professor of Philosophy, Allahabad University, is teaching ethics from the very beginning of his teaching career, in Ranchi University. Dr. Guha was awarded Visiting Professor of UGC (1994-96) in Jadavapur University, Kolkata. He was awarded Major Research Project (1997-2001) on 'Applied Ethics in Indian Context', which was published in six volumes, under the series "Practical and Professional Ethics". In addition to it, he also authored a book entitled 'An Enquiry into the Case of Pain and Suffering'. Dr. Guha is internationally known for his books and articles published in national and international journals.

Avinash Kumar Srivastava, Professor and Head P.G. Dept. of Philosophy, Magadh University Centre, Nalanda College, Biharsharif, competed M.A. from Patna University and Ph. D. from Magadh University, Bodh-Gaya, on the topic of 'comparative study of the concept of Samadhi (Yoga) in Early Buddhism and *Bhagavad-Gita*'. He received the research scholarship of Nava Nalanda Mahavihara for his said research. He was awarded Minor Research Project of U.G.C. on the topic of 'Adaptable Nature of Buddhism'. He has authored two books, 'Bharatiya Darshan ki Mool Samasyaen and Living Buddhism'. Besides he has edited three anthologies, 'Ethics at the core of Globalization', 'Bauddha Darshan : Adhunik Sandarbh' and 'Tulnatmak Dharma Darshan'. Dr. Srivastava is a prolific writer and widely known scholar, with more than forty research papers published in India and abroad. He was Joint Secretary and Secretary of Akhil Bharatiya Darshan Parishad, General Secretary of Bihar Darshan Parishad and Vice President of Indian Society for Buddhist Studies. Besides he is member of editorial board of several Research Journals.

Issues in Ethics and Applied Ethics Series

Volume-V
Part – II

Normative Ethics and Virtue Ethics

Edited by
Shiva Nath Prasad
Debashis Guha
Avinash Kumar Srivastava

CONCEPT PUBLISHING COMPANY PVT. LTD.
NEW DELHI-110059

ISBN-13: 978-81-8069-976-4 (Series)
ISBN-13: 978-93-5125-152-1 (Volume-V) (Set)
ISBN-13: 978-93-5125-154-5 (Volume-V, Part-II)

First Published 2018

Published and Printed by

Concept Since 1974 **Concept Publishing Company Pvt. Ltd.**
A/15-16, Commercial Block, Mohan Garden
New Delhi-110059 (India)
T : 25351460, 25351794
E: publishing@conceptpub.com, W: www.conceptpub.com

Cataloging in Publication Data—*Courtesy:* D.K. Agencies (P) Ltd. <docinfo@dkagencies.com>

Normative ethics and virtue ethics / edited by Shiva Nath Prasad, Debashis Guha, Avinash Kumar Srivastava.
pages cm. -- (Issues in ethics and applied ethics series ; volume-V, part - II)
Contributed articles.
Includes bibliographical references and index.
ISBN 9788180699764 (series)
ISBN 9789351251521 (vol. V-set)
ISBN 9789351251545 (volume V, part-II)

1. Normativity (Ethics) 2. Virtue. 3. Ethics. I. Prasad, Shiva Nath, editor. II. Guha, Debashis, 1956- editor. III. Śrīvāstava, Avināśa, 1955- editor. IV. Series: Issues in ethics and applied ethics series ; volume-V, part - II.

BJ1458.3.N67 2015 DDC 170.44 23

Foreword

I have read with pleasure different contributions of new and old teachers of moral philosophies in different Universities in this edited work on Issues in Metaethics, Normative Ethics and Virtue Ethics and some applied concerns of ethics. Editors Sarvashri Shiva Nath Prasad, Debashis Guha and Avinash Kumar Srivastava must have been working hard on this project for couple of years. I felicitate them on its completion.

Studies of ethics down from the ancient age of Socrates, Plato and Aristotle, to our modern age refer to normative, critical and metaethical issues. History of Moral Philosophy had its well-known milestones in Western thought by seminal thinkers like David Hume, J. Bentham, J.S. Mill and Immanuel Kant. Lately in last century, we had significant revival of ethical studies in the light of newer departures about analysis of concepts. Cambridge Professors Henry Sidgwick and George Edward Moore made novel critique of concepts of Good and the nature of Human Value Concerns. They sought to reconcile contemplative deliberation with moral intuition as well as fusing public utility and rational individualism. This agenda of theirs led to contemporary ethical theories in several original formats.

Besides, these beginnings in our times nature of Logic of moral discourse and Language, kinds of Value Categories and their conceptual articulation and grounds, nature of good-reasons in moral arguments or persuasion marked the various topics making analytical Metaethics, today. These undercut traditional Normative Ethics that was divided on contrast of the Concept Right/Wrong (Deontology, Duty Ethics) with concepts such as The Good

Summum Bonum and various other Goods (Values) that Normative Ethics seeks to formalize in Man's Moral Life in the community of his peers (Teleology). Lately, some philosophical Metaethicists wish to sidestep the above theoretical dichotomy of concepts, i.e., of the Right and the Good. They underline the ethics as deliberation on what they visualize to be the constituents of truly virtuous character or different Virtues that could either together or singly make us the virtuous person. This makes Virtue Ethics particularly sensitive to praxis in specific situations (Acts), rather than the old concerns with general universal Moral Rules/Principles. In this sense Virtue concept emphatically tries to liberate ethical deliberation of these A-Historical Norms or General Principles of conduct that fail to guide in concrete Praxis of living. Actually, the agent faces Moral dilemmas, casuistry, naturally, dominates such Praxis.

For instance, the innate sense of Justice conflicts with our compassion. Indian Tradition furnished several Challenging Moral Dilemmas. Only three, here, are mentioned below, one Yudhishthira in *Mahabharata* faces a moral dilemma about his vow of speaking the Truth while committed to wage his just war against unassailable enemy Drona. Two, Personal Agony of Harishchandra exacting Cremation Fee from his spouse Tara, who is having no money for cremating their own son – child Rohitashva. Lastly, the most controversial dilemma of Desertion by Prince Siddhartha his young and nursing wife Yashodhara and son Rahul at midnight to seek the Middle way to eliminate the generic *Duhkha* of our Human-Condition. Very obviously, despite of passage of aeons from times of Epics, now, today's Existentialism such as of Albert Camus "Outsider" or to Twentieth Century Classic of GE Moore's *Principlia Ethica* the Dilemmas and contrarieties of human Praxis hardly get any better solution. Should one fight for the freedom of one's country over nursing one's terminally sick Mother? Moore argues that intrinsic verities likes of justice, generosity, intelligence, compassion or truth-speaking could never be optimally co-realized. So, we have to make choice of Verities-profile and order and bear the responsibility for the heart-breaks each involves.

Now consider the last letter a character Inspector Javert writes to Prefecture of Paris (*Les Miserabillis,* Victor Hugo's Classical Novel) before committing suicide for failing in his duty to send a Jail Fugitive Jean Valjeon back to prison because he cannot ignore the marvellous great noble deeds the said fugitive has been putting up for the underdogs and wretched of the Metropolis, while he himself, failing in his own duty. He seeks way out of this impasse by committing suicide... Quitted his Existence.

Clarity and conceptual architectonic as different contributors have reviewed with considerable skill in different sections of the present work on Ethics Normative, Analytical, Virtue Ethics of various scholarly schools like Existentialism and Linguistic Philosophy as well as some themes in Indian Moral Philosophies, is monumental. It is comprehensive survey of world's ethics-scholarship. Fabulous, Kierkegaard, Sartre, C.L. Stevenson, Utilitarians Rule/Act theorists Philippa Foot, R.M. Hare, Wittgenstein, GES Anscome are all exposed sufficiently in this Work. This treatise though edited and a compilation is still way highly useful to even serious graduate students, researchers and Faculties in the area of Philosophical studies in Indian Universities. All those interested in seeing A regeneration of interest in Humanities in the face of obliteration threatened by Social and Managerial Studies in our times should welcome this publication.

Dharmendra Goel

Retd. Prof. & Head, Panjab University

Chandigarh (Panjab)

Introductory Note

A Note on Normative Ethics, Virtue-Ethics and Metaethics, and their inter-relationship

In order to understand the above topic it is necessary to understand first what is Ethics. Ethics is a discipline which prescribes rules for the conduct of human beings. It is only these beings for whom any rule of conduct can be prescribed. Such rules are the 'norms' according to which any human being ought to perform his or her action. Thus, Ethics is a *Normative Science.* Positive Sciences such as Chemistry, Physics, etc., are not normative, but are *descriptive.* So, they are not normative, but are *descriptive* or *positive sciences.*

What, then, is Virtue Ethics? Here one ought to understand, first the distinction between a '*rule*' and a '*disposition*'. A rule is formulated, but a disposition is either innate or acquired. In a sense, a rule is external but a disposition is internal. To illustrate, a legislative body can formulate a rule of action, say, 'while walking always keep left'. And this would be norm of behaviour in connection with walking. But, anger, kindness, envy, etc., are tendencies or dispositions which have their locus in a mind. Now, when such dispositions give rise to actions which are beneficial to humanity and/or entire existence, they are 'virtues', and when they are harmful, they are 'vices'. Many moralists would lay stress on virtues, rather than on norms in connection with the implementation of actions. So, their Ethics would be characterized as 'Virtue Ethics'.

But, over and above the aforesaid two types of Ethics, there is a third type which is called 'Metaethics'. The business of this third type of ethics is to examine the reasonableness or otherwise of the first and the second types. This third type, viz., Metaethics is, therefore, just a critique. Its only business is to critically examine the tenability or otherwise of both 'norms' and 'virtues'. I shall explain this point by giving two concrete examples, one for norm and another for virtue.

There was a norm, and at many places it still is that a child must be married in childhood itself. But after critical examination it has been established beyond doubt that child-marriage is a curse. So, norms, if necessary can very well be changed. Now, in the case of virtue I shall give an example from my own experience. At Oxford, one day returning home from the university library, I met a well-clad adult-healthy gentle man who begged me one shilling. I out of kindness gave him one shilling. And then the very same evening I narrated this event to my land lady. She at once rebuked me and told me that I committed a crime by helping that beggar. Such kindness are not at all beneficial for society. So, kindness in the above example is not a virtue, but a vice. Thus, it is clear that the concept of virtue is very much context-laden. No virtue is a virtue straightway. And it is *Metaethics* which decides when a so-called virtue can be regarded as a genuine virtue.

It should also be clear by now that all the three types of ethics mentioned above are very intimately related to one another.

N. Mishra

Tilka Manjhi Bhagalpur University,

Bhagalpur (Bihar)

From Editor's Desk

It is conventional among philosophers to formulate definitions of its branches that would satisfy you in understanding what is their nature. However, most of time a cut and dried definition fails to satisfy our purpose of nature—clarification of the branches of philosophy such as ethics, epistemology and so on because the said definitions do nothing but state some of the task of these branches, which remain either incomplete or scrappy, or else, the definitions are figurative or subjective exhortations of what should be done in ethics. Hence, the most important aspect of thorough clarification of "tasks" of the branches of philosophy remains neglected, which, however, should not be the case. It is desirable, therefore, that for the clarification of the nature of ethics or what ethics amounts to, we need to state what are "tasks" undertaken by ethics or moral philosophy.

A number of things are done under ethics, the most important being, the critique of ethical *language* or what call *"metaethics"*, the study of norm or bases of evaluation of voluntary human actions for their moral worth, which is known as "normative" ethics the study of moral values and virtues or "*Virtue ethics*", and the aspects of practicability of ethics in individual, social and professional life, which are, practical and *"professional"*, ethics. More than this, we speak of the *"descriptive"* and the *"empirical"* tasks of ethics, the former, more debatably takes up the task of description of the psychological basis the ethics, the latter deals in the empirical study of the individual and social interactions to collect data and analyse them to find out what are their moral repercussions. The field of ethics is ever growing, we need to be careful to study the extending tasks and include them as well. It may be troubling for some of us not to include environmental ethical, bioethical and some other tasks under ethics task because the value laden environmental, biological and some such issues call for practical resolution whether through application of standard norms of ethics or through social discourses.

After a cursory statement of the tasks of ethics, that gives us a fair idea of what ethics is or what ethics consists in, we need to clarify the tasks a little more so that the readers of this work nurture no confusion about what awaits them in the following four sections of the work. *Metaethics* is also called *second order* ethics, the *first order* being the 'normative' or, which is *standard* ethics. The second order task, *vis-à-vis* the first order task is so called as it *moves beyond (meta)* the traditional normative discussion or the discussion of the value, evaluation and criteria of evaluation of intended human actions that affect a number of beings and things either adversely or favourably and are thus judged to be either desirable or undesirable, good or bad, right or wrong, just or unjust, a duty or not a duty, an obligation or not an obligation, a responsibility or not so, that is whether the human actions have a "moral worth" or a "moral value", not simply a drab "practical" or "emotive value". In this sense, *metaethics* as a second order moral inquiry is not about moral worth of human actions, rather, inquires about the nature, meaning and truth of the statements of moral value or the moral judgements. In this sense, *metaethics* is as '*after inquiry*", an inquiry that turns not to be concerns of value and evaluation but the "*language of value and evaluation*", which is more basic to philosophical inquiry, says many. Apart from the conceptual and language clarification, *metaethics* taken interest in the basic *logic of proving and justifying* the norms of the standards of morality that has been advocated through the ages as monolithic and sacrasanct *ideals,* most notably in the names of *teleology* and *deontology,* having a wide range of varieties of these norms. *Metaethics* is thus an "after inquiry" that turns to argue why or why not certain ideals are based on either a weak logic or a stronger one.

Traditionally, ethics has been dealing with values and virtues, that is, it is concerned about the human values and virtues in particular, not about the general theory of values (or axiological thesis of values) because moral worth of human demand which decisions and actions are truly worthwhile or have a value. Among a number of the assumed values, are the "virtues" or "dispositions of character", again, not one but many. However, there has been long debates over the relative merits or pragmatics of these assumed values (including virtues). Nevertheless, broadly there are *aretaic* and *deontic* values and virtues, that is values and virtues of human character and duties, which always makes good cases of inculcation among humans truly so called. There has been a lot of hue and cry about the transcendental or *spiritual* values and virtues as well, as is the case with *social* or *community* values and virtues, and even in the cases of non-spiritual, and anti-spiritual values and virtues. There is a good debate about the replacement of normative theories by inculcation of values and virtues because the artificial following of a norm in life and its adoption for all sorts of moral evaluation is thought to be absurd and unpragmatic, Hence, the clarion call is to shun normative theories (which is a anti-theory stance) and thus embrace value and virtue inculcation among humans. However, many of us argue that a return to theory without begging a norm of norms is equally absurd because without norms, to call something a value and a virtue is impossible.

In the midst of the controversy, of late, grew parctical and professional ethics. In fact, the practical and professional ethical tasks were udertaken since a long time in ethics, but these fields grew in prominence and late as 1960s. There is a lot of confusion about what exactly is practical and professional ethics. Many ethicists thought that practical ethics, is nothing but ethicists' dynamic involvement in applying one or more ethical norms (as seen above) to resolve one or more practical problems which are also value-laden, that is, they raise distinct questions of moral worth or value. Similarly, professional ethics is nothing but resolution of professional value-crises by applying standard ethical rules and codes; of late, ethicists thought that apart from these dynamic concerns involving norms, ethicists should take up necessary theoretical inquiries as well, such as dealing with the modes of application, logic of normative application, weighing strengths of normative application and so on.

Professional ethics takes up theoretical inquiries about the nature analysis of profession, professionalism, ethics of a profession and ethics of professionalism. Interestingly, both practical and professional ethics came closer to meta-inquiries as nature analysis and logic of justification of these fields were urgently needed. Gradually, critiques of artificial or engineering model or application of norms by ethicists in resolving practical and professional problems paved way for new way for applied and professional ethics demanding involvement of ethicists, non-ethicists and those directly or indirectly involved in a value-crisis for resolution, in which not one or more theories are applied as mere tool or tools rather, in which spontaneity of moral opinions and arguments resolve crises, which, when analysed after a dialogue by ethicists, give us the norms of ethics which were dynamic or applied in a unique non-engineering manner.

Ethicists classify value crises troubling persons of occupations and professions needing resolution and their theoretical analysis as environmental, bio-medical, educational, economic, business, administrative, managerial, and social and political in the main, thus giving us environmental ethics. We also have engineering ethics, nursing ethics, war ethics, accounting ethics, financial ethics and many more.

This book takes utmost care to do justice to unravel the said tasks of ethics through the thirty seven papers that were contributed by authors of our times in India. It is testimony to the fillip that ethics has given to the Indian ethical diaspora. The essays are thus carefully arranged moving from the second order to the first order tasks of ethics, and then to virtue ethics.

The series on Ethics and Applied Ethics is a very ambitious multi-volume scheme and an outcome of painstaking and careful selection of papers contributed by the noted Indian writers on Ethics, which is as broad as covering the first and second order ethics, as well as virtue ethics, and practical and professional ethics. The selection and arrangement of the contributed papers was based on both merit and pragmatics, Special care has been taken to include papers concerning key issues and problems in the field of ethics.

Shiva Nath Prasad
Debashis Guha
Avinash Kumar Srivastava

Preface

The present multi-volume series "Ethics and Applied Ethics" is an ambitious enterprise and is intended to bring man, to the right rails of morality as the basic end of life, society, as also to wed morality, to all departments of knowledge, framed, created, and developed by man. Since all developments are for man, and man always aspires to be at the centre, so to devoid man of morality, would be nothing more than devouring the same man, who, being at the pivot of everything, development of all arts, science, crafts, knowledge, by his own hands through rational deliberation. Is this not great malady and a tragedy, indeed?

The present world is ridden with multitudinous crisis, i.e., crisis in the plural and the main anxiety of man in the recent scenario of moral destitution, is to end the crisis that has created an impasse or halt in several ways and man now is feeling suffocation of the worst kind. His heart - felt desired need is, naturally, to make all out efforts to resolve the crisis forthwith. But can it be possible? This is a question, which once tackled and solved, the other thing would be normalized naturally and bring a scope for peaceful sailing of life.

In this context, it would be essential to know the meaning and the content of the very word "crisis", which is eating into the vitals of every man, whether the common man on the street, or those who are enriched enough to avail all luxury. Fortunately, the word crisis is a good word and it is not incorrigible too. The word crisis has been defined as a "process of transformation", so to mean, crisis is not close-ended, but on the contrary, it is open-ended. When crisis is not close ended, it would signify that crisis as process can be reversed in order to amend, if the very process is wrong, thus, by reversing the process, one can reach at the right point, rather than remain in the state of flux or helplessness. But who can reverse this process; it is only man, who can help himself. Man's omissions and errors can be amended, set right, or rectified by man himself.

In this context, it is essential to make a distinction between crisis and natural disaster, or natural calamity, like earthquake, tsunami, flood, etc. Natural disaster is caused by nature's fury or any supernatural causes, as it is commonly understood. But contrary to it, most of the crises are man's own making and what man has done, it can be amended by man alone, it is within man's capacity to either control the crisis, or remove it altogether for all time. But the tragedy is that, man has become confined in the cobweb which man himself has created, out of his venom, out of his own wilfulness, out of his devilish desire of discrimination, divisiveness, angularities and everything that is evil in him, lying dormant, every moment, goading man to behave in wrongful ways. The question then is, can man succeed in destroying the fetters of multitudinous crises like social, political, economic, psychological and technical and spate of others? The answer is a positive assertion of "YES", but how?

Earlier, it was believed that God created everything, to top it all, He created man as the crown of His creation and in His image, but having created man, he also made a provision for sin, owing to man's disobedience, in not eating the forbidden fruit. Thus God also created sin and disobedience too. He violated his own limitations and constraints. Man was created by God, but man out of his own mental capacities and imaginations, created the image/ photograph/ idol of God and God was fettered in his own creations, he became captive to his own made prisons of limitations. Man also created many things, many arts, artifacts, art, crafts, sciences, technologies, society, wealth and thousand of things, thousand types of knowledge, but the result was that he became captive to his own creations and now that he wants to set free, from his own cobwebs and cocoons. Man can free himself, provided he wills firmly, resolves firmly. All this involves a process, to develop faith, trust, reliance in himself, to change himself to bring a total regeneration by removing what are evil aspects in him, his needs, his limitations, his envy, jealousy, instincts and impulses, anguish and angularities, his wants, his hankerings, which are really captivating him and not giving a way for moral upliftment, to make him see every thing as divine, to take all as equal, brotherly, friendly and humanly. This is really a lack of moral sense, that is causing moral crisis, which is the mother of most of the crises, if not all. So by inculcating moral sense, man can rise to the level of perfection, often attributed to the Divinity. With the advancement of knowledge, there has been enlargement in the domain of ethics and ethics with its lots of theories have enriched its stock. The volumes to come would take up separate department of knowledge–sciences and try to examine how the crisis caused and crept therein, can be rectified by the touch of magic-wand of moral ideals, which have now come to the lowest ebb, or placed in a state of stupor and now, by ridding which man can create a new humanity on earth, a spiritual moral globalization, rather than bring about a consumerist culture of material globalization or global competitiveness, callousness, cold war, terrorism, fundamenta-lism, barriers to humanity, dividing man from man. If our efforts succeed even a little bit with the ethical discussion presented in these volumes, we will feel prized beyond all bounds and rewarded amply.

Shiva Nath Prasad
Debashis Guha
Avinash Kumar Srivastava

Acknowledgements

We acknowledge our deep sense of gratitude to all the scholars, who have taken pains to contribute their choicest papers, to the present volume, entitled "Issues in Metaethics, Normative Ethics and Virtue Ethics"; not only for submitting papers after deep deliberation, or for taking pains to write for us, but for the prime reason, that they had to wait for years to see their papers published. We have no words of apology commensurable to the ordeals of the great scholars, who have contributed their papers. Anyway, it is hoped that very soon they will have the book in their hands (as assured by the publisher) to console, "better late than never", but till then, we feel guilty. Once again, we humbly beg apology to all the scholars, as well as, our well-wishers, our elders, guardians, as also the youngsters, friends, relatives and all others, who have in any way, in any form, helped, cooperated us in this great academic adventure for bigger, valuable, pious missions and goals, at least.

We are thankful to Shri Shailesh Kumar Sinha, who very sincerely has computer-typed the manuscripts, correcting the print errors time and again, with extreme patience, as also with extreme sense of responsibility and humble meekness.

At the end, we express our sincere thanks to Shri Ashok Kumar Mittal, Proprietor of Concept Publishing Company Pvt. Ltd., New Delhi, who agreed to publish the series "Ethics and Applied Ethics" voluntarily, in the greater interest of academia, the researchers, Professors as well as, the general curious readers of the country and feel aware that Ethics is not only a part of university syllabi of Philosophy, but it is also an inseparable part of each and every man's practical life, as a key to safe sailing of life's boat, amidst the troubled waters of turmoil, discord, regrets and remorse, it teaches man, how to inculcate sense of contentment, rid of malice, avarice, scorn, hate and the like and to remain faithful, sincere, truthful friendly, sympathetic to all human beings of the world, since life is the precious gift, life is precious to all and sundry and no one has the right to disturb or harm anyone for one's own petty-interests. Man is born naked and dies open-fisted, with nothing to catch. So, the question is, "Why discord at all? Life is great, life is gigantic, a part and parcel of Divine spark. So, everyone is equal. Hence, the principle of "Live and Let Live", live peacefully and joyfully, is the key principle of Society and "Community". The word "community" "may be interpreted as" "common-unity", which is the guiding principle of "Ethics".

Shiva Nath Prasad

Avinash Kumar Srivastava

Contents

List of Contributors

Chakrabarty, Dipasikha— She did her Ph.D. in ethical topic, under the able guidance of Prof. Debashis Guha, Ranchi University—Prof. Guhas is now Prof. in Allahabad University (U.P.) Deptt. of Philosophy.

Chakravarty, D.K.— Retd. Head of the Deptt., of Philosophy, Guwhati University, Assam. An outstanding writer, brilliant teacher, specialised in Metaethics, presented about one hundred papers in different seminars—also a member of ICPR and committed academician.

Chincholkar, L.G.—Retd. Prof. of Philosophy, Nagpur University, Maharashtra. He has been an established scholar in ethics, wrote several books, published not less than 100 papers, he is still too active in writing, he is also an established writer in Marathi. He may be contacted at–Back Road, Congress Nagar, Napur, Pune-440012, Maharashtra.

Ingallali, R. I. — Retd. Prof. & Head of Philosophy Deptt. Karnataka University, specialised in Nyaya/Navya Nyaya Philosophy, also writing for Multi-volume prestigious Encyclopaedia of Indian Philosophy, being edited by Mr. Karl Potter. He is known nationally and internationally for his great scholarship has written several books on Nyaya Philosophy, also a Book on Values, Philosophy of Action. More than hundred papers are to his credit. He lives in Dharwad.

Kapoor, Veena— Prof. Deptt. of Philosophy, Panjab University, Chandigarh, she has specialised in Ethics. A reputed brilliant writer on almost all topics related to Ethics. Her writings are marked by extreme clarity of vision, contributed lot of papers in several Jounrals.

Kumari, Ranju—She completed her Ph.D. on ethical topic, under the able guidance of Dr. Debashis Guha, then in Ranchi University, her writing is quite clear.

Mishra, Nityananda—Retd. Prof. Deptt. of Philosophy, Bhagalpur University, he is known nationally and internationally, several of his books are taught throughout Indian Universities as well as abroad, he has written books both in Hindi and English–a scholar exemplary—more than hundred papers published from India and abroad. He lived in Bhagalpur and recently died.

Prasad, Pradeep—He Completed his Ph.D. from Ranchi University in the able guidance of Prof. Debashis Guha, then in Ranchi University, now Prof. Deptt. of Philosophy, Allahabad University.

Prasad, Shiva Nath–Chief Editor of this series Issues in Ethics and Applied Ethics contributed papers in Prof. R.I. Ingallali, Prof. S.P. Dubey and Prof. R.C. Guha's Felicitation Volumes and author and edit on or books on Philosophy. Also contributed materials on Applied Arts and Aesthetics for IGNOU MA Course (MA Philosophy).

Sarin, Indu— Presently in Deptt. of Philosophy, Panjab University, Chandigarh specialised in Existentialism, a prolific writer, published some books in English and other languages–a very brilliant writer, contributed large number of papers in research Journal presently. She is posted in the same University.

Sebastian, V.T.—Prof. Department of Philosophy, Punjab University, Chandigarh (U.T.)

Shaida, S.A. —Retd. Prof. I.I.T., Kanpur, Humanities Deptt., lives in Allahabad, 34, Kazmi Street, Randi Mandi, Allahabad—A prolific writer specialised in Existentialism, Phenomenology, Ethics— a rare scholar, contributed large number of research papers in several Journals.

Sharma, Chandra Kanta— Head of the Deptt. of Philosophy and Principal of Women's College, Tinsukhia, Assam did her research works under the guidance of Prof. D.K. Chakravarty, Assam. He contributed good number of papers and authored some books.

Singh, Shiva Bhanu— At present, Head of Philosophy Deptt., Ewing Christain College, Allahabad, (U.P.) he is a very good scholar, specialised in social, political and philosophy on which he has written several books which are taught in Indian Universities—he specialised on Sartre also. A good number of research papers have been published in Journals and books as well as in Felicitation volumes.

Sinha, M.N.— Retd., Head of Philosophy Deptt., BRA Bihar University, Muzaffarpur—a very brilliant teacher, wrote several books, published a large number of research papers—very social and of helping nature to any one who approach him for any academic or personal help, lives in Muzaffarpur town, near University Campus.

Tandon, A.K.— Though not in academic post, he has done a great service to philosophy. His research is on Sartre, Gramsci – Voracious some books – about one hundred reader and writer papers are to his credit.

SECTION – I

NORMATIVE ETHICS

Chapter – 1

Nicomachean Ethics

Veena Kapoor

Aristotle's fundamental purpose in Nicomachean Ethics is to discover and analyse what the good life actually is. He starts with the commonly held view about good conduct to find out what makes a good life for man. His contention is that to become a good man, you must behave like a good man and consequently you will know what goodness is. Aristotle never seems to talk of individual's good apart from the good of the society. What then is the best kind of life that an individual may live in a society? The generally agreed conception to call the best life is the Happiness, the final good according to Aristotle. The final good for him is that at which all things aim[1].

But the problem lies in finding out the true nature of the Happiness. What sort of life could appropriately be called best life? Aristotle opines that the solution to the problem can be found in the efficiency of the function of the man that he undertakes.[2] The efficiency lies in the excellence of human character or virtue of man and in the action itself. For excellence of human character and action are not isolated from each other[3]. In the practical or calculative life, unlike scientific knowledge, there is no one demonstrative rule or principle to tell the truth but many varied conceptions regarding what to do. Therefore, in order to find out the right principle one will have to understand what goodness of character is and to understand goodness of character, one will have to understand the way in which it is *actually* produced.

As such, in order to live a happy life one must be familiar with (i) a good judgement as to what a right principle is; and (ii) one's appetites, desire and emotions must be so trained that they obey the right principle. Perhaps, Aristotle suggests that nature endows us with impulses and emotions which are neither good nor bad in themselves.[4] And it is through training that the indeterminate and neutral emotions develop into fixed habits. It is by repeated performances of right way of acting that we acquire right kind of dispositions and as such right kind of conduct; as the dictum suggests it is the 'Like activities produce like dispositions'.

Aristotle's claim undertakes the position that dispositions are the trained emotions and to be considered as a matter of habit. It may be argued it is not merely like activities that produce like dispositions but also like emotions produce like activities. Activities and dispositions are not different from each other because dispositions are the activities to which a person gets accustomed by performing them time and again whenever circumstances require man to do so.[5] Now, what about those who are of ill-tempered, selfish and unjust nature? In such situations how to hold a man responsible? And again, how to hold a person morally bad for his action, when he claims it to be the result of his present circumstances, which themselves are the outcome of his previous actions which he was incapable of making distinction between good and bad? Or, in other words, suppose, there is a person who is by nature attracted to all that which is vicious or is brought up under such an environment that leads him to do what is evil? What sort of justification can we provide to call such a person bad? Following Aristotle, such actions should be treated as actions done under compulsion or in ignorance.[6] If so, then man cannot be accounted for any of the actions that he performs. But on the other hand, since it is a disposition, that a person gets used to, can be characterized for the attitude that he holds which could be taken account of him for good or bad.

According to Aristotle, all our actions are the manifestations of our deliberate choices, which are directly related to our desires, i.e., the moving principle. When a man acts in a virtuous way, he must be in certain frame of mind, he must act in the full consciousness of what he is doing; he must will his action, and will for his own sake; and the act must proceed from a fixed and unchangeable disposition.[7] Not only the man of practical wisdom knows what to do but he also does that.[8] Deliberation is characterized as the working out of means to ends already adopted during the course of acting.

It is not clear what Aristotle means to say that an action must be willed for its own sake. It is something self-evident? If it is so, then what could Aristotle do about this problem of choice? Are we really and genuinely free according to Aristotle, i.e., can we say that we are not controlled in one-way of taking decisions? If we agree to it that there are some actions which are good in themselves then we will have to start from what is known absolutely to us. But Aristotle will never be for such an understanding of human conduct because he advocates practice rather than theory. For him ethics is the science of behaviour which cannot be studied in the Platonic conception of absolute Good, the eternity of the Supreme Form.[9] Again, if we were to say that an action is to be done for its own sake, then certainly we cannot talk about free will or ask; could we have done it otherwise?

For Aristotle, "there are in the world three things which determines or influence actions and the discovery of truth; sensation, the reasoning power, desire or appetition, of these, sensation is never the source of considered action as may be seen from the fact that the lower animals have sensations, but exhibit no trace of such action . . . . that moral virtue is a habit of making the right choice in conduct and that such choice is a reasoned desire . . . . thus we view choice either as thought wedded to desire or desire wedded thought."[10] The question is as to what constitutes my action? Is it the desire or the deliberated choice? For my desire is certainly not equivalent to my deliberate choice. Choice, according to Aristotle entails disposition of character as well as exercise of reason and the cause of action is will or deliberate choice.[11] It may be contended that desire is in a natural causal sequence which is provoked by the thought, perception or imagination of some object of attraction. But, for a choice is not to be explained in causal terms but in rational sense. Aristotle includes in desire the exercise of reason (thought) to constitute on action.

It appears that Aristotle tries to define virtue on two different grounds (1) on the basis of what is done requires the deliberate choice to be good, and (ii) Virtue is something which is chosen for its own sake. These two views do not seem compatible with each other. Must acts be deliberately chosen if they are ascribed self-evident? For Aristotle, decisions in individual cases require a judgement or insight analogous to eyesight. "The goodness of your eye is not only that which makes your eye good: it is also that which makes it function well."[12] For, it is by the excellence of the eye that we see well. Therefore, Virtue of a man is a state of character which makes him do his work well. Applying Aristotle's conception of goodness in terms of the efficiency in the function performed by the person, we can say that if a person is virtuous, he will act in the virtuous manner. Aristotle has given us a misleading analogy. The action of an individual cannot be justified in the like manner as man's functioning or eyesight. The two acts refer to absolutely two different phenomena. On the one hand Aristotle is making reference to conventional values to be taken for granted which do not leave room for responsibility and obligatoriness, and on the other, he recognizes that a man of practical wisdom is under an obligation to determine what is right or wrong.

The problem is as to whether moral virtue comes first or practical wisdom, to determine the nature of action. Or is it the case that moral virtue originates out of the habit in accordance with practical wisdom? Practical wisdom, says Aristotle, helps us in finding out the right means towards the end and a virtue is an end.[13] As such, practical wisdom can be taken as an instrument to pursue the end that it stands in relation to. It means that there is one self-evident, ultimate end, which could be achieved by man of means. If we could mark the *ultimacy* of an action to such an extent which could be taken as self-evident, then perhaps it is only the action which matters and the significance of practical wisdom is little. By making use of whatever means one may get good results. What a man does, does for the sake of action itself because it is good to do it.

A man of practical wisdom (Phronimos) is described by Aristotle as a practically wise man having good moral character.[14] And a good or a virtuous man is the one who has good moral character with practical wisdom. For, a virtuous person is indeed he who knows what moral virtue is and knows its application too. And a prudent man is one who knows how to act rightly. Does Aristotle see a difference between rightness of an action and goodness of an action? It appears, as if Aristotle is here confusing the two terms. A prudent man is described as a man of high moral character. It implies that there is a picture of (or notion of) good moral character before man of practical wisdom, which he could approach. That is say, that there is a preconceived idea of virtue which could be taken as a standard or criterion to justify whether a man is prudent or not. If so, then Virtue could be defined irrespective of the means that a practically wise man could make use of. Whereas, Aristotle emphasizes the interrelation of the two to that extent that one cannot be defined without the other. If *phroanesis* and virtue are so related that one could not be defined without the other, does not it imply that there is only one possibility of making a distinction between the two terms that of conceptual possibility? For, the defining characteristics in both the cases, are the same, Aristotle makes difference between a clever man and a practically wise or a prudent man. A prudent man is unselfish, bears a good moral character and desires a right thing.[15] This, again leads to the same kind of contention as if for Aristotle, there are certain things to be desired for their own sake, in other words, good in themselves. But on the other hand phronions is defined as, practically wise man having good character, and good is defined as having good moral character with practical wisdom, therefore, no difference between the two, except the conceptual one.

Next, it is not clear from Aristotle's view who is to be called a virtuous person. There are several virtues. Is it in the unity of all these virtues that we call a person virtuous? The fact is that it is the complexity of situations and the complexities of human nature which to a great extent determine human conduct. Therefore, the situation will be such that an action considered to be virtuous in one sense may not be taken to be virtuous in another, or in other words, we can say, that no activity appears to be good enough to be called virtuous on its own account. For Aristotle, "goodness is one, evil is multiform."[16] Now, the question is, if there is only one way of being good, can I always have such a fixed disposition that I will always act in the similar way? And at the same time can I prescribe the same disposition to others to possess to behave rightly? The right means is not same for everyone, but the final end is the same that is the goodness. In one particular sense, virtue or moral goodness is inseparable from the action, still in another sense they are different, for virtue is the final end, whereas action is a means to be performed in virtue of practical wisdom for the attainment of the end (i.e., the virtue) which is rather too difficult to make distinction between the two, because sometimes virtue and action seem to be having interchangeable expressions and something virtue stands unaffected by the action having its own qualities.

Now, if we leave it up to the understanding of a practically wise man to pursue his final good then each and every person could prove himself to be acting in right manner in one way or another. The right means are different from person to person under different situations. There will be as many ways of conducting moral and social issues, as many are there situations and persons to deal with them. There is certainly a difference between right way of acting and good way of acting. A case of theft may be certified for not being a matter of good action but a right one when made by a starving man. Aristotle, in its practical realm, takes an action to be done rightly when performed under the supremacy of reason. Reason helps us in justifying an action to be called a right action under certain situations but not for its being good. Aristotle does not seem to be making a distinction between the two.

Aristotle takes good action and end synonymously. He says

"while making has an end other than itself, action cannot, for good action itself is an end".[17] He shows the distinction between doing and making. But the question which may arise as to the nature of action itself. Is it not like making something? Does not an action consist in taking steps to bring about some change or outcome? Cannot we apprise an action in two ways : (i) Meaning the will of the individual; and (ii) in terms of the effects of the action, i.e., if a doctor gives some medicine to a patient to save his life but fails to meet with the anticipated effects. So, as a result the patient may become more ill, or even die, but the will of the doctor and the kindness of his action certainly does not depend upon whether he achieves his end. How can we then say that action is not different from that of an end. Whether it is the 'will', to do something is to be called good in itself or the effects of the actual performance. For Aristotle, the will of the individual is to be seen in the action itself.

Following Aristotle can we at all claim a person to be good who wills to do something good but cannot do because of the lack of resources? It seems that virtue not only lies in action but also in willingness to do it even when a person lacks resources (Physical, psychological or material, etc.). And again, how do we come to know that an action was an unintended, unwilled act though it is discharged and reflected in perfect moral sense? For Aristotle, it may be contended that an action — if it is done reluctantly and from the fear of consequences — then its rightness is merely accidental for such an action would be neither voluntary nor involuntary but non-voluntary.[18] But how can we know that the person acted reluctantly if he himself does not disclose the fact? Suppose, a man returns a sum of money, deposited with him by someone, from fear of consequences, can we say that the rightness of the action is just accidental? Is it that the agent is not behaving in the right way? Aristotle would suggest that he is not, because the motive behind the action is not appropriate. Now, again, it follows that the motive of an action is more important than the action itself. The two cannot be taken together. Aristotle seems to be confusing the two issues by taking action and disposition simultaneously. But even if we say that the goodness of our action lies in the validity of the motive itself then how can we sort out the validity of the motive itself? And here, in such cases, the agent is fully aware of the results and the means adopted by him to do the action, how can then the action be considered incidental only?

Aristotle says that it is the agent who is to be held responsible, or praised or blamed for his voluntary and not for his involuntary actions. An involuntary action as defined by him, is an action done under compulsion or in ignorance, or when it originates from outside and the agent has nothing to contribute.[19] And a voluntary action is one that originates in the agent himself when he knows the particular circumstances in which it takes place. A voluntary act includes the awareness of the agent, the act done, the person or object whom it concerns, the instrument employed, the manner and the effect of the action.[20] If a person is ignorant of any of these factors his action is claimed to be involuntary in nature. But how do we know that it was a voluntary action or an involuntary action, for an agent can posit all sorts of reasons to make it appear either as voluntary or involuntary.

Aristotle divided human soul into two main parts (i) rational, and (ii) irrational, and further subdivided the rational part into two faculties — one which enables us to understand the first principles of knowledge and admits or variations, and the other is concerned with practical knowledge that we deliberate about, which does admit of variations and change, subsequently may be called scientific and calculative faculties. It is through the calculative faculty that a man can know moral goodness. In so far as we are talking about thought and truth in conduct, speculative thought is not in question because it has nothing to do with action or Production. Practical life is concerned with the human affairs, therefore, may lead to various approaches to human problems. But in the end of *Nicomachean Ethics,* Aristotle has a way of saying something different what he said in the beginning. He says in his first book happiness "the end to which all our conscious acts are directed, is found to be something final and self sufficient . . . . we might arrive at this if we could grasp what is meant by the function of a human being . . . . the good for man is "an activity of soul in accordance with the best and most complete form of goodness".[21] But he concludes in tenth book by saying, "we find after all there is still a higher life open to man than that of public affairs, i.e., the life of leisure.[22] All the practical affairs are undertaken as means to getting leisure just as civilized men go to war not for the sake of war but for peace. The wise man can do more than a temperate man and the brave man and so on. He can speculate all by himself, and the wise he is the better he can do it. The activity of contemplation "is the only activity that is praised on its own account because nothing comes out of it beyond the act of contemplation, whereas from practical activities we count on gaining something more or less over and above the mere action."[23]

The life of leisure, according to Aristotle, does not need external accessories. It calls into play the highest Capacities of our soul, i.e., intuitive reasoning. The activity of this faculty is accompanied with the purest of all pleasure, Life of contemplation is related with the best and purest self. And, he says, this life is such which we live not in virtue or practicing human life but in virtue of having something divine in us. The end is to be sought in human life. It is not a condition, not a state of mind or disposition of character. It is a form of activity desirable in and for itself. It is not in need of anything still self-sufficient. Such an activity, therefore, will have a speculative or contemplative character—the most continuous and highest form of activity. Here, it seems as if Aristotle is making a distinction between two types of good, (i) the good that an individual reaches through virtuous action and the final good that a person may approach merely through contemplation. He maintains that actions which are in conformity with goodness or virtue, though desirable in themselves need external accessories. The 'Final Good' attained through contemplation does not aim at any end beyond itself. But since a man is constituted of appetites, desires, and intelligence, such life of contemplation is too high for him to attain, for it will not be lived by him in his merely human capacity but in virtue of something divine within him. Gods, according to Aristotle enjoy the most complete blessedness and felicity, for no actions can be attributed to good except for the contemplation.

Now, the question is as to what is the nature of this divine element? Whether this element of divinity is same with intelligence of faculty of intuitive, reasoning in area. If the two are not same then, is this element of divinity poured in man from outside? Aristotle does not clarify the issue. If the final end — the happiness– and the activity of the divine or intuitive reasoning (if the two could be used inter-changeably) is one and the same then the question my be raised what noble deeds contribute in the pursuance of the final end? And if we say the divine element is not same as intuitive reasoning then can we say that man is not capable of speculation for it can be attributed to goods only in a mysterious sense. At the most, a man can be happy only in the secondary sense, that is, by performing virtuous actions or by living a good life. Actions that are done in conformity with goodness or virtue may lead to a different kind of happiness than that of a attained through contemplation.

Sometimes, it appears, as if Aristotle is equating the two concepts pleasure and happiness. Actions, he says, must be accompanied either by pleasure or pain and the contemplative activity is the one which is always accompanied by the purest of all pleasures. Is there any distinguishing mark between the purest of all pleasures and happiness? If happiness, as if Aristotle is pointing out the qualitative difference in pleasures and not quantitative. For all pleasures are perfect at any moment but not every pleasure is to be desired, these being distinguishable from the good pleasures. But the question that may arise can we say that there are some pleasures that are bad and some good? Is not it that the action of an individual to be called good or bad, right or wrong and the agent to be accounted for his good or bad intention may accompany pleasure but it is the intentions that differ from each other and not the pleasures. Therefore, we cannot refer to the qualitative difference but sometimes we do say that at this moment "I am very pleased" which refers to the qualitative difference in the pleasure. For qualitatively pleasure will be the same in all the cases.

Aristotle, finally says that animals and children are not capable of being described as happy because, they cannot contemplate and not free to make decisions. Is it that since animals are not capable of theoretical thinking, therefore to be distinguished from? The difference, perhaps, lies between the two not only because of the lack of theoretical thinking but because animals are incapable of practical thinking also.

Aristotle says, by any chance—a person—even a slave can enjoy the bodily pleasures no less than the best man; but no one can assign to a slave a share in happiness unless he assigns to him also a share in human life—for happiness does not lie in such occupations but in virtuous activities. If there is something divine, man that he shares with gods then how can we ignore this with slaves who can by all means have it being human beings. In so far as divine element is there in rational human beings, it must not matter whether the person is a slave, or master or whatsoever, so long he is capable of contemplation and, therefore, can seeks the *highest* good — the happiness.

REFERENCES

1. Aristotle, *Nicomachean Ethics, The Ethics of Aristotle,* Tr. By J.A.K.Thomson, Penguin Books, 1952, p. 38.
2. Nancy Sherman, *Making a Necessity of Virtue, Aristotle and Kant on Virtue,* Cambridge University Press, U.K., 1997, p. 223.
3. Aristotle, *Nicomachean Ethics*, p.99.
4. *Ibid.*, pp. 154-155.
5. D.J. Allan, *The Philosophy of Aristotle*, Oxford University Press, London, 1957, p. 184.
6. *Ibid.*, p. 185
7. Aristotle, *Nicomachean Ethics,* pp. 100-101.
8. *Ibid.*, p. 104.
9. Edwin T. Mitchell, *A System of Ethics,* The University of Texas, p. 391.
10. Aristotle, *Nicomachean Ethics,* p. 28.
11. Edwin, T. Mitchell, *A System of Ethics*, p. 391.
12. Aristotle, *Nocomachean Ethics*, p. 104.
13. *Ibid.*, p. 145.

14. *Ibid.*, p. 146.
15. Nancy Sherman, *Making a Necessity of Virtue, Aristotle and Kant on Virtue*, p. 223.
16. Aristotle, *Nicomachean Ethics.* p. 145.
17. *Ibid.*, pp. 148-149.
18. *Ibid.*, p. 151.
19. *Ibid.*, p. 151.
20. MacIntyre Alasdair, *After Virtue – A Study in Moral Theory*, Duck Worth Land, 1985, p. 147.
21. *Ibid.*, pp. 28-29.
22. Ackrill, *Aristotle's Ethics*, Faber & Faber, London, /1973,
23. David Gauthier, *Morals by Agreement*, Clarendon Press, Oxford, 1986, p. 157.
24. Stephen D. Hudson, Human character & Morality, Reflections from the History of Ideas, p. 50.
25. Aristotle, *Nichomachean Ethics*, p. 142.
26. Allan, D.J., *The Philosophy of Aristotle*-OUP- 1957, p. 180.
27. Nancy Sharman, Making a Necessaty of Virtue, Aristotle and Kant on Virtue, Combridge Universty Press, U.K., p. 55.
28. *Ibid.*, p. 74
29. W.W. Fortenbaugh, *Aristotle on Emotion Duckworth*, London, 1975, p. 80.

Chapter –2

Aristotle's Concept of Justice

Veena Kapoor

Justice is a socio-political and moral virtue that all rational beings tend to seek and achieve. Aristotle contends that virtuous nature of man may be grasped by exposing the peculiar function of a human being exclusively exhibiting his nature in actions. The concept of justice can be understood in the light of the division and function of the human soul in rational and irrational parts. He asserts that man is not a bundle of appetites seeking their satisfaction, but a decision making, a choice making and a judging authority as a rational being. Man is capable of rational understanding, making moral judgement and action, creation and contemplation, understanding the value of the emotional activities of compassion, sympathy, love and affection and holding human relations meaningfully. A just society enables men to make best of their capabilities and capacities in dignified manner. In order to be fully human, man is given the opportunity to develop his character and personality in right direction. Each person is important for the welfare of society. He contends :

> "The mere act of living is not peculiar to man — we find it even in the vegetable kingdom — and what we are looking for is something peculiar to him. We must, therefore, exclude from our definition the life that manifests itself in mere nurture and growth. A step higher

> should come life that is confined to experiencing sensations. But that we see is shared by horses, cows, and the brute creation as a whole. We are left, then, with a life concerning with which we can make two statements. First, it belongs to the rational part of man. Secondly, it finds expression in the actions."[1]

His analysis of human nature points out that dignity of the individual is safeguarded by the sense of justice and moral obligation. It is the duty of the individual to exercise his best self for the development of the society as a whole. The life devoted to reason is just and fair. Reason is the supreme authority and rational life is the noblest. However, he does not rule out or underestimate the significant role played by the emotions if guided and trained by reason while making decisions regarding principles and their application in practical life. So prudent or the man of practical reason can contribute to the good of the state in best way and can also guide other members in right direction. Acting according to reason is to lead a just life; for a rational man can understand his own psyche as an agent in relation to other persons' psyches who might be affected by the consequences of his actions, the means by which the action can be performed, i.e., the circumstances, the quality of action, etc. Aristotle while analyzing the concept of justice lays emphasis on practical wisdom to make deliberations and reflections on practical affairs of human life in right and just manner. For him, best are the persons of intuitive insight, and philosophic wisdom, and of scientific understanding of first principles as they live for such high ends, whereas a man of practical wisdom understands the practical affairs and can set rules and regulations for governing the city-state in a harmonious order.

Justice cannot be merely an expression of feelings or emotions. We may agree with this contention that man is a rational animal and his rationality may be considered as the defining feature of mankind. Man cannot be identified with gods either, because gods are supposed to be perfect in all respects, whereas human beings err in actions and are imperfect, however they partially share divinity with gods on the one hand, and passions with animals on other. It is only human beings' conduct is subject to evaluation and judgement. Human beings alone need a value theory to judge actions and seek justice and fairness while interacting with others. Being social is inherent in their character and must interact with each other. Animals do not have voluntary purposeful activities to perform, they cannot foresee, they cannot imagine to act according to a preplanned schematic order in social and moral sense. Human beings are action and purpose oriented beings, performing actions in a harmonious order. Animals are conditioned to behave only on the instinctive level. Man alone is capable of making use of his potentialities lying in his rational, inventive, aesthetic, moral, social, etc., capacities leading to the purpose for which he is there.

The rational nature of man is such that no one would like to be treated less than any other human beings, i.e., unjustly. Justice is a virtue that we realize in our conduct in relation to other human beings. But what do we understand by just conduct? When does the question of justice arise? and to whom and under what conditions is justice demanded? What is the criterion to judge whether an action is just or unjust? We may say, that a person who understands, reflects and is capable of making judgements can seek justice. All rational beings have a sense of justice, even when their rational capacity is at the very low level. A child may not be able to conceptualize justice but still he can show, by his overt behaviour, that he is not being treated at par with his fellow-beings. Justice, Aristotle claims to be a supreme virtue exhibited in virtuous actions.

> "Unlike the other virtues, it has less to do with a motivating range of feelings, which produce wrong actions and which like at the extreme of some mean, than with the external aspect of our actions as it relates to another."[2]

Actions done in ratio and proportion are both good and just. For Aristotle, virtue is a habit or a disposition that we develop by performing like activities in the like manner, time and again under certain situations towards certain persons for achieving some goal or purpose. A just man's purpose or goal is to maintain equality and equilibrium among unequals and discriminated persons to establish a good society. Virtue, Aristotle defines, is a mean between two extremes of emotions in their application in deliberate actions. For him, the two extremes are vices and evils whereas their mean is a virtue and good action and, therefore, is just. To be just is to be virtuous and fair in one's dealings. Justice, thus, is a mean between two unequal parts. It is a virtue which is somehow inherent in all social and moral actions. It is pre-eminently social and moral manifested in social relations between human beings. Thus, justice is not a personal virtue. For Aristotle, justice is a virtue, which unlike other virtues does not directly apply to simple actions and feelings of human beings, but consists in a proper proportion between the merits of two or more persons and equal distribution of goods, honour, rewards, wealth and freedom, etc. For him justice is.

> "... that kind of state of character which makes people disposed to do what is just and makes them act justly and wish for what is just, and similarly by injustice that state which makes them act unjustly and wish for what is unjust."[3]

Justice is founded on our moral reflection which is a mental operation that seeks to determine the moral worth of human beings, their intentions and actions in institutional framework. We can apprehend justice in what one ought to do, and that requires freedom from any constraints and unequal treatment. Justice may be understood in acting freely and treated equally with other rational human beings while enjoying rights and opportunities. But, freedom from what and equality in what sense? When are we treated unequally? We cannot conceptualize justice without referring to its opposite. We can understand the concept of justice by reflecting over the conditions which make actions and agents unfree and unjust? A man enslaved by others and conditioned by environment may be called unfree and being treated unjustly. 'Man is a social animal' is a platitude; and being so he is liable to act in some set patterns of social order. Not only that he is a social being, rather is a rational, free and conscious being too. Injustice emerges in giving less of good and more of evil to oneself or others. Aristotle defines justice and unjustice in the sense that :

> ". . . just behaviour is a mean between doing injustice and suffering it. For to do injustice is to have more than one ought and to suffer it is to have less than one ought. And justice may be regarded as a mean though not the same kind of mean as the other virtues for it is not, like them and like injustice, related to the exremes, but is a permanent attitude of the soul towards the mean. Or we may describe it as the disposition in virtue of which a just man is said to choose deliberately to do what is just."[4]

Injustice means to inflict injuries to oneself or others. To redress the injustice the affected person may ask for reward of punishment to the unjust man, and he himself be given what was due to him or be compensated for which he was deprived of earlier. So, the one thing that justice would claim to have, would be law or legislative power. The just then, is the lawful and the fair, the unjust the unlawful and the unfair. Law places people at par, however, not overlooking the differences in their capabilities and capacities. Justice presupposes equality not in the sense of division of something in two parts in mathematical sense, rather of ratio and proportion between talent and his achievement.

> "Justice is ranked as a virtue of character and the general theory of the Mean is applied to it, though with a difference . . . . But in this instance Aristotle evidently finds it impossible to preserve the separations between the moral virtue and the accompanying excellence of judgement . His essay on Justice is largely concerned, not with the emotional disposition to accept or reject the Mean, but with various quasi-mathematical operations whereby a just Mean is ascertained."[5]

Men are not equally deserving, therefore, equal shares, in the literal sense will not do justice. In so far as men are not of equal worth, therefore, they ought not to be treated equally in absolute sense. Some men are naturally born slaves or masters. Only those who are capable of doing administrative works should be given authority to govern, whereas others who are technically talented should be given work suitable to them. It will as a result promote good of the society as a whole besides good of the agent. So, there are artisans, soldiers, and ministers and so on, all pursuing good of the society in parts. For Aristotle good of society is greater than good of the individual.

Justice is done if all are given equal opportunities to promote their talents, and if someone hinders others from pursuing their ends then that person may be dealt with the law of Courts. In this sense justice would mean dealing members lawfully, i.e., the human conduct in a state is determined by Law. Dealing lawfully and justly seem to be having interchangeable expressions. Demanding or seeking justice implies the application of certain rules commonly acceptable to all the members of the institution and as and when it is felt that someone is being treated otherwise, then their actions may be evaluated in the light of set rules. D.J. Allan rightly points out with Aristotle that :

> ". . . the adjectives just and unjust are used, at least in Greek, in a wider sense, to describe every form of right and wrong conduct in so far as it brings a man into relations to his neighbours, e.g., an act of cowardice, which from the agent's point of view is a fault, may be viewed as an act of injustice in so far as he abandons others to danger. The term 'just' is in this sense, synonymous with legal, for it is precisely with this aspect of our actions that the law is concerned."[6]

Defining justice in terms of law is partial because it does not cover all human actions. Justice cannot be explained fully in the sense of conformity to law. Violation of law is not always unjust under certain conditions, place and time. Laws are the policies adopted by the legislators for a particular kind of city-state; for they are conventional and cannot enjoy the universal status. For example the law of India may not permit its members to hunt deers but the same may not be applicable to some other countries where deer hunting is permissible. For what a man may be punished in India, he may not be treated so in the other countries. So this kind of justice is particular in nature.

Aristotle makes a distinction between *universal justice* and *particular justice*. Universal justice refers to the natural rights of the individuals that all should be treated equally and given equal freedom. This is the form of perfect justice which finds its content in the concrete situations. The formal and universal nature of justice may be so expressed and articulated in the form of particular justice in a concrete situation. For him :

> ". . . evidently all lawful acts are in a sense just acts. . . that tend to produce and preserve happiness and its components for the political society. And the law bids us do both the acts of a brave man (e.g., Not desert our post nor take to flight nor throw away our arms), an' those of a temperate man (e.g., not to commit adultery nor to gratify one's lust), and those of a good tempered man (e.g., not to strike another nor to speak evil), and similarly, with regard to other virtues and forms of wickedness, commanding some acts and forbidding others, and the rightly framed law does this rightly, and the hastily conceived one less well. . . . This form of justice then, is complete virtue although not without qualification but in relation to our neighbour. And, therefore, justice is often thought to be the greatest of virtues, and neither evening nor morning star is so wonderful and proverbially "injustice is every virtue comprehended. And it is complete virtue in its fullest sense, because it is the actual exercise of complete virtue."[7]

Justice thus, may be articulated in particular actions by taking one's due share and giving others their due. Taking more or less than one's due, or giving more or less than other's due is to act unjustly.

> "... just man is the doer, by choice, and distributes goods what is equal in accordance with proportion, and similarly in distributing between two other persons. Injustice on the other hand is similarly related to the unjust, which is excess and defect, contrary to proportion, of the useful or hurtful... proportion may be violated in their direction. In the unjust act we have too little is to be unjustly treated, to have too much is to act unjustly."[8]

We find that law cannot grasp universal justice completely. We may interpret justice as a value in the light of which we evaluate laws and change or modify them according to the needs and goals of members of the city-state. So, we may say that sometimes, it is justice that determines law, and sometimes it is law that determines justice. Law itself may be just or unjust, therefore, we cannot give interchangeable meanings to law and justice. For example, although Socrates raised a voice against the existing corrupt laws of his times, still kept acting according to them for he believed that it would be immoral and unjust if he acts against the prescribed law of his city-state. However, the laws could be revised, and he asserted that the freedom of a person lies in evaluating the existing laws. Pointing out the wrong and corrupt practices, is in a way, doing justice to the humanity. What the law is and what it ought to be are the two different issues. The existing law is a matter of fact; whereas universal justice as a value looks for the rules which will be applicable to all rational beings equally. Thus, justice may be understood as a perfect virtue or as law abiding rule.

Now if justice is explainable in legislative and law-abiding directives then what sorts of laws should be instituted? It may be the laws which distribute goods, freedom, positions, offices, responsibilities, privileges, etc., on the basis of merit and basic needs. In a city-state all are supposed to bear the burden in a certain law fixed way. The legal distribution has to be in accordance with the law in a just manner. It may be pointed out that justice is realized through legal rules but not necessarily always so. Justice, not only distributes happiness among people but also pains, not only gives freedom but burdens and lays responsibility also. Mitchell argues that :

> "The rules of law are stated in completely general forms. Cases, on the other hand, are always particular with all kinds of unique circumstances and qualifying conditions. It is impossible for a law to take account of all these factors, and yet they are relevant to the case. The strict application of the law may easily result in substantial injustice. Then again there are conflicts between laws, or between the statutory law and the constitution, or between the constitution and ideal justice. For these and other reasons it is well to have special courts, called courts of equity."[9]

Aristotle is convinced that without morality politics cannot be fair in the application of its rules. ". . . . For those whose desires and actions have a rational basis a knowledge of these principles of morals must be of great advantage. . ."[10] Ethical principles are the foundation of political affairs. Moral rules govern human conduct in general, whereas legal rules govern behaviour of the members of a particular community. Justice in moral sense may cross the limits of legal rules, i.e., the legal rules may be questioned for justification. Aristotle takes recourse to equity to overcome conflict situations in the application of law. We find :

> "Aristotle's discussion of equity is brief and rather obscure, but one gathers that a court of equity would supplement the law, especially in cases not specifically covered, and in doing so would apply first principles. Underlying the concept of equity is the assumption that there exists or subsists a standard or perfect justice to which all enacted laws and constitutions are only approximations. It thus appears that Aristotle, in spite

> of his more empirical approach, was not as far from Plato as he thought."[11]

We may say that justice without liberty and equality would be reduced to nothing. Aristotle realizes that justice lies in between two inequalities, so equality is that absolute point which transcribes the concept of justice. In common sense and in social and legal too, justice promotes equality in the distribution of rights and duties, rather is resolved in equality. Justice and equality go hand in hand, however, the criterion to determine equality will have to be pin pointed. Will this equality leave a room for privileges to be given to some selective people, and burdens have to be imposed on to some other? For instance, we find that a governing authority is given security whereas a common man may not be given. Is it to treat some people unjustly? On the other hand the distribution can be made on the basis of colour, creed and religion. Is it a just distribution? So what can be called just distribution? The criterion, that people are unequal because they belong to different classes, they have different colours, castes and creed cannot be rationally justified and they are supposed to be treated equally according to some norms generally acknowledged and standards having rational basis. In absolute sense justice implies that if one is treated by applying one principle then other persons too, ought to be treated alike. The equality pursued for justice cannot be absolute in nature for it would not leave any room for special rights and privileges given to some special persons having merit, authority or position in the society. All laws cannot affect all equally and laws affecting all equally may not be just. Reasons have to be given while treating someone unequally to justify the action.

For Aristotle, the society is the cohesion of unlike persons in their nature, dispositions, qualities, talents, actions, interests and so on. A man cannot do everything for himself and has to depend on others to fulfil his needs and lead a purposeful social life. Within the differences, the social life of individuals requires an institution, which could do good to all without irrelevant discriminations. The differentiations have to be considered and determined for the good of the society as a whole by giving positions, rights and duties to the individuals. State is prior and pre-condition of man's achieving his rational goal. An institution is the prerequisite of bringing all at par with each other, thus, doing justice to all. Aristotle, we find, distinguishes between two sorts of justices, general and particular. General is the complete virtue, the righteousness. Particular justice, he classifies, under two heads *distributive* and *corrective* or *remedial justice* that he finds in ratio and proportion of common goods such as wealth, honour and merit. He contends, that

> "... Just man is the doer, by choice, and distributes goods what is equal in accordance with proportion; and similarly in distributing between two other persons. Injustice on the other hand is similarly related to the unjust, which is excess and defect, contrary to proportion, of the useful or hurtful... proportion may be violated in either direction. In the unjust act to have too little is to be unjustly treated; to have too much is to act unjustly."[12]

Aristotle believes that an unjust man is not contented to have equal share with others. Because the unjust thing is the unequal part, it is obvious that there must be a mean between more and less equality. He argues,

> "If then the unjust is the unequal, the just is the equal; everyone accepts the conclusion without demanding a reason for it. But, since the equal is the mean, the just must also be a mean."[13]

He asserts there to be

> ". . . minimum of four terms in which justice finds expression—two *persons* and two *shares*. And the equality of the second pair will be reflected in the equality of the first. The ratio will be the same in one case as in the other, because, if the persons are not equal, their shares will not be equal."[14]

Thus, he defines distributive justice in ratio and proportionate division of social goods, wealth, honour, position, rights and duties amongst members of the society, and accordingly classifies it in its various forms. The transactions and contracts are determined on the basis of work, the ability of the individuals which, he says, can be transcribed in terms of fair deal, fair wages and so on. Corrective justice is another kind of particular justice which takes care of the redressal of the injustice incurred on an individual by an unfair means by other person in their dealings with each other.

> "Unlike distributive justice within Aristotle's scheme, corrective justice depends not on merits as one of its criteria but purely on the transactional nexus of the parties. The parties are sufferer of the same injury. They stand related to one another simply in terms of their actions."[15]

For him, the distributive and contractual and corrective justices are based on proportion, i.e., each is to be given according to his needs and merits. So, the principle of equality applicable here is not the equality in the sense of division of something in two parts in geometrical sense, rather of ratio and proportion. Men are not equally deserving, therefore, equal shares will not do justice. However, if all are given according to their needs only then it may be a case of compassion and pity and not of justice necessarily. If men are not of equal worth then they ought not to be treated equally in absolute sense. Corrective justice is shown in private transactions or business deals, where it serves the purpose of correcting any unfairness that may arise.[16] Corrective or emendatory justice works for fair deals, buying, selling, loaning money at interest or without interest, pledging, depositing, hiring out, etc., and awarding punishment for theft, adultery, poisoning, killing, insulting and so on.

> "Injustice done to someone is redressed by a judge what the judge aims at doing to make the parts equal by the penalty he imposes, whereby he takes from the aggressor

> any gain he may have seemed. The equal, then, is a mean between the more or less."[17]

Aristotle's contractual justice or justice of exchange with regard to wages, exchange of goods and commodities was possible through the medium of money. Money is the common denominator to exchange commodities. The value of the commodities could be determined by money, based on the worth of skill, labour, demand and intellect and so on. The worth of something can be measured not only by the time factor but by the intellect as well. For instance, an architect who makes blue prints of a building, is paid more than a labourer who works manually and mechanically. The determination of the value of commodity is not universal, it is different for different societies depending upon the merit of products and necessity of the city-state. However, determining the merits of two classes of producers and their products is vague. Absolute justice, cannot be realized fully in human actions, although it may be the goal of human nature. His principle of justice, relative in nature referring to the merits of the individuals, is quite intelligible. However, while determining the merit of individual talents one may go wrong and do injustice to someone intentionally or unintentionally. Injustice is giving less of good and more of evil to others and hurting and inflicting injuries to them.

For Aristotle, the notion of justice is also applicable to those actions which lie beyond the sphere of lawful acts, i.e., to the private life of the individual, where equal distribution of praise, affection, love and immaterial goods may be in question than wealth, merit or honour which Aristotle calls *domestic* and *reciprocal justice*. In personal cases, we may have certain psychological claims regarding love and affection, respect and dignity, care and support resulting from the reciprocal relations.

> "There is another form of Justice . . . between master and slave, and between father and child . . . there can be nothing in their relations which is politically just or unjust . . . . on terms of equality. . . . It is in fact justice between

husband and wife that is the true form of domestic justice, although it too must be distinguished from 'political justice'."[18]

There is a relation of parents and children, husband and wife, of friendship and so on. For these relations there might not be fixed laws but still we claim some favours from each other and if our expectations are not satisfied we feel subdued. Reciprocal relations depend upon give and take phenomenon. What one does or gives something to another does not imply that the latter would do or give in return the same to the former. For example, in most of the cases, parents out of affection give all that what is required or demanded by their children, but in return they may not expect anything material, but respect only. Reciprocal justice is not bound by some rules and regulations in strict sense of the term. We can explain it in psychological terms. Domestic justice does not have fixed and well pronounced laws which if not carried out would impose penalty on the person who fails to perform according to expectations of others. Legal justice is different from conventional and customary justice. Customs keep going on even when laws change with the changing policies of the state. One finds oneself bound by the traditional way of life and feels obligated to perform actions in the conventional way only. Conventional ways of acting may not completely and rationally comply with the changing life discourse. Justice will be done only when the customs are changed according to the changing life styles. Thus, justice expects something to be done as a duty, or respect or affection. Legal justice expects duty to be done by the citizens to promote good of the society. Reciprocal justice expects respect, trust, cooperation from each other in one form or the other; and domestic justice expects affection for each other among the family members or friends. We cannot make strict claims in reciprocal or domestic justice.

The ideal or absolute justice is embedded in the equal rights be given to all the human beings because they are homosapiens. In the concrete situations the ideal is carried out in the equal distribution of privileges to grow in individual faculties and talents, their right to live life of their choice, however, without frustrating others' interests. Justice demands that all persons should be given natural or human rights; that they are not used as means, nor they themselves use others as means. But this is not applicable in all cases. As Aristotle discriminates women and slaves against other persons living in society. He says :

> ". . . If a man in authority strikes somebody under him, it is wrong for the latter to return the blow. But if he strikes his superior officer, it is not enough that he should be struck back; he should receive some extra punishment."[19]

It may be pointed out that Aristotle was in favour of giving equality of freedom and justice, to specific people than all. However, on the other hand, we may believe that conception of justice is possible in giving meaning to oneself and others as subjects and not as objects. Neither one nor others are to be treated as objects. The notion of otherselves leads to the reciprocal relations and equality between selves, at the same time giving rise to a series of obligations to each other in the form of duties and equivalent corresponding rights. Human actions can be evaluated and judged as good or bad if performed consciously and willingly by the agent making him worthy of respect or hatred in reciprocal relations, and just or unjst in socio-political and moral sense.

Formal principle of justice may be taken as the basis of law. Legal orders presuppose certain general rules, otherwise, they will be arbitrary and temporary subject to change every now and then. The general rules have to be impartial and applicable to all persons. Justice, thus, implies disciplining human relations in harmonious manner by applying impartial rules without infringing anyone from acting freely and willingly. For Aristotle, just is the form of the 'equal', which implies that like cases should be treated alike. Justice, thus is defined by lawfulness, impartial application of laws or general rules, rational justification of rules, freedom and equality.

Formal justice can be fully grasped and understood in actions when actually performed. Equal and impartial treatment of the like cases may be the motive of justice and that is the principle to be worked on. Thus, whether justice is done or not will require us to analyze what we understand by '*alike*'. In what sense actions are alike and individuals are alike? Why or under what considerations be treated differently? To what extent circumstances be considered for differential treatment and evaluation of human conduct? Aristotle's relative approach to human conduct in terms of golden mean does not seem to be free from objections. He may be criticised for not giving us more than an empty sermon, "nothing too much and nothing too little". Does Aristotle give only a formula empty of content? We may support his method of deliberation and cultivating emotions and desires. We can act virtuously by avoiding the extremes by rational deliberations. MacIntyre asserts :

> "Nonetheless it is Aristotle whose account of virtues decisively constitutes the classical tradition as a tradition of moral thought, firmly establishing a good deal that his poetic predecessors had only been able to assert or suggest and making the classical tradition a rational tradition, without surrendering to Plato's pessimism about the social world."[20]

Justice presupposes freedom in action without interference by others. But the question is what is meant by interference? Is interference always unjustified? In most of the cases we do not perform actions for ourselves only, rather they are subject to some ends or purposes which are other-oriented or in relation to others. In such cases how far a person can act freely. Evaluation of an action does not refer to subjective or personal activity but an act as it ought to be performed by all rational beings. Thus, justice will first presuppose a system of rights and duties binding people together in a social and political network which will rule out arbitrariness altogether. Freedom, thus, is a conscious activity and its rationale will equate one's action with another generally. The body of rights and duties will give meaning to equality and freedom, and injustice is the instance of discrimination between human beings on irrelevant differences. Norms, legal or moral, are relevant to social actions. Efficiency of law in attaining its purpose is the justifying criterion of making judgements in favour of just actions. Thus, existing law in actions must be in conformity with the notion of justice.

Justice can be fully understood in practice than theory. For Aristotle, an action is neither absolutely rational nor merely an expression given to one's emotions of approval or disapproval rather they are the results of deliberate choices well reflected before their application. One who believes that justice is an expression of approval and attitudes of individuals cannot have certain general principles to judge others' action as just or unjust. We may say that Aristotle contends that morality, and justices for that matter, is experienced in our practical life in relation to others, but he will not assent to the view that this experience is merely based on individual approval or disapproval of something. Moral experience is something more than mere emotive experience. Men not only make choices because they approve or disapprove of certain things but because they reflect on them and have a reason to believe why should they choose and judge certain actions as good or bad. Thus, Aristotle, does neither believe that just actions are the mere expressions of emotions, nor that they are *a priori*. Aristotle is not giving an emotive meaning to justice, however, he gives emotions their due place in determining the rightness or wrongness of an action. The emotive theory of judgement is not acceptable because judgements are subject to rational tests of consistency, clarity and coherence. A just action cannot be explained in terms of the emotions of approval. Moral judgements have empirical basis and normative accountability. Justice, while referring to both what we desire and what we ought to desire will take recourse to the rational basis. However, social and moral outlook widens with human sympathies, pity, compassion, love, affection, trust and so on, on the one hand, and needs, purposes, desires on the other. And what is just is not known *a priori*, for it has a meaning in psychological and social situations. Justice is required to reconcile the conflicting interests. Morality may seem to be emerging from the fulfilment of desires, interests and needs and purposes but their fulfilment on subjective basis would lead to conflicts and their resolution is possible by some principles which could take care of interests, not only of one or some persons but of all. The desires have to be guided rationally. This guidance leads to the way to grapple with the problems in an efficient manner by specifying rights and duties to be assigned to individuals in a society. Thus, justice is an expression of what ought to be done than what is done. We may object to the view that rights and duties in legally just actions conform necessarily to rationally justified actions. All such rights and duties are determined in their schematic framework and may not necessarily be rationally justified for all. For example the duties of a slave to his master, or rights of the master may not be rationally justified and may be proved unjust.

Justice demands an enquiry into the existing rights and duties in a society in the light of equality and inequality. Justice does not have to consider equalities only but inequalities as well. Aristotle very rightly points out that justice can be based on ratio and proportion of equality. The relevant differences among people cannot be overlooked. The differences in needs and capacities would determine responsibilities and actions of the individuals. Differences are as much important as alikeness while deciding for what ought to be done by one in a society so that interests of all are protected to secure best results. Thus, rights and duties have to be thought and rethought in changing situations. Although Aristotle's standard of justice is implicit in the notion of rational morality but in certain cases he seems to be overlooking the criterion, e.g., master-slave relation. Aristotle may say that taking side with emotion or reason in isolation of each other to act in a just manner would not be free from errors. Justice will be meaningfully advocated if man is considered to his complete self in actions and judgements.

In Aristotelian view, we may say that the structure of rights and duties, position and status of individuals in the society, moral or legal, should be based on an individual's talent interests, needs, purposes in relation to other's interests, needs and purposes. Out of conflicting interests, needs and purposes, the reflective nature of man points out some commonly accepted principles which could generally take care of interests of most of the people. For example, Aristotle introduced the notion of currency for the just distribution and transaction of the goods among the members of the society. Justice involves rights and duties to adjust individual beings interests through comparative evaluation of their actions to resolve conflicts. The core idea of justice is to bring harmony and adjustments in the conflicting ideas of human beings while working together. And if someone is harmed or hurt, then his losses be redressed. The redressal may be in various forms, i.e., in the form of money, apologies or physical punishment and so on.

Thus, according to Aristotle a just society requires basic rights and freedom be given equally to the individual members belonging to the society; and obligations parallel to such rights are also acknowledged. All are to be given equal opportunities to participate in society according to their worth. Justice requires basic principles be equally applicable to most of the members of the society and if someone is not treated at par with others, or is deceived, injured, battered or harmed then he can make an appeal in the court of law, and legislator or judge as a mediator may redress the injustice by giving his due to the losing person by taking the excess from the unjust man, or by punishing him. Legal rules should be objective in nature to deal with individual and social problems. Freedom to make deliberate choices should be limited within the law-governed society, i.e., one cannot break the law, one cannot harm or injure others, one cannot take away other's property; one cannot misuse one's position and power. Justice is explained in arithmetical proportion by imposing punishment on the wrong doer and benefiting the sufferer in the form of money or honour and so on. In general, we can say with Aristotle, that justice is done to the humanity as a whole by living well and faring well in our different walks of life and pursuing happiness—the supreme good.

> "Since every activity involving some acquired skill or some moral decisions aims at some good, what do we take to be the end of politics—what is the supreme good attainable in our actions? Well, so far as the name goes there is pretty general agreement, 'It is happiness', say both intellectuals and unsophisticated, meaning by 'happiness' living well and faring well."[21]

So, to be happy implies living a virtuous and just life. We may recapitulate that, Aristotle analyses the concept of justice in its various forms and their correlated meanings and uses. He points out that the formal and universal justice is perfect and is articulatable in living well and faring well while dealing with others. He classifies justice in universal and particular sense. Particular justice is further divided in distributive and contractual or justice in exchange of goods. Contractual justice or justice in exchange is based on proportionate reciprocity, e.g., calculation of exchange value through money. Distributive justice is explainable in geometrically proportionate division of wealth, honour or goods according to the merit, talent, needs and status, etc. Besides them, he refers to domestic and reciprocal justice. Emendatory justice is law abiding to treat persons equally and redress the discrimination made against them in terms of loss and gain. Of course, abiding by law is right in legal sense however, it may be questioned whether abiding by law is always morally good too. Laws are conventional and are in accordance with the policies of the city-state which do not necessarily involve universal good. Many a time political justice clashes with moral goodness, and we are forced to raise a voice against law because we find it to be corrupt and it is unjust to act in accordance with it. Perfect or universal justice in its formal sense is absolute good; but particular justice is bound by the time, sort of person, motive, occasion and so on, therefore, it is relative in nature and would vary from state to state, person to person and time to time. Particular justice is contextual, spatio-temporal, relative in nature and having social and moral significance. For Aristotle generally acceptable rules applicable to all the members of a society in particular circumstances we may have. However, we may point out that we make deliberate choice while doing actions, therefore it is not merely to act according to a set pattern of rule always. We do the action from a particular motive and disposition. It is not always so easy to do the right action; for right action itself is to be understood through practical wisdom in existing circumstances. We may question his conception of justice related to what is lawful.

> "How does this form of justice—obedience to the law—differ from moral virtue in general? . . . . And does not a good man often do things not required by law? And is motive as crucial for attributing justice as it is for attributing moral virtue to a man?[22]

It is difficult to know and find which laws express natural justice, for no two persons deliberate about crucial issues alike. Even if we say that an action or a person just is because it is generally believed to be so. But cannot there be an instance where majority could be found unjust in relation to a decision of the minority? So long as man can choose to be virtuous or vicious, he can indulge in just or unjust activities voluntarily. But can the sufferer treat himself unjustly voluntarily? Aristotle says that not only the doer is unjust to others, but also that he may be equally unjust to himself if he suffers it knowingly. We may agree with him that one can treat oneself unjustly if one does wrong by taking less good than due and giving more to others. Justice is a public virtue that one realizes in one's course of actions in relation to others. A sagacious or prudent man alone can be just, for he can safeguard his own interests without harming others. Just actions promote goodness and happiness of the society. Gauthier holds the view, similar to Aristotle, on justice that it is a disposition to deal fairly. "Each person's choice must be a fair optimizing response to the choice he expects the others to make, provided such a response is available to him . . . ."[23]

We may conclude by saying that Aristotle comprehends justice as a virtue in its various forms, in relation to others in different fields. Being a virtue it finds its 'mean' in between inequalities, the two vices to be avoided. Equality, for him, lies in the ratio the proportionate division of common goods, wealth, honour to be enjoyed by members of society. For him, good of the society is greater than good of the individual. A virtuous and just man is prudent who reflects on the common good while promoting his own good. The goal of individuals is to seek their own good, i.e., the happiness without interfering in other's pursuit of happiness. One does justice by treating others at par with oneself while striving for the common end, the happiness. Aristotle broadly surveys the field of humanity and appeals to reason to act well and fairly and promote good of the society as a whole. Since virtue or moral goodness can be viewed in terms of actions performed by individual in a group the justice that takes stock of all of them while judging can be construed as the supreme or perfect virtue. Justice is acquired not in the exercise of particular emotions in action through reflection, rather it deals with various emotions and their application in a proportionate order in situations while coming into contact with others. Freedom of choice, moral goodness, responsibility, all these terms have meaning only in so far as they are in relation with other persons and objects. One cannot be held unjust and responsible for the actions which have no bearing on others. A just man trains himself by acquiring virtuous life in actions, to be fit for citizenship and goodness of the society. Justice as a golden mean is followed by the reason. Justice, thus is the character or quality of mind acquired as the result of effort and principle with reference to our own particular nature.

Justice, thus we can say, opposes lawlessness, uncertainty, partiality, inequality or discriminatory attitude and irrelevant differences. The formal account of justice that like cases be treated alike, does not always lead us to a right direction, for to find a mean between extremes is rather a difficult task. It is not always possible to say on what grounds the unlike people, under different circumstances, be treated in certain order. What one wants or desires is a psychological and factual matter but what is morally desirable is normative which considers distributive and corrective justice in fair deal. Fair deal is pronounced in social and political rules and justice follows a procedure accepted by most of the people. Justice lies in conformity with rules, however, the fairness is procured by the desirable results. Thus fair deal is just if it produces such results which include equal distribution of material goods, honour, rights and duties, position and authority according to merit, capability and capacities of the individuals.

REFERENCES

1. Aristotle, *Nicomachean Ethics, The Ethics of Aristotle,* Tr. By J.A.K.Thomson, Penguin Books, 1952, p. 38.
2. Nancy Sherman, *Making a Necessity of Virtue, Aristotle and Kant on Virtue,* Cambridge University Press, U.K., 1997, p. 223.
3. Aristotle, *Nicomachean Ethics,* p.99.
4. *Ibid.,* pp. 154-155.
5. D.J.Allan, *The Philosophy of Aristotle,* Oxford University Press, London, 1957, p. 184.
6. *Ibid.*, p. 185
7. Aristotle, *Nicomachean Ethics,* pp. 100-101.
8. *Ibid.,* p. 104.
9. Edwin T. Mitchell, *A System of Ethics,* The University of Texas., p. 391.
10. Aristotle, *Nicomachean Ethics,* p. 28.
11. Edwin, T. Mitchell, *A System of Ethics*, p. 391.
12. Aristotle, *Nocomachean Ethics*, p. 104.
13. *Ibid.* p. 145.
14. *Ibid.,* p. 146.
15. Nancy Sherman, *Making a Necessity of Virtue, Aristotle and Kant on Virtue,* p. 223.
16. Aristotle, *Nicomachean Ethics,* p. 145.
17. *Ibid.,* pp. 148-149.
18. *Ibid.,* p. 151.
19. *Ibid.,* p. 151.

20. MacIntyre Alasdair, *After Virtue – A Study in Moral Theory*, Duck Worth Land, 1985, p. 147.
21. *Ibid.*, pp. 28-29.
22. Ackrill, *Aristotle's Ethics*, Faber & Faber, London, 1973,
23. David Gauthier, *Morals by Agreement*, Clarendon Press, Oxford, 1986, p. 157.

Chapter – 3

God as Experience of Value

Indu Sarin

The aim of the present chapter is to reject naturalistic approach towards God and to show that realization of God involves experience of value. I am not holding a position that values emerge from metaphysical or transcendental source. Values are not God-given, they do not exist prior to human experience. To create an experiential foundation of value is to make room for the transient actualization of value, which presupposes freedom, commitment and striving by the individual.

Before analysis of the term God, it is important to highlight the nature of value experience. At the outset, it should be noted that value experience is not to be confused with biological or psychological experience. The realm of value transcends the milieu of physical life. Further; value is not to be identified with habits, drives or inclinations. No doubt, value experience is not possible without the individual but it is not limited by the psychological correlates of the individual. Value is non naturalistic, it cannot be identified with empirical conditions though empirical condition are presupposed by it. Value presupposes a supervening notion not necessitated or entailed by the conditions through which it is supervening. Suppose *B* is a supervening concept expressed or manifested by the empirically stated conditions called *A*, then neither *A* is identical with *B* nor *B* is identical with *A*, which means none of these entail each other. But *B* cannot be without feasible sets of *A*. Similarly, value cannot be without empirical conditions but empirical conditions do not entail value. The factual object, as such is not the value object. To say that 'this is valuable' and 'this is here' (factual object) are not identical, i.e., what is valuable cannot be reduced to what is. Value and fact are disparate; one cannot be substituted by the other. Value neither exists as a material object nor it is eternal or abstract. The being of value is neither real nor unreal but irreal — not yet, a dispositional prototype correlated to its transitive realization in successive states. Value experience is not mere collection of what is given, it implies articulation and transformation of the given to a not yet state (contra-factual). The given must be appropriated and judged by the individual. Value implies a creative act which transcend the given and thus makes room for creative invention of future possibilities. Thus it involves double transcendence, i.e., subjective and objective condition; personal inclination, on the one hand and natural order on the other.

Value experience cannot be explained in abstract or conceptual terms. It is volitional and conative. It implies the ideal and formulates the standard of judgement. The gap between these two functions of value is only at the level of imperfection, i.e., when the ideal is not actualized. The actualized ideal involves an explicated standard. When the ideal is realized, the individual judges it as worthwhile. Value is not a utopia, or an abstract ideal, it must press for its realization. It is an ideal to be aspired for which shows worth and desirability of the ideal. It is to be realized in decisions choice and actions.

From the foregoing discussion, it emerges that value presupposes the following elements:

1. Man (valuer) who appropriates pre-axiological elements ascriptively, posits them as supervenient norms and thus reacknowledge and appreciate their value.
2. Content of experience. It includes act of desiring,

appropriation of the value sought as well as action to be done and assurance of the intrinsic worthiness of the value sought through the performance of the correlated act. Value experience entails interrelated acts, decisions, evaluations and is prescriptively obligatory to the person. The above content of value experience is not descriptive, the obligatoriness is not derived from pre-existing rules, laws or nature of things but emerge from the satisfying awareness of value-worthiness of the conditions seen as correlated with stipulated or intended ideal

3. Objective correlative — the terminus of seeking. It is that which is valued or which makes value experience possible.
4. Having analyzed the nature of value experience, it is important to explicate the term God. While discussing the term God, two questions may be posed : the first is about the reality of the existence of god, the second is about our knowledge of god. If God exists, how can we know Him?- this is an abiding question of traditional and contemporary philosophers of religion and the answers are given from different standpoints. The other questions are : What type of reality can be ascribed to God? Is God ontologically real or just intended? Must we understand God ontologically or axiologically? What is the nature of religious experience? What is the relation between God and Man and between God and the external world?

Religious rationalism intended to look at the whole problem from an objective and impersonal standpoint. God is regarded as a reality being ontologically independent of human experience. He is known objectively and through reason. A case in point is the natural theologian's belief that a natural explanation of the existence of God is possible in the same way as explanation of the existence of other objects. To regard reason as an appropriate instrument to apprehend the Divine is among certain philosophers who attempt to explain God (to find a place for God) in conformity with their philosophy in general.

The natural theology is often called the rational theology because it asserts that knowledge of God is possible by man of reason unaided by revelation. Since the end of last century quite a few philosopher, scientists and theologians found 'a place for God' in their system, the Gifford lectures delivered in the various universities of Scotland have mostly been of the nature of armchair approaches to the problem of religious experience. The tendency of theology and metaphysics to propound like science in objective set of doctrines is not to be traced. However, only to the nineteenth and twentieth centuries, when science and scientific ways of thinking had begun to overwhelm human civilization. Long before the advent of modern theoretical science, theologians have advanced arguments for the existence of God, passing from a discovery of order and purpose in the physical world to a knowledge of a creator, a divine architect, a divine purpose. God is interpreted in terms of an analogy which is no doubt symbolic but far too inadequate to represent His nature.

Existential approach towards God is vigorous reaction against rationalistic theology. For the religious existentialists, religious experience cannot be separated from authentic individual experience, pure thought cannot serve as the foundation for the knowledge of God. Religious experience unlike scientific knowledge is direct, non-inferential and based on personal experience. God is not an object to be grasped and analyzed. He is to be experienced by the subject. The individual does not conceptualise about God but rather address Him directly and in a personal manner as 'Thou'. This is what is meant by saying that 'I or Thou' relationship to God takes us above the inauthentic conception of Him as an objective reality. God cannot, therefore, the made the object of any argument or of any inference. The categories of logic and epistemology cannot be applied to religious experience. A scientist uses deductive or inductive reasoning to establish or refute the truth of a proposition. He has a definite procedure, a technique or verification and methods to test a hypothesis. As religious experience is non/discursive these procedures are irrelevant. The rationalistic method may be adopted in dealing impersonally with things in the world. The rationalistic arguments start with the idea or essence of God and come down to explicate various attributes of reality. This method could be justified if we are able to grasp God's factual existence. But religious claim about the existence of God is not a factual claim. It is based upon faith.

Religious belief is not equivalent to factual belief. Factual belief is cognitive and it can be true and false. Religious belief, on the other hand, is non-cognitive. Suppose a person says, 'I believe in God' and the other person says, 'I do not believe in God', we cannot say that the first statement is true and the second statement is false as it is not a question of disagreement about the facts. 'I believe in God' is neither a descriptive statement nor the act of believing a simple conceptual act. It is partly an act of constituting a firm disposition to visualize a perspective about the world and our place in it, commitment to will in a way. God is not a being to realize what is unique and undetermined. The realization of God through cipher is to break objective determination and enter into the realm of freedom and creativity. The cipher cannot be tested on verified, it can be understood only through faith. Faith for Jaspers cannot be expressed into definite form, it is a venture of 'radical openness. Jaspers again continues, we can neither compel faith by arguments nor prove it by factuality. All we can do is to think on its basis, or in its direction' Further, faith is not bestowed on men as a gift of grace, it cannot be described by a line pointing 'downward from God to man'. Faith is a human achievement which may be described by a line pointing 'upward from man to God'. The function of faith is regulative, it regulates and transforms the life of the person.

Upshot that emerges from the foregoing analysis is that religious experience is neither exhaustively grasped through speculative nor psychological type of analysis, it is rather existential, inward free and, therefore, valuational. Religious experience cannot be conceptualised, yet it is different from a mere emotional experience. The individual rises above petty egoism through an inward decisive act. The indubitable transpersonal experience is divine experience which is the realization of meaning and value. It is a quest for total and ultimate meaning of existence. The fruitfulness of this experience is self fulfilment and satisfaction. It commits the individual to the action he ought to be performed and he is obligated to act or refrain from acting in a particular way. The individual judges the worthiness of the action and which is recognizable by others too. The realization of God thus calls for : (1) axiological universality, (2) Praziological obligatoriness, and (3) should act as standard of judgement of ultimate intrinsic worth. God is the terminus of seeking. The individual is aware of his limitations and finitude, he posits God as the highest value. The divine experience consists in man's commitment to the highest value—the locus of all perfections and source of self-enrichment and self-realisation. It is the organization of experience into a living totality in which all the conflicts are harmonized.

God becomes the principle of reconciliation of diverse values which are historically incompatible, confliction value are integrated into harmonious schematized value, which does not satisfy one person but aims at optimal and inclusive satisfaction of all individuals. God is not one value but is the foundation of embedded unity of disparate dimensions of value, which satisfactorily encapsules satisfactory value-profiles. Man as a historic being is driven by conflicts. One cannot have simultaneous realisation of values in history. This is not to say that value-conflicts are redundant or trivial, they are rooted in the very being of man. 'Man's quest of God is search for axiological optimality, i.e., homogeneous realisation of values; it is to overcome axiological relativism and dissatisfaction arising out of non-realisation of some values in history. The ordinary individual experience is marked by the *trichotomous* division of (1) agent, (2) process of actualization of the ideal, and (3) the ideal. But this *trichotomous* division is in truth merely a distinction, which needs to be fused and coalesced into authentic uplifting divine experience, which transforms the mundane experience. Objects and events are experienced as worthy or unworthy in terms of this emerging ultimate meaning. The individual is profoundly involved and affected so that the whole course of his life is changed.

REFERENCES

1. John Hick: *Faith and Knowledge*, Macmillan, 1967, p.3.
2. J. Hick: *Philosopy of Religion*, Prentice Hal, INC, 1963, p. 71.
3. K. Jaspers: *Why to Wisdom*, Trans. R. Manheim. Jule University Press, 1960, pp. 45-46.
4. K. Jaspers: *Philosophy*, Vol. I, Trans. E.B. Ashton. The University of Chicago Press, 1969, p. 255.
5. S. Hoim: Jaspers's Philosophy of Religion in *The Philosophy of Karl Jaspers,* P.A. Schilpp. (Editor). Taudor Publishing Co., New York, 1957, p. 669.
6. The issue of valuational antimonies has been discussed by N. Hartmann in his book *Ethics,* Vol. II, Moral Values. The Macmillan Company, pp. 76 ff.

Chapter – 4

God as Experience of Value

A Different Approach

Veena Kapoor

The chapter on "God as Experience of Value" is a reflection on value experience and experience of God and seeks to bring forth similarities in their characteristic features and that realization of God involves value-experience. Both are stated to be non-naturalistic and as such are neither biological nor psychological experience. Value is non-naturally experienced and presupposes a supervening notion. It has been argued that Experience of Value and Experience of God are non-natural because they fall under a category, which does not refer to facts and their descriptions alone. Value terms, as has been stated, also transcend the milieu of physical life and hence they are non-natural in nature. Values are non-natural not only because they transcend objective conditions but subjective conditions as well. With regard to God several questions have been marked out in the chapter. (1) What is the reality of the existence of God? — whether ontological or merely intended. (2) What is our knowledge of God? (3) What is the nature of religious experience and its relation with God and man and the external world? Dr. Sarin rejects the rational and teleological approaches to religious experience. Religious experience is ascribed to authentic individual experience, which is personal and based on faith. It is agreeable that religious belief is not equivalent to factual belief, which can be shown by applying the principle of verification. It is stated that belief in God is a voluntary act of faith. The way of realization of God is made possible either through existential attitude or by free choice. The author states that, "the *indubitable transpersonal* experience is divine experience which is the realization of meaning and value. It is a quest for total and *ultimate* meaning of existence". (Italics mine).

The Chapter is open to various questions while trying to show the realization of God as value experience. First question that strikes the mind is whether value is experienced or realized through understanding. if it is said to be an experience then what is its nature? And, how can such an experience have an affinity with the experience of God? Do we supervene the factual situations while using value words or transcend them? Do the two terms: 'supervenience' and 'transcendence' mean the same? However, no one can deny that values cannot subsist without persons and conditions. Whether supervenience is a notion or property of a term, which is neither natural nor supernatural nor non-natural. Supervenient property of a term or a value-word is realized in the factual situations-internal or external. We may say that supervenient property of a value-word is realized in and through factual conditions as a consequential epithet. What is called good is an object, which is subject to certain conditions, and its accountability as good is supervenient. Something as an object does not have a property of goodness in itself, for, goodness is the property of the term good and not of the object which is evaluated as good. On the other hand, the ascription of the property of goodness to an object is feasible only in certain conditions, situations and circumstances. no moral notion is complete in meaning apart from man's freedom and the factual conditions. To support one's free-rational choice is to look for its application in the conditions without reducing it to facts. To state a fact that twenty civilians were killed by terrorists is certainly not evaluative, but 'killing of civilians by terrorists is wrong' is evaluative. We do not come across this conclusion just by stating the fact but by the prescription, i.e., 'killing of innocent people is wrong'. The two statements are not entailed by each other however value content cannot be understood independent of its application in the relevant situation. If value is not naturalistic it cannot be non-naturalistic either. For, non-naturalistic approach would imply that value words have non-naturalistic property known to us immediately or intuitively or through rational insight. But supervenience is a property of a value word, which is not to be confused with non-natural property or rational insight.

It is not only a mere coincidence that various things are called good. When we come to honour, sagacity and pleasure, the notions that we have of them in respect of their goodness, are different and distinguishable. Therefore, good is neither a general term known to us naturally and empirically and corresponds to a single form, nor it is absolute and *a priori*. We call various things good without their being identical. Goodness does not make them identical because they are good. If good predicates many things which are separable from each other then good is something having its own independent meaning: and as such value cannot be realized in action or acquired by an individual; it is realized in evaluative practice under certain circumstances that speak for supervenient character of value terms. Value words are not realized through faith but by their supervenient property, which we realize in facts and their consequences that they bear in our practical life. As Aristotle says that pleasure is a state of mind, which supervenes upon human activities.[1]

Metaphysical assumptions may be kept out of a theory which deals with good and bad. There are no absolute first principles from which conclusions could be deduced. Are good things called good because they come under a single category and are to be sought entirely on their own merit? Can they be realized in the same manner, as colour white is recognizable in snow and milk? Goodness in pleasure, intelligence and prudence is not comparable to colour in different things. Goodness cannot be realized as a single and isolated element in actions. Goodness is realized in what makes an action worthy of practice and its merit differs from one action to another. For instance, Aristotle maintains that in medicine it is health, in military science it is victory, in architecture a building and so on.[2] So goodness can be realized only in what is doable, which could be practised in terms of what ought to be done in accordance with rational decision. Ought implies can. We cannot make use of the concept ought unless what we believe to be morally good and can also be put into practice. It is only in practice that goodness is realized. Value is different from fact but is inseparable from it, e.g., intelligence itself does not change anything in material sense unless it is put into action, i.e., potentiality lying in intelligence is realized through action. Here, actions in concrete situations and principle in respect of which they take place are fused together into a complete unity. Situations change but actions remain inseparable from their principles; as they may be conceived as co-existent. Situations do not change principles as such; nor one principle changes another principle; but a new or modified principle may fashion the action in situations. A principle is the purpose, having a potentiality to be actualised in action. Value consists in actions, e.g., an action is virtuous only if it involves virtue. Goodness consists not in possession but in exercise of a rational principle. It is the direction of the reflections on sound moral principles that makes us modify them to make actions worthy of doing.

It is not always easy to make up our minds as to what is our best course of action in choosing one of the two alternatives; or still harder it is to stick to our decision when made. You cannot have some first principles, which are not having foundation in rational deliberations because facts are there to qualify principles. Desires and actions have a rational basis. Indeed value experience is not abstract and wholly cognitive in nature because it is primarily volitional and conative. Supervening property is realized in facts through decisions regarding principles. To say that they are only volitional and conative is to reduce them to emotive expressions, which can be objected to. Any decision regarding principle presupposes certain factors to be kept in mind such as facts of the matter and possible effects, which might take place with the application of principles. One's decisions regarding principles have to be reflective in nature so that the decided principle could become a type rather than remaining at the individualistic level. Realisation of principles in terms of decisions renders its applications universalizably which is logical in character.

Indeed, values cannot be reduced to facts but do not have any relevance without facts. The two are not casually or logically related, however, a rational bridge between the two cannot be denied. Facts having descriptive meaning are liable to judgement as true or false and may also be liable to value judgements because of their supervenient property, as good or bad. Value words are efficacious only because of their universalizable factor, which we realise in facts as justifying or supporting reasons. Value experience, therefore, is not individualistic; it is something which may be subject to rational justification.

Now let us examine how God could be assumed as a value experience. It is indisputable that God's existence is not a factual claim because it is purely a matter of faith. However, many arguments may be given in favour of the existence of God for its justification. And we find that no absolutely satisfactory rational justification can be given. However, it is possible in the case of values. The conception of God, which is necessarily affective-conative in nature, cannot be paralleled with value-words. Value-experience is certainly not based on faith, for it is not a blind step taken in favour the principles of value. Values are not created as ideally possible standards but are said to locate their status in facts, which justifies their supervenient property. God is something above finite natural phenomenal reality whereas values are very much engrossed in facts. If God is extra temporal and voluntary act of faith then how can it be evaluative? Evaluation involves both prescription and description. God's experience is not open to evaluation whereas value-experience is necessarily evaluative. What is possible in the arena of ideals is not subjective, but something which is realized by someone in the process of actualisation of the possible latent dispositional prototype in value which is certainly not to transcend the given but to actualise something which was already there as a disposition or potentiality. Value has a potentiality to actualise the possible, to transform itself according to its model other than what it appears to be; as for example a seed has a disposition to grow like a tree but that is not irreal or a contrafactual state. Faith is the basis of religious experience but reason is the basis of value-experience. No understanding based on faith is valuational. To say that religious experience is free because it can be realized only by faith is to make a mockery of freedom. Decisions or arguments based on faith can never be free. Faith may or may not commit one rightly to action which one ought to perform or finds obligated to perform or refrain from acting in a particular way. Any judgement pertaining to the worthiness of an action which is acknowledged by others too, certainly is not based on faith but on reason which makes it prescriptive and regulative in nature. Any standard of judgement having intrinsic worth is understood rationally, intuitively or through rational insight but not by faith.

The existential way of realizing God by free choice is open textured and raises questions on the nature of such a free choice which is based on sheer faith. It is presumed by the author that divine experience is indubitable and transpersonal in character. Such a claim obviates the necessity to enquire as to what exactness and certainty can we talk of its indubitability and to what extent can it be a transpersonal experience? If experience of God is personal and founded in faith then how can it be transpersonal? If it is based on faith then such expressions as total and ultimate meaning of existence becomes pseudo. Another problem that arises in this chapter is: Whether such a transpersonal experience of God can be realized through actions. Be that as it may then how can such a personal experience of God speaks for, (1) axiological universality; (2) praxiological obligatoriness; and (3) should act as a standard of judgement of ultimate intrinsic worth? (p. 85) Do we realize it through actions with such an ultimate standard that we start or perform? Will it not create a vicious circle? Are we saying that first there has to be an ultimate and existing reality to be realised through transcendence of phenomenal existence and then talk of value-bound issues in its light? Do we realise first values in conflicting situations and then experience of God in their framework? I find myself totally confused due to the several terms used by the author without defining them adequately. Other terms like 'will' and 'irreal' also need further elaboration in their use and application.

To sum up I would submit to the view that it is only through the consciousness of man's limitations and finitude that man can posit God as the highest and infinite being. The idea of incompleteness suggests the idea of completeness not as a matter of faith but as a matter of understanding through reason. The conception of perfection, as a highest value I think is not to be called as divine experience. Highest value may be regarded as the locus of all perfection and source of self enrichment and self realisation and this need not be God. Do we really require God for this perfection which may be conceived as an ideal for reconciliation of diverse values, which suggest as an ideal of harmony? Such a harmony can be thought of without there being God. Supervenience does not suggest anything divine or perfect in nature. Therefore, we may say that God and Value are conceived independent of each other. Values are not something that we experience individually but are also found to be appropriate for judging human actions of a type and, therefore, they are prescriptive and universalizable. Whereas God may be conceived by faith, which abandons any kind of judgement through rational justification. My contention centres around the point that the relation between the two is superficial and the supposed bond between them is insignificant and uncalled for.

REFERENCES

1. Aristotle, *Nicomachean Ethics,* Tr. By J.A.K. Thomson, Penguin Books, 1963, p. 269.
2. *Ibid.,* p.36

Chapter – 5

Sigmund Freud on Morality

Chandra Kanta Sharma

Sigmund Freud has brought about an approach to the problem of morality from quite a new angle. For the first time the individual psyche has come to be analysed less with the object of salvation than of sanity. He generalizes on his own limited experience; his empirical data are his mentally deranged patients and on this basis, he builds up a theory of psychology of morality, without stopping to consider whether he is justified in generalizing from pathological to normal. Yet, Freud recognizes that the odd way in which his patients have expressed their symptoms is an indication of the alienation. Compelled by a desire to understand, he probes deeper and is the first to demonstrate the shortcomings in the attempts to understand individual and social behaviour on the basis of human reason and intellect alone.

Freud has always been receptive to new ideas; that is why he has continually kept modifying his theory according to his experience and learning. His psychological concepts are, by a strange historical development, fused with many scientific concepts of the nineteenth century, and at the same time he tries to fit them to his philosophical postulates. The Freudian system has developed in a historical period in which hope in science had reached its height, whatever its real achievement might have been. Science had become an object of worship—a *weltanschauung*. The belief that Freud retains till the end that science is the prime solvent of world ills tends to displace the hope that has been built of religion, political action and philosophy. Yet, Freud has not completely eliminated his science, the ideas of 'purpose', 'intuition', 'ideas' and 'morality' as expressed by his pleasure-principle and unconscious motivation. He opines that the conscience ridden person is in the grip of certain presuppositions of which he is unaware, human beings have an ineradicable social heritage of guilt. The great religions are attempts to solve the problem of guilt. It is at a bottom an attempt to reconcile the injured other through delayed obedience.[1]

While not denying the natural development of a moral sense, Freud offers little support to the religious conception of it. In this usage, conscience is an instrument of parental dominance. It is precisely the religious view of conscience as intelligent and reflective as well as passionate that here comes under attack for Freud argues that conscience is furnished by social authority and remains unreflectively at its disposal. Freedom of conscience is a contradiction in terms. "Freud's critique of conscience derives from his conception of it as a deposit of inhibitions and ideals expressive of authority originally located in the parents. But as parental authority was determined by their super-ego. Since parental authority was determined by their super-ego, the problem is referred back from ontogenesis to phylogenesis."[2] In other words, morality is based partly on necessities of society and partly on the expiations which the sense of guilt demands. Thus, Freud has an empirical conception of the origin of morality. Morality has no claim to be based on rational operation. Like religion, it is wholly the result of the formation of association and projection, because the only foundation of morality is an exterior prohibition introjected into the unconscious.[3]

Morality begins in childhood as a part of the personality development. The first source of morality is an external power, the parental authority which inhibits pleasure seeking impulses of the children. Parents influence their children by affection and punishment; punishment affects in two ways — as a threat of pain and a loss of love. This state of affairs is carried over by adults into their religious beliefs. People believe that there is a superior father-like power that rewards and punishes them. Thus, for Freud, ethics and religion have a common stem, *the father complex* originating in the Oedipal situation.

This is also applied to the phylogenetic development. The primitive man was forced by the society to restrain his pleasure seeking impulses. The norms set by the society for the protection of its members became internalised in the minds of the individuals. Conscience is basically the fear of society; it is the inner restraint of the individual who is "virtually an enemy of the culture" imposed on him.[4] Moral restraints stem from without and "majority of people obey the cultural prohibitions on these points only under the pressure of external coercion as long as it is to be feared".[5]

According to Freud, the rules of ethics should have no connection with religion, if it has to remain unmutilated and advantageous. Though religion helps in the growth of morality, it is imperative for morality now to win its own autonomy. There are various reasons for it. *First*, morality based on religion is primarily negative. This kind of morality consists of prohibitions and avoidances. *Secondly*, religious morality is too archaic for it deals with sex-taboos. And then it is too inflexible as we find in the laws of Moses and Manu. *Lastly*, religion being a mass neurosis is bound to be outgrown by man and if morality remains wedded to it, then with the disappearance of religion, morality is also likely to disappear and this would mean serious loss to human culture and civilization.[6] Human helplessness and anxiety, in the face of the dangers of life, becomes endurable by the assumption of a Providence. The function of religion is one of balancing the renunciation and satisfaction through which man tries to make his harsh life tolerable. We *believe in God for three main purposes*, viz., for exorcizing the terrors of nature, for reconciling man to the cruelty of fate and for bringing about group solidarity. Thus, God, to Freud, is a *fictitious idea* produced by self-seeking motivation.

Freud gives a violent shock to the moralists, by tracing its origin in the Oedipus complex. He shares Kant's awe and wonder at the starry heavens alone, but as for the moral conscience within us he says that "God has been guilty of an uneven and careless piece of work, for a great many men have only a limited share of it or scarcely enough to be worth mentioning". Freud's critique of conscience derives from his conception of it as a deposit of inhibitions and ideals expressive of authority originally located in the parents. But, as parental authority is determined by the super-ego, the problem is referred back from ontogenesis to phylogenesis. Thus, when we hear the censorious voice of the super-ego, we really hear some phylogenetic echoes of primitive men. Freud, thus exposes the primitive cruelty of our morality. He opines that the conscience ridden person is in the grip of certain pre-suppositions of which he is unaware. Human beings have an ineradicable social heritage of guilt. The great religions are attempts to solve the problem of guilt. Morality thus stands under the sign of guilt. It is at bottom an attempt to reconcile the injured father through delayed obedience. Man is a remorseful killer and *religion is the history of guilt*. But, why guilt at all? To this Freud opines that when an instinctual trends undergoes repression, its libidinal elements are transformed into symptoms and its aggressive components into a sense of guilt.[7] However, the guilt about which Freud speaks is above all the 'sense of guilt', a psychological, *not a moral fact*. In Christianity, the sense of guilt is characteristically a sign of augmented moral delicacy; in Freudian psychology, the sense of guilt is a source of private illness. So, as Rieff says, Freud's meaning and that of Christianity are close but completely at odds.[8] The sense of guilt as defined by Christian culture seems to Freud a sandy foundation of morality. According to him, Morality, the sadism of the super-ego, appears as a stupid alternative to "the will to power", the sadism of the ego.[9]

Freud opines that emotional ambivalence is the basis not only of taboo conscience (taboo sense of guilt) but also of the moral imperatives as formalized by Kant. Taboo conscience is probably the earliest form in which the phenomenon of conscience is met with and that is why the explanation of taboo throws light on the nature and origin of conscience. Thus, Freud regards morality as homogeneous with obsession. he sets out to determine its psychological roots. He begins by considering one of the most essential prohibitions of sexual morality — the ban on incest and asserts that the veto against incest is in the nature of a taboo.

Among the numerous controversies which are aroused by psychoanalysis, the question of Freud's negative attitude towards morality plays no minor role. Freud's morality opponents find it easy to draw the rather superficial conclusion that psychoanalysis is basically irreligious and the psychoanalysis are all atheists. Freud's view on religion are accepted or rejected too uncritically and too readily.[10] He is being attacked by the critics on moral, aesthetic, theological as well as scientific grounds.

Freud's opinion on values is often criticized on the ground that he has no right to a realm of thought not his own, because science in general has nothing to do with morality. Critics find no satisfactory reason for Freud's sudden jump into the field of morality, of values and of normative discussions, when he is basically a scientist. Moreover, the way he attacks the traditional religious theories, has damaged his image as a true scientist. This charge is definitely baseless, for we cannot fix up the boundaries of discussion for any thinker. It is impractical to think of maintaining any watertight compartment in the world of knowledge. Apart from that, religious beliefs, emotions and attitudes are part of the mind of man. Values happen to be the facts of mental life and psychology, since its task is to study the mental life, is also concerned with the examination of values as parts of aspects of mental life. How can we expect from a psychologist to pay attention only to one side of human psyche, ignoring the others, simply on the ground that they are not supposed to be as phenomenal as the others, but rather characterized to be spiritual.

Freud's views have often been misunderstood. In fact he exposed the foundations of our pseudo-morality. What goes by the name of morality is blind and irrational. It directs us to repress the instincts and produces conflict. A conflict-torn man would not have the energy for any higher striving. But Freud does not advocate triumph of instinct over moral feelings. While it is true that Freud shows evil impulses in human being, it is no less true that he also shows the powerful forces within the personality making for their censorship. Flugel suggests that according to Freud there is a higher morality which is associated with our true self. It is the morality of reason that works through the ego.[11]

A profound humanist and libertarian, Freud looks on the world only from the point of view of the individual. He sees true values only in the individual's creative forces and in his normal existence, in his aspirations for a better life. He is the great representative of the Renaissance. Broad philosophical systems and the inner empire of religion are of little value to Freud, because in them the individual seems to be lost. Anything that threatens the autonomy of the individual is treated with scepticism. He leaves the question of values to be answered by the healthy individual himself.

REFERENCES

1. Freud, S, *New Introductory Lectures on Psychoanalysis*, p. 84.
2. Chakravarty, D.K. *Self in Psycho-Analysis*, p. 38.
3. Freud, S. *Totem and Taboo*, p. 195.
4. Wolman B.B. *Contemporary Theories and System in Psychology*, p. 274.
5. Freud, S. "The Future of an Illusion", SE XXI, p. 11.
6. Mashih, Y, "Freudianism and Religion", p. 207.
7. Freud, S. *Civilization and its Discontents,* p. 132.
8. Rieff, Phillip, "Freud; The Mind of the Moralist", p. 34.
9. Freud. S, "The Economic Problems of Masochisms" Collected Papers Vol. II, p. 267.
10. Zilboorg, G. *Psychoanalysis and Religion*. p. 20.
11. Flugel, J.C. *Psychoanalytic Study of the Family*, p. 154.

Chapter – 6

Revaluating Karl Marx's Ethical Scepticism

Ranju Kumari

In the Marxist philosophy, morality has been considered as a particular form of social consciousness. The intention of Marx is very offensive as regards to traditional ethical discussion and about absolute ethical value. In other words, its approach towards traditional morality is negative, and that is why Marx is very cautious in expressing his views regarding 'duties', 'values', 'right', etc. in his ethical writings. After formulating some ethical rules in the "First International", he apologized to Engel's "though I have used words like 'duty', 'right', 'morality', etc., but the use of these words will not have any negative impact on our philosophy"[1]. It is clear that Marx did not easily accept the traditional explanation of words like 'duty' and other value concepts because he felt that the value concepts are mainly based on some ideologies which are in themselves not acceptable and as such in the very beginning of Marxist thought there appears some scepticism about traditional meaning affixed to moral language. He does not mean to say that there is no possibility of moral language in the use of terms like 'duty', etc., but in his views, the way in which their meaning has been fixed in bourgeois ideology is unacceptable.

In the modern western ethics, the study of scepticism is very important because it makes a logical effort to establish futility of normative and practical ethical discussions. Those ethicists, who accept the value of normative and practical ethical discussions, will certainly oppose this negative effort. My effort in this essay is to discuss the value of a specific ethical sceptical thought and not to clarify the usefulness of non-sceptical thought. I have, therefore, selected the Marxist sceptical views for discussion. The main reason for such selection is that the Marxist ethical scepticism is of a different nature as compared to other sceptical thoughts, because Marxist thought regards the usefulness of the normative, the metaethical and the practical ethical discussions based on a particular socio-economic philosophy which is known as "Historical Materialism". This materialistic view is also based on his unique philosophical thesis, which we call, "Dialectical Materialism".

What is unique about Marx is that he believed in an ethical discussion, which is based on a class ideology. In his views, class ideology based morality serves the purpose of capitalists. As such Marx has not only denounced capitalist morality but also all types of traditional absolute class based morality. According to Marx, as the communist revolution destroys capitalism, so also we should destroy all ideologies and ideological ethics. In views of Marx, the unnaturality of moral language is owing to ideology and so it is essential to be abolished in totality from its roots. By abolishing it, the ideological standards, which are parts of capitalistic morality, will also be abolished. In this essay my aim is to reflect upon the view that Marx should either be considered as a supporter of normative value and practical ethical scepticism in a special sense because he has never completely denounced the possibilities of normative ethics as well as ethical values, virtues and ethical application. When Marx denounces morality, he, in fact, trashes a specific ideological morality. He does not completely disregard values or value based decisions. Actually, Marx talked about complete abolition of specific morality in view of the materialistic view of the history, and nothing more than that.

According to the historical materialism, all epochs in which human society exists, it is dependent on special types of production corresponding social relations and the class division. According to the materialistic view, change in society is essential because productive capacity of the society is not static but moving and always changing. The concept of revolutionary social struggle or total revolution may be had in the background of this class struggle. It is a known fact that in a class struggle, the society breaks into classes and the situation of such a break-up is dependent on the role of different classes in production, the physical means of production and the power to control production. Thus, in the society, an ideology regarding class struggle takes birth. Hence, in an ever-changing state of social struggle, the morality of classes takes birth, and that is why Marx had to declare that "morality is just an ideology". In true sense, ideology is a dilemma, a false consciousness and as such we may call it a form of bondage. As a result, the ideologies established by the people as absolute truth by other classes. So, the capitalistic morality and normative theories established by intellectual class cannot be accepted as universally accepted ideology and it is in this context that Marx is against moral norms and values set by the capitalist class but that does not amount to his rejection of morality and moral value as such, because some of them may be free from class-ideology.

According to Ellen Wood, a critic of Marx, the ethical scepticism of Marx is based on rejection of capitalistic normativism, or it is scepticism towards the ideology of a particular class and, therefore, not scepticism at all. The problem arises if Marx accepts the common ideology of a particular class, as unethical then Marx must have to accept that in future communist societies, a number of such ideologies will develop which will be universally acceptable. But, how Marx will accept the stable universal ideologies of the future communist societies as there moral principles are themselves ideologies of working class? According to Marx an ideal communist society is a classless and exploitation free society. But in that society there will be a class of labours who will have an ideology to get total freedom from exploitation. Can we not consider this as an ideology or moral principle of the labour class? In this context, Marx holds a materialistic view to deny the existence of any specific ideology for the labour class, but so far as the fact of exploitationless state is concerned, does Marx has any way to escape from such an ideology? Can Marx deny the responsibility of the exploited class to revolt against exploitation and an ideology to get freedom from exploitation? We shall be able to get answer to these questions only after discussing the anti ideology principle of Marx.

According to Ellen on the one hand, Marx has denied Kant's morality and in this way he has denied traditional normative morality as well. But, on the other hand Marx has stressed revolution as a means of the proletarian society to achieve their desirable highest goal. This, in a wide view, is not in accordance with the Marxist non-ideological principle. From this, it is clear that though Marx did not attempt to establish any absolute ideology, even then it is not easy to call him anti-ideologist. Certainly Marx has not accepted the moral principles or ideologies established by the ruling class as a standard, but the principle he has established for the freedom of the proletariat from bondage or exploitation and for the future of the humanity is also an ideology. We cannot deny this by mere play of words or distortion of Marx.

According to Kai Nelson, Marx has certainly accepted that morality in any form such as moral socialism if it is forced upon any society, how much great that may be, it will always misguide the proletariats because they will be in illusion that this ideology of freedom is absolutely necessary and sufficient and thus, they will not develop any revolutionary thought and cannot progress on the path of total Revolution by themselves.

From the above discussion it is clear that there is contradiction in the normative thoughts of Marx. We can say that the normative scepticism of Marx nurture contradiction between ethical and anti-ethical, ideologies but in reality does not shed little doubt on ethical ideals or norms. Thus, this view of Marx in connection with proletariat ideology is concerned with the expansion of the ideology of socialists and not with the expansion of the ethical normative principles we know. Hence, it appears that scepticism of Marx is not similar to what we call normative scepticism, because in the normative scepticism there is formal non-acceptance of absolute moral standards and not of the non-existence of moral standards of a particular class.

Nelson says, "In social anthropology, to talk about a society's ideology is to talk about a society's belief system."[2] If the views of Nelson are acceptable, then it will become essential to explain the ethical scepticism of Marx in the context of recent analysis as only scepticism related to bourgeoisie ethical faith.

For this reason Nelson argued that "have morality, like law and religion, does ideological work and has a conservative system supporting role through an extensive and beguiling mystification ideology, while purporting to be the exact opposite, is one of the techniques of domination of the ruling class. Ideology helps in various ways to reconcile people to their fate in the established order by convincing them, among other things, that any hope they have for substantive change is a wild and possibly dangerous utopia"[3]. Ideology in the form of superstructure or in the form of ideology does only one thing in human life, either it can give a holy instruction or for a better world it can become a decisive holy purpose. In this sense morality is our fate and we have been compromising with the fate. Though, originally this is the view of Freud, Marx has presumed this as an ideology of ruling class. From this point of view, Marx has called morality an ideology and in his view the total trust (or stock of) morality has been scattered and broken because it is not the real morality but merely the ideology of a particular class serving its purpose.

In my view, in the statements of Nelson, two things are clear — firstly, there is no need to consider Marxist view of morality as immoral, subjective, relativism; and secondly, in the views of Marx, only value related objectivism is classified and as such it is somewhat difficult to call him metaethical sceptic. Nelson has described Marx as a "Contextual Objectivist". According tc Nelson — "Historical materialism supports a contextualism that in turn is compatible with a robust objectivism in ethics. If these "eternal principles" are thought to have any determinate substance, they will not sit well with historical materialism. But this is not at all to reject a contextualist objectivism" [4]. However, in the context of historical materialism, non-legitimacy of capitalistic system has been accepted by Marx and by that denying the capitalistic moral system, Marx himself established a new system according to which ethical scepticism has a particular meaning. We may say that Marx did not consider any moral standard (normative) such as traditional teleology because it is essentialistic. He had doubt as to whether these ideals of exploitist class will serve any purpose of exploited class. But from any angle, he was not an opponent of ethics (In the words of Ellen Wood). In a specific view (as Nelson said) – Marx can be considered as a founder of "Socialistic Moral" and actually in this sense he established "Communistic Ideals" and took value-based decisions.

On the basis of Nelson's views, a number of writers in enthusiasm have called Marx as "*Manavtavadi*", and also supporter of communistic ethics. They say if the views of Nelson are accepted then can we not call Marx in a special sense as "*Prayojanvadi*". Has he not accepted his absolute goal as "total liberation of man from exploitation", "freedom of man" or establishment of the great communism? Did he not take value-based decisions and did he not explain the meanings of words like holy and duties in view of these standards?

In my view, many over-enthusiastic ethicists, if they understand the views of Nelson properly, there is hardly an ethical scepticism in Marx. Nelson has classified that he considered Marx as a supporter of "Communalist Ideology" from specific socialistic view and not from the current normative ethical view. It cannot be equated with a normative ethical thought such as teleology. In reality, Marx has opined to abolish traditional absolutist teleology and deontologist which are to him superstructure or ideology of a particular class denied from traditions and they are the sources of dehumanization and alienation by accepting these ideals as source of alienation. It is clear why Marx declared them as immoral and why for this matter, Marx cannot be called as anti-moral. On this basis it is understood that to call Marx hurriedly as a supporter of ethical theory such as humanism is mistaken. Similarly, according to Marx, these are never absolute universal ideals which can be accepted as stable superstructure in all changing systems and can be thus taken as the basis for evaluating human voluntary actions. Further, communism as such is not a teleological normative theory; rather it is a non-ethical ideal from social, economic and political standpoints. However, on this basis, we cannot say that, therefore, Marx is anti-moral or ethical sceptic.

Now, if we accept this non-ethical ideals of Marx, then can we call Marx as sceptic from a practical moral view or is he a sceptic in a specific sense only? We have to understand that a solution of value based practical problems such as abortion cannot be found in Marx, who mainly aimed at the exploitation free society. Naturally, if all the absolute normatives have been eliminated then how can there be a solution of these problems? When the freedom from exploitation is the social, economic and political goal, then by accepting this as an ethical standard, how there can be a solution of practical problems?

According to Marx when moral problems surrounding the society can be understood only by knowing the situation of man in the context of production and exchange, the problem is, how does he solve ethical crises like abortion? In reality, Marx has challenged for complete freedom from exploitation and not for the solution of one or many value based problems. According to Marx, there can neither be freedom from exploitation nor solution of value based practical problems on the basis of any ideological revolution. Now on the basis of these thoughts, can we call Marx as a supporter of ethical sceptic?

Ethicists of the era of established ethical normativism talked about the solution of practical problems in the contemporary ethics either by artificial thought experiments or by ethical corroboration. As I understand, in the normative scepticism of Marx, all value based practical problems cannot be solved on the basis of socialist ideology. As Marx is completely anti-ideological, there is no question of artificial thought experiment in his ethical system. On the other hand, it is useless to talk about experiment in any normative discourse or normative ethical discussion in the society.

Marx has never denied that value based decisions cannot be taken if the freedom of the proletariat from exploitation is possible.

According to Marx, ethical crises in slavery, human exploitation, suffering, alienation, separatism, sin as disvalues are totally unfortunate and improper. But, this does not mean that he has taken this decision on the basis of any ethical norm and that all the practical problems have been solved on that basis. We have to remember that as a part of revolution of thoughts, if the solutions of value-based problems are to be found out through social discourse, then the primary thing is the freedom from exploitation, which is possible through complete social and political revolution. In this way when exploitation free society exists in order to prevent all unethical practices, ethical discourse is needed, but for that there need not be any absolute bourgeois ideology.

In this way, the practical ethical scepticism of Marx is scepticism in a specific sense. It is actually to express doubt about the practical value of bourgeois ideology. To conclude it is improper to call Marx as ethical sceptic, a subjectivist, relativist and authoritarian. Hopefully, we also get the answer that Marx has not established any fixed ideology for the freedom of proletariat from exploitation.

REFERENCES

1. Readers may find this discussion in Peter Singer (ed.) *A, Companion to Ethics* in an essay by Ellen Wood entitled "Marx Against Morality", Blackwell, p. 511.
2. Nelson, Kai, *Marxism and the Moral Point of New Morality, Ideology and Historical Materialism*, Westview Press, London, 1959, p 123
3. *Ibid.*, p. 128.
4. *Ibid.*, p. 130.

Chapter –7

Ethics: An Existential Approach

Indu Sarin

Existentialism puts forth the problems of ethics in a new perspective, challenging all the traditional standpoints. Existential fundamental standpoint is presented in sharp contrast to conventional morality. It rejects cut and dried formulations in the realm of morality. Existential ethics can be called an '*ethic of openness*', which does not usher in moral principles fixed and crystallized in advance. Consequently many of the ethical problems analyzed by the ethical thinkers, have not been tackled by the existentialists or seen differently. The existentialists abolish the distinction between the ontology of man and analysis of morals. The being of man is characterized in terms of his decisions, choices and actions.

Existential philosophy is a protest in the name of individuality against the traditional rationalistic thought. It reflects on the problems that are directly related to concrete human existence rather than on those that are abstract and speculative. According to it, philosophy does not merely involve the principles of pure ratiocination or deductive procedure out of certain postulates and general principles. It is also a quest for man's creative worth

Existentialism is a philosophy from the first person perspective, i.e., it is an exploration of the interiority of human existence. Its aim is not the achievement of a self-consistent closed system of ideas. It rather attempts to awaken man to his own authentic human situation. Any attempt to schematize it [human situation] exhaustively is the falsification of situation itself and destruction of individual authentic possibilities. It rejects the very idea that the individual reality can be merely grasped through intellectual construction, however logically sound such a construction may be.

The individual is ever constructing and reconstructing himself by acts in concrete situations and defies by his dynamic character, any characterization. He is not merely a spectator but an actor who is actually engaged in the problems. It is the whole spectrum of existence known directly and concretely in the very act of existing that the Existentialists are trying to explore. Man is not only a thinking subject but also an initiator of action and centre of feeling.

In Existentialism, subjectivity is looked upon as the pre-condition of all analysis of objectivity. Man is viewed as the creator of all standards and evaluations. The often quoted statement of Kierkegaard – "truth is subjectivity" implies that truth is not something that is outside the individual, as an end product. It is to be realized within the subject, to be assimilated in inwardness. Subjectivity is not to be viewed in psychophysical dimension. It is characterized in terms of creative acts.

Man's intrinsic worth is not the result of the material body or a mere rational ability but is the outcome of autonomy, authenticity of the individual and his genuine encounters with others, which constitute the groundwork of Existential ethics. The individual is in continuous process of transcendence, which is a transition from being an object to pure subject. There is a shift from heteronomy to autonomy, from passivity to creativity. To be a person is to be one's own distinctive self and to be one who relates himself to others in an authentic manner. Existential ethics advocates the intrinsicity of man in treating him as well others as ends.

Existentialism avoids errors of both the approaches — naturalistic and idealistic. The former equates normative assertions to factual assertions, the latter reduces values to fixed patterns.

Both the approaches fail to recognize the autonomy and creativity of the individual. Values are not transcendent given independently of human subjectivity. They are rooted in human historicity. There is no *a priori* ought or obligatoriness in existential ethics. This view of morality imparts a good deal of responsibility to the individual who is to act in accordance with the inner urge that impels him to act. The ability to give a creative response to the situation is the essence of human freedom and responsibility.

In the analysis of existential freedom, the Existentialists are not interested in the controversy of determinism and indeterminism. The deterministic picture of man completely denies free will. The scientific picture of man as mentioned in the chapter on human condition is deterministic. It attempts to control and modify the different aspects of a human being. Though the Existentialists reject the deterministic picture of man yet they do not advocate indeterminism, which may lead to anarchy. Freedom for them, implies self-determinism in the sense of self-control. The individual is responsible for what he does. He is gifted with free critical self-reflexive nomothetic [rule making] capabilities.

It is the individual's choice and freedom that gives meaning to the situation. Laws and rules are considered to be external impositions, forcing the individual to a predetermined pattern and preventing him to realize his unique authentic selfhood. To be authentic is to choose oneself [the choice be not imposed on the individual] and to own the responsibility for one's actions. To be authentic is to confront oneself and not to take shelter in excuses. Authenticity is the cornerstone of existential ethics.

Existential ethics is a creative quest of man's authentic being. The whole question of ethics revolves around the question — 'how can I become an authentic individual?' To become an authentic individual is to become aware of the innermost depth of one's individuality. What this authenticity means to the individual is ceaseless rising above dogmatism or conformity to an abstract formulation of roles and obligations. Acts demanded of me by external norms are not mine. Hence, they are inauthentic. Any attempt at submerging oneself in collectivity is a flight into inauthentic existence, which is a state of 'being outside oneself'. Since man is explained in terms of decisions, choices and actions, there is nothing like 'I am' or my 'intrinsic being' over and above what I do in the course of my striving. Authenticity is realized in decisions and actions. It is man as a distinct being who is free and authentic, defines his existence through choices.

A free act is not arbitrary, the individual knows what he is doing and without such knowledge there is no freedom. Freedom does not mean lawlessness. Existential choice is not conformity to the external norm but it does not mean that it is irrational. To be free means to rise above one's impulses and act in a rational way. The non-capriciousness is analyzed by Jaspers who holds that the 'decision for reason' is also the 'decision for freedom'. If one renounces reason, he renounces his freedom also. So it is wrong to think that Jaspers thinks irrational acts to be free acts. For him, if one renounces the 'freedom for reason', one loses one's capacity to appreciate and think of freedom. Existential choice is grounded on self-imposed principles.

Jaspers holds that there are three conditions of freedom — knowledge, arbitrariness and law. But freedom cannot be reduced to any one of them. A free act is based on knowledge of the whole situation and one's own self but mere knowledge does not make one free. Freedom is revealed in the unique and temporal decisions of the individual. Arbitrariness is the condition of freedom in the sense that a free act is not calculated, it is spontaneous but it is not capricious even. For Jaspers,"knowledge does not make me free as yet, but without knowledge there is no freedom".[1] A free act is based on the knowledge of the whole situation and one's own self but mere knowledge does not make one free. Freedom is revealed in the unique and temporal decisions of the individual. Arbitrariness is the condition of freedom in the sense that a free act is not calculated but it is spontaneous. According to Jaspers, ". . . . arbitrariness does not amount to freedom but without an arbitrary act there is no freedom.".[2]

Freedom presupposes law in the sense that it is not mere conformity to an external law. To Jaspers, "A rationally unequivocal formula cannot but become rigid"[3]. There is no choice without decision, no decision without some kind of ought and no ought without a being, and our being is always capable of reflecting an alternative to any well justified decision.

The achievement of freedom is a continuous process, it has to be renewed constantly. Freedom is given in the beginning but a great struggle is required in order to keep it. I have to find myself upon the decisions consciously taken by me. The individual is endowed with the freedom to choose, he can adopt for himself whatever life he wants, whether the life of reason or the life of passion, it is for the individual to keep his freedom or lose it.

Freedom implies commitment and responsibility. Jaspers implies that the greatest urge that man in the modern age is, the "urge to be freed from freedom". He wants to seek shelter in objectivity and hand over the responsibility for his action to some causal necessity.

Existential norms are not universal in general sense. They are universal-specific. First, they are universal because they have got potentiality of being realizable by each individual. Secondly, existential norms are specific because they have to be realized by the individual in his concrete, specific situations.

It is the choice of the individual in situation that is most important to Jaspers. The individual for him is ceaselessly in situations. One situation may give rise to the other. The question is — what is the situation? The situation is a state of affairs in which the individual finds himself. It can be natural as well as man-made. Situation for Jaspers is "a sense-related reality — neither psychological nor physical, but both in one". It can be seen as advantage, opportunity or obstacle. It may involve beneficial factors, undertaking risks, shortcomings, failings, possibilities and impediments in the diverse phases of human existence. The situation is not something fixed, one can modify or change it or create new situations.

Existential ethics is called as *situation ethics* in which the course of action is in accordance with the unique situation in which the agent finds himself. It is dynamic and future-oriented, i.e., choice and action is in accordance with the new situations. Each situation is unique, it is to be viewed from its own perspective

Human actions are associated with one situation or the other. Different people can view the same situation from different perspectives. For example the biologist, economist, anthropologist and historian views the same situation from different angles. The situation is not completely surveyed. It is very difficult to have full knowledge of the situation. In retrospect, one may come to know some of the possibilities, which one may not have visualized earlier. The advanced knowledge also may help the individual to control and modify the situation but one cannot know the situation completely.

Values cannot be justified in terms of rational methods. In case of value conflicts, it is not possible to have an objective criterion for articulating value-profiles. How to prefer one value to the other? No amount of empirical knowledge helps one to make the preference unproblematic. Thus, preference made is not in accordance to any objective paradigm as there is no common denominator to judge the diverse value-profiles. Realization of value is the realization of one's self in making choices and doing actions. Because of the complexity of the situations, it is difficult to have a rigid framework of values.

Value is not an abstract ideal, it is to be realized through temporal encounters of one's being. Sartre takes the example of a student who faces the moral dilemma between the choice of attending his sick mother and joining the French forces. No Christian doctrine can help him to make the choice. He himself has to take the decision. The moral dilemma occurs when one has to choose between two intrinsic values. There is no conflict between the intrinsic values *per se*. The conflict arises only in the situation. All the values cannot be simultaneously realized.

The individual has to encounter the condition of preferring between two intrinsic values. In the problematic situations, the individual himself has to take the decision without a higher court of appeal. The self-reliant individual is not just a creature of impulses and habits, he makes his decisions resolutely in a responsible manner. He is guided by his conscience illumined by the knowledge of the situation. He impartially pursues the best in the light of the values chosen by him.

Subjectivity of norms, however, does not relegate the ethical issues to the realm of arbitrariness. Subjectivity is not to be viewed in psychophysical dimension that is impulsive and follows the natural inclinations devoid of deliberations. It appears to be free but in fact it is determined by the psychophysical dimension of man and can lead to wrong actions. It is constantly hankering after the things — possessed with the desire to get one thing or the other. The unfulfilment of these things is a source of agony to the individual. The reflex activity of the organism results in involuntary actions. One becomes the victim of the succession of sequential episodes of one's empirical life. The psychological will is not clear of its goal and is unable to make a distinction between illusion and reality.

Subjectivity thus is exercise of freedom both from psychological determinism and objective social order. Although man is necessarily linked to the world and cannot withdraw from it into some self-contained region of being, which is purely his, he should not get lost in the world and sink to the level of brute material object. Man's circumstances are given to him but his attitudes and perspectives for confronting them are undetermined. The meaning of the world is constituted by the subject.

Subjectivity is characterized in terms of creative acts. The individual deliberately chooses a particular course of action, he is aware of his choice and action. This makes ethical choice meaningful and authentic. Ethical choice implies commitment and responsibility by the individual.

Existential freedom is the exercise of volition; it involves deliberation by the subject. Jaspers says,

> Freedom exists as volition. The will is not just the forward-driving activity; its freedom is that it wills itself.[11]

Volition enables one to rise beyond the realm of empirical existence. The former is in contradistinction to the instinctive and impulsive activities, generates intrinsic values. The will that wills itself is volition that involves free will. It has a freedom to choose between good and evil. The question of evil arises at the level of free will. The good will remains free in the real sense, as it is not bound by the psychic or external factors, it frees itself from the chains of historicity. The evil will gets bound by the historicity. It is only through choice that the question of good and evil arises. One can lose freedom by choosing evil or retain it by choosing good. Jaspers maintains :

> To opt for good frees it for infinite unfoldment, to opt for evil, freely to relinquish freedom, entangles it in a negation of all being out of itself.[5]

The free will can will not to will. It can will and nil the willing. It can generate good as well as evil. The question of evil arises only where there is free will. It has a choice to choose good as well as bad. Existential choice is not motivated by the strongest motive. Jaspers states :

> Existential choice is not motivated by the strongest motive. A choice is not preponderance of a force — for I can decide for the psychologically weakest motive. . . a choice is a decision I make on grounds of see-sawing reflection. . . . At this moment, I am not moved by motives but face to face with them.[6]

Existential freedom is the expression of free will. Since it is not at the empirical level, it cannot be scientifically analyzed. There cannot be any calculus for measuring existential freedom. The latter is in the realm of Existenz distinguished from the empirical existence. The "will that wills itself" is the intrinsic power of Existenz governed by the idea, which is the outcome of self-reflection. This is grand will. It is important to recognize close convergence between critical self-generating values and their progressive discovery of their praxiological force and self-actualization. In this sense, what Jaspers is calling "willing the will" is intelligible and it is this which is the progenitor of both" self-transcendence" Existenz and the grand vision of one's moment in eternity. The "will that wills itself" implies self-awareness implying clear consciousness of one's strivings. Jaspers says :

> . . . the will that wills itself is the active assurance of being which my volition of something derives from the ground of freedom. . . My will is no mere sense of reactivity or striving insistence, nor is it the pragmatically indifferent visualization of an objective content. It is the union of both, rather: the lucidity of the goal at which my striving aims.[7]

Reason in contradistinction to impulses plays a significant role in articulating purposes and goals, discriminating between illusion and reality, good and bad. But it is not merely an intellectual formal exercise. The idea [mentioned above is not objectified timeless idea, it rather works in and through historicity. Volition for Jaspers works only with the discriminating thought that results in actions. The grand will gets content from Existenz. It has a passion to concretize the decisions. Jaspers holds :

> The grand will, too is impassioned, but never by finite goal alone, its passion comes within the goal, and simultaneously with it, from a never adequately objectified idea.[8]

The grand will is a strong will, which involves (1) intensity [that moves the individual to take the decision], (2) tenacity [persistence in the course of time, sticking to a thing and carrying it through]. (3) vehemence [taking into account the situation, taking sublime risks and decisions and not conforming to anything fixed], and (4) unconditioned volition [intrinsicity]. The strength of the moment, tenacity and vehemence flows from the unconditionality.

The grand will does not indulge in fanciful imagination but takes decisions in confrontation with reality. It is aware of the fact that it has no power over the entire world. It has a horizon and commands no absolute insights into reality. It rests on seeing, not the whole but perspectives in the whole — and on seeing them not in entirety but in time. Perspectives are tied to historicity.

The grand will is aware of its limitations. It is to be exercised in temporality and historicity, which reveal the finitude of human existence. One can will this thing or that but not everything at once. One occupies a particular place in the whole. To quote Jaspers :

> I cannot will everything at once. There are also good many things, which exclude each other in the sequence of time. The situation requires spatial and temporal choices. Since we cannot will the whole, since we are capable only of willing within the whole — for anything else would be an empty wishing unrelated to reality — we are real only at our place in the whole, in the active performance of our narrow, finite realization. It is consciousness of this irremovable limit that lends depth to Existenz.[9]

The grand will listens to the voice of conscience that discriminates between good and evil. Free will is the source of both good and evil. The conscience discriminates between good and evil. The grand will chooses the good. For Jaspers, the voice of conscience is not the voice of God. He states :

> The voice of conscience is not God's voice. It is precisely when conscience speaks, the deity is silent, that it remains hidden. My conscience points me toward transcendence but leaves me on my own.[10]

The resolution is the answer to the voice of conscience, which must result in a fulfilled absolute consciousness. Jaspers further adds,

> Conscience is the supreme authority at the turning point, but it is not what fulfils us. We depend upon another source. . . . the original factor, stirred by the thought movement and subject to the authority, is reflected in a fulfilled absolute consciousness.[11]

The fulfilled absolute consciousness is the realization of the certainty of unconditionality. It is attained through imagination, love and faith. Imagination here does not mean indulging in fantasies. It means that one is not tied to the facticity but goes beyond it. It signifies contra-factuality of human consciousness. It subdues the dissipation of locality through creative reflexivity. One can visualize alternative perspectives. There is suffering in the world but one can see beauty in it. The experience of love is fulfilling and implies the unconditional presence of the other. It involves passion and yearning for the other. It implies personal relationship transcending egotism — transcendence in immanence. Faith implies certainty of one's being and its goals. There is no room for doubt.

For Jaspers, unconditionality does not involve rejections of the conditions of life by taking the absolute step of suicide or by religious denial of the world in search of Deity. It means confronting the situation and not to be victimized by it.This is transcendence in immanence. It is the act of transcending that makes consciousness as absolute leading to the realization of meaning and value. The absolute consciousness is realized historically through freedom.

The absolute consciousness is the embodiment of axiological praxis in terms of projects and ideas that constitute the person's overarching identity, which formulates through his self-deliberating pursuit of values. It is what Jaspers calls 'willing oneself', which is intelligible and progenitor of both 'self-transcendence', Existenz and the grand vision of one's moment in eternity. It is at the same time the realization of limitations. The individual does not enjoy absolute freedom.

REFERENCES

1. K. Jaspers, *Philosophy*, Vol. 2, trans. E.B.Ashton, The University of Chicago Press, Chicago, 1970, p. 156.
2. *Ibid.*
3. *Ibid.*, p.157.
4. *Ibid.*, p.133.
5. *Ibid.*, p. 151.
6. *Ibid.*, p. 134.
7. *Ibid.*, p.133-34.
8. *Ibid.*, p. 141.
9. *Ibid.*, p. 143.
10. *Ibid.*, p.237.
11. *Ibid.*, p.241.

Chapter – 8

Sartre and Ethics

A.K. Tandon

Sartre's greatest impact was as a passionate moralist, yet he failed to provide us any complete work on ethics. Though committed himself and ready to judge in most scathing terms, the behaviour of others, he finds no objective ground for his judgements. It is not that he did not recognize the need to construct an ethical theory to come out of this ambiguity. In fact, he promised for such a work in the concluding paragraph of his 'Being and Nothingness' and tried to work it out thrice, in 1945, 1965 and 1975 respectively. But he considered these attempts as failures and never intended to publish those notes. He even abandoned his highly effective manifesto of 'humanistic ethics'. 'Existentialism is Humanism'. But Sartre's posthumous publications can certainly throw some light on the dilemma faced by him in defining his ethics. In this chapter, an attempt is being made to find out if a coherent theory of ethics can be constructed on the basis of all his writing published before and after his death.

What discouraged Sartre from publishing his theory of morals apart from his political preoccupations was his awareness of the futility of such project? In 'Being and Nothingness', Sartre recognizes the philosophical impasse produced by an attempt to derive prescription from description when he says:

"Ontology cannot itself formulate moral precepts."[1]

Sartre expresses clear doubts about the value of what ethical systems seek to establish:

> "The ethical moment aims at culminating itself on behalf of a calm plenitude. The contradiction of ethics is that it requires its own disappearance ultimately, the prescriptions of the ethical will become social reflexes; the identity of Being and Good, which existed at the starting point and which one finds again at the finish will entail the disappearance of values."[2]

In an important footnote to Saint Genet, Sartre states the impossibility of living an ethical moment:

> "Any ethics which does not explicitly profess that it is impossible today contributes to the bamboozling and alienation of man. The ethical 'problem' arises from the fact that Ethics is for us inevitable and at the same time impossible. Action must give itself ethical norms in this climate of non-transcendale impossibility."[3]

Thus, 'morality', Sartre proclaims, takes place in an atmosphere of failure. [4]

Moreover, Sartre's refusal of an essential human nature renders any attempt to ground a universal ethics inappropriate. Keen awareness of dangers involved in such an exercise kept him away from publishing a major ethical study. Yet his three abortive attempts, one after "Being and Nothingness"[5] another subsequent to 'Critique of Dialectical Reason[6] and finally in collaboration with his friend Benny Levy[7] few years before his death, bear testimony to his concern for moral questions and dilemmas throughout his whole life. We can read Sartre's whole work as a long meditation on the subject.

As there is no standard version of Sartre's ethics, his thoughts on morality can be culled from his conception of freedom, values, and human relationships and of ideal society. As such, *we can identify three distinct phases of his ethics*: earlier *ethics of authenticity*, later social ethics of dealienation, and last *ethics of the 'Family Idiot'* and last interviews. For Sartre, moral questions are also political questions. Hence, his moral views should be studied in this perspective only.

Sartre, in his earlier writings, does not accept the objectivity of morality. He, not only denies moral absolutes in involving Reason or God, but also determinism of any sort which often accompanies such denial. Morality, for him, is purely a human affair.

"Whether God exists or does not exist, morality is an affair 'between men' and God has no right to poke his nose in. On the contrary, the existence of morality, far from proving God, keeps him at a distance, since it is a personal structure of human reality. The second consequence is that there is no way to determine the prescriptions of that morality, except by determining the nature of human reality. We must take care here not to fall into the error, which consists in deriving values from facts. For human reality is not a fact.[8]

Thus, value for Sartre, is not a fact of this world but is only developed in the activity of human life. Man gives meaning to his life as it is lived and this meaning is related to value. But there is no natural choice for a particular value. Its foundation is freedom of man. Sartre admits that his ontology cannot formulate ethics. As there are no absolute values and no eternal rules of conduct, it is impossible to guide the actions of an individual. Only an action chosen in the intensity of the experience of freedom is moral and an action not chosen in this way is immoral. Sartre calls it authentic action and defines authenticity as following.

"Authenticity, it is most needless to say, consists in having a true and lucid consciousness of the situation in assuming the responsibility and risks that it involves, in accepting it in pride or humiliation, sometimes in horror and hate."[9]

But, such a concept of authenticity fails to distinguish moral from immoral choices made in social situation and converts the individual into purely subjective witness. A criminal's act can be as authentic as that of a priest. Probably, realizing this difficulty, Sartre hints in the 1946 essay: "The choice of authenticity appears to be moral decision."[10]

But to be called a moral concept, it has to be one of uttermost inwardness without any social content like Kant's categorical imperative. It still lacks concrete objective criterion for identifying and prescribing authentic acts. It seems that here Sartre is *offering us an ethical style*, not the content. His essay, *Existentialism is a Humanism*, though disowned by Sartre later, is an attempt to provide a positive content to his earlier ethics of authenticity. The argument runs as follows: Man is absolutely free and makes his own nature by his free choice, he is totally responsible for his choice, in choosing for himself he chooses for all mankind. This optimism is in direct contrast to Sartre's earlier pessimism of man as a useless passion. It gave wide popularity to his humanistic ethics. But it was left with the objection that willing one's own freedom need not entail willing that of everyone else. Thus Sartre, here fails to provide systematic foundations to its startling pronouncements. But, as pointed out by Flynn[11] *three value concepts — humanism, solidarity and a new understanding* of freedom — developed by Sartre in other essays can fill conceptual gaps.

In 'Cahiers pour une morale' Sartre sets his task of evolving an atheistic ethics which recognizes its paradoxical nature and is concrete. He refers to a paradox between *lukewarm moral* instinct and *self-centred moral analysis*. Moreover, no amount of reflection can ever produce moral certainty. But this very impossibility, in Sartre's opinion, makes human morality possible. The experience of failure in various forms may lead us towards purifying reflexion, which in turn may lead to authenticity. This, failure can be a possible route to conversion. In 'Cahiers' Sartre replaces negative quest for being of 'Being and nothingness' with a project of action which easily overcomes the dialectic of sincerity and bad faith Sincerity involves an attempt to be true to oneself which is for Sartre merely an imaginary construct. Authenticity, on the other hand, involves a recognition of one's project, Sincerity is ruled out because it focuses on what I am. Authenticity focuses on what I want . . . . It is the refusal to define myself by what I am (Ego), but rather by what I want. [12]

The definition of Authenticity as project changes the pessimistic ethical picture of 'Being and Nothingness', which can be said to contain description of human relations before conversion. As conversion seems to be a distinct possibility, Sartre elaborates potential relations with others in some detail and writes at length about love, joy, generosity and sacrifice. Now, human conflict is no longer viewed as an ontological necessity. It is seen rather associated historically with alienation. Sadomasochistic character of love is not denied but considered to be only half the picture, the other half being authentic love which involves recognition of the aims and world view of the other without any attempt to appropriate them.

On page 486 of 'Morale' Sartre posits a hierarchy of values leading up to freedom. Values (purity, innocence, race, sincerity, etc.) that crush freedom under being are at the lowest level. Intermediary value (nobility, virility, sexual values, etc.) and social values come in the middle. Values of subjectivity (passion, pleasure, responsibility, creation generosity etc.) that enhance freedoms are at the top.

In 'Cahiers' Sartre accords important status to 'conversion after which morality will be possible. In the first page he writes:

> 'One cannot carry out conversion on one's own. In other words morality is possible only if everyone is moral' [13]

Conversion no longer appears merely as a kind of purifying reflection of an individual, but rather a social phenomenon with clear political implications. Thus, ethics cannot be considered to be an individual enterprise.

Sartre accepts that social revolution depends upon moral conversion but refuses to give primacy to either. It is utopian to expect conversion of all at once. Social change must make moral change more likely which may, in turn, bring about social revolution. Here Sartre distances himself away from Marx Kant and even Hegel for their disregard for individual specificity due to totalizing aims. In 'Saint Genet' he brings out the incompatibility between absolute moral imperatives and complex society. Sartre uses Genet to show the inadequacy of both conventional morality and Kant. To him conventional morality is alienating and acceptance of an original foundation would mean the end of freedom. Therefore, a pure morality is not only impossible but also unthinkable.

Our discussion of Sartre's earlier ethical reflection reveals the internal contradictions of an attempt to find an existential ethics. In Being and Nothingness, Sartre is a pessimist describing inauthentic existence. 'Cahiers' is an attempt to describe post conversion ethics that sounds optimistic. But a morality though desirable is perpetually deferred. The only possible morality is "to prepare for the kingdom of Ends by a revolutionary, finite and creative politics". [14]

The grave difficulties Sartre faced in elaborating his notion of authenticity forced him to reconsider the relation of social existence to freedom. In his later writings, Sartre situates human freedom in the social context and favours the concept of 'limited choice' in place of free and total choice among various possibilities available in the social situation. The evil reality of scarcity, need, class inequality and alienation casts its shadow on the freedom of the individual but Sartre asserts. Though the choices are tragically narrow, one cannot escape the responsibility of choosing oneself. Thus, Sartrean concept of freedom, even in its later phase can serve as a basic supposition of moral action since without free choice from various alternatives, there can be no moral action. Therefore, Sartre's own definition of freedom as *both a value* and '*sources of all value*' [15] is the source of his ethics.

Growing awareness of social constraints to the freedom of man, forces Sartre to espouse social ethic of desalination in his later writings. Desalination, for him, is the removal of sources of otherness in human relations, leaving out non-objectifying otherness 'free altarity'— obtained in group-in-fusion. He pleads for rooting out all structural factors, which separate one individual from the other and from his own self. Here, he comes closer to Marx but goes deeper in his analysis of alienation. *Practico-* inert qualified by the fact of scarcity is the source of all human conflict, according to Sartre. He supports Marxist plan of destroying capitalist form of society but questions its claim of abolishing all forms of alienation with that. Given the fact of scarcity in human condition, we cannot hope for disappearance of all forms of alienation, Sartre asserts. Thus, he accounts for the abiding alienation in the socialist states and shows the limitation of Marxist ethics.

After discussing the negative side of Sartre's ethics of desalination, we can grasp his positive vision of 'true inter-subjective community. Flyn has unpacked three interrelated values[16] of reciprocity, transparency and community which constitute the conceptual backbone of Sartre's later ethics. Positive reciprocity emerges as the supreme expression of human freedom after Sartre's experience of French Resistance. It is a far cry from his earlier understanding of human relations as perpetual conflict. What Sartre hints in his post-war imaginative literature. (The Devil and the Good Lord) culminates in an open declaration in 'The Family Idiot :

> The true relation among men is reciprocity which excludes commands properly speaking.[17]

Sartre considers it necessary to end all forms of authority for which he demands changes in socio-economic conditions and replacement of political leaders by direct democracy. The twin values of socialism and freedom make him a libertarian socialist.

Transparency is another value, which seems integral to Sartre's socio-ethical vision, though it does not figure as prominently in his remarks. It means complete openness and honesty in social relation. Secrecy and privacy, for him are the forms of power which undermine positive reciprocity. Though Sartre fails to meet the demand of the rationalist for an objective criterion in these relationships except trust and faithfulness yet he imagines the day when two men will have no more secrets from each other. Thus, transparency too belongs to future when man will be free from the yoke of scarcity.

In some interviews[18] published shortly before his death, Sartre seems to attach a lot of importance to the related value of fraternity and even recommends it as an ideal for demoralized left. By it, he means not only sharing of goods like Marx but also mutual support and an affective identity. Experienced first in the family, it stands for him as a model for all interpersonal relations. It is more basic than the productive relation emphasized by Marx. But again true brotherhood will prevail at the end of a long historical development. There seems to exist some uncertainty about the true relationship between fraternity and violence. On the one hand, violence (terror) seems to be necessary to guarantee brotherhood in the conditions of scarcity on the other, violence can never further the advent of 'Man' of his final interviews.

Thus, Sartre's ideal society is one of fully disalienated individuals, voluntarily engaged in non-hierarchical relations based on moral values of openness and brotherhood. In the absence of any concept of human nature reciprocity serves as a criterion for judging 'human from inhuman' in Sartre's ethical reflection. His ideal for the fully human relationship can be consistently used as a moral norm, because Sartre gives primacy to praxis to change our inhuman lives, perpetuated not only due to force of circumstances but also because of our abuse of freedom.

The theme of Sartre's last conversations is that of hope which is a constituent part of acting. His appeal for an ideal future society is a value choice as it does not yet exist and one can easily choose to collaborate with existing reality. To achieve this ethical ideal, Sartre hints to construct *'an ethic of we'* in contrast to the *earlier ethics based on the 'I'*. It will be based on new ontology of consciousness and man's 'desire for society'. Thus, the *final picture* of his ethics is essentially the *'ethic of relationships with the other'*.

However, one cannot deny some modifications in Sartre's thinking on morals in his last days when he asserts:

> "One must attempt to learn that one can seek one's (own) being one's life only by being *active for others*. This is the truth. There is no other".[19]

Despite of our living present subhuman conditions, Sartre recommends one to go beyond oneself and enter 'in the circle of men'. What he calls moral consciousness is "this self considering itself" as self for the other, having a *relationship with the other*. Though aware of the hurdles (war, exploitation, etc.), Sartre's moral vision of what man can be together gives us hope in the future when men will be brothers. But Sartre's words, "we must ground this hope" sound as a call to bring it about. This is Sartre's legacy to us.

Our discussion of Sartre's unfinished ethics can be concluded by pointing out some of the ambiguities and unsolved problems left unresolved in it. Sartre himself acknowledges them in his discussions with Beny Levy. If failure is inevitable, there is no point in developing an ethics. The relationship between violence and brotherhood is also not very clear. And it is necessary to find the meaning of history as defined by Marx and Hegel somewhere else. But these are not the only problems. Though Sartre in the 'Critique' accepts definite limitation to man's freedom, he fails to tell where the limits exactly are. Never failing to raise his voice in protest against injustice, Sartre presupposes a conception of social justice, which he never fully elaborates. He fails to provide an objective criterion for selection of values, which remain a matter of man's arbitrary choice. Though for himself, values like freedom, equality and brotherhood are absolutes, he seems to espouse a situational ethics and categorical imperative at the same time. The dual role of freedom is also not proved.

In some of the recent works, an attempt has been made to answer some of the criticisms levelled against Sartre's ethical views. Though a full discussion of them is beyond the scope of this chapter, contribution of Christina Howells[20] and David Detmer[21] need to be specially mentioned for defending the legitimacy of Sartrean ethics.

REFERENCES

1. Jean-Paul Sartre, *Being and Nothingness*, Tr. Hazal Barness, New York, Philosophical Library, 1956, p.720.
2. Saint Genet, Tr. by Bernard Frechtman, New York, George Braziller, 1963, p. 371.
3. *Ibid.,* p. 186,
4. Jean-Paul Sartre, *Cahiers pour une morale*. Gallimard, Paris, 1983, p. 19.
5. Michel Contat and Michal Rybalka, *The Writings of Jean Paul Sartre,* Northwestern Uni. Press, Evanston, 1974, p.15.
6. *Ibid.,* p. 26.
7. *Ibid.,* p. 426.
8. Jean-Paul Sartre, *War Diaries*, verso, p. 109.
9. *Anti semite and Jew*, Tr. Backer; New York, 1865, p. 90.
10. *Ibid.,* p. 141.
11. Thomas R. Flynn, *Sartre and Marxist Existentialism*, University of Chicago Press, Chicago, 1984, p. 42.
12. *Cahiers pour une morale, op. cit.,* p. 496.
13. *Ibid.,* p. 16.
14. *Ibid.,* p. 426.
15. *Being and Nothingness, op,cit.,* pp. 627-28.
16. Being Marxist Existentialism, *op. cit.,* p. 190.
17. Jean Paul Sartre, *The Family* Ideot, Vol. 3rd, University of Chicago Press, Chicago, 1981, p. 48.
18. Quoted by Herbert Spiegelberg in Sartre's last word on Ethics in *Phenomenological Perspective in Simon Gelyn* (Ed.) Sartre: An Investigation of Some Major themes', Averburge Aldershet, 1987, pp. 37-54.
19. *Ibid.,* p. 44.
20. Christina Howells, Sartre: The Necessity of Freedom,Cambridge University Press, Cambridge, 1988.
21. David Detmer, Freedom as a Value: A Critique of the Ethical Theory of J.P. Sartre, La Salle, IL, Open Court, 1988.

Chapter – 9

Man and His Destiny: Marx and Sartre

A. K. Tandon

The problem, of man and his destiny has been discussed by various thinkers in different times and ways. In the classical rationalistic view, inherited largely from Greece and Rome, what most distinguishes man is the fact he is a rational being. Reason is the highest faculty of man and its function is to guide human conduct. For Socrates, Plato and his followers, the intelligent man is the virtuous man. To know the right is to do it. The goal of human effort and the meaning of progress are the harmonious development of all of man's functions and capabilities through the supremacy and perfection of reason in man and society. Though Democrats, Epicures and Lucretious treat man as wholly a part of nature, yet they too do not deny the importance of reason, they merely interpret it in more naturalistic and mechanical terms. Middle ages saw the dominance of Judaeo-Christian view of man. From this stand-point, man's uniqueness is not based on rationality but on being created by God. For St. Thomas as Aquinas man is an embodied spirit. He is an expression of the intelligence and moral purpose present in the universe. He cannot become himself till he devotes himself to the highest, i.e., God. The failure of rational natural and religious traditions paved the way for a tradition of will and artifice in

Hobbes, Locke and Rousseau. But their individualistic concept of man met a serious challenge in the collectivist view of man in the philosophies of Hegel and Marx. Along with the development of industrial society, there arose positivistic, analytic and functionalist schools of thought, which converted man into mere abstraction. Thus man was thrown out from the centre of philosophical discussion of human destiny. Then there emerged a movement of protest in the thought of existential phenomenological group of thinkers, such as Kierkegaard, Husserl, Heidegger, Sartre, etc. which restored some of the lost glory to man. But the final solution to the problem of man and his destiny still eludes us because in each phase of history, the problem is raised from different perspective on account of changed socio-economic conditions. Hence, always there is need to look into the problem afresh. This chapter focuses mainly on the contribution of Karl Marx and Jean Paul Sartre for both are profoundly concerned with the condition of man and his freedom to shape his destiny here in this world and their influence on twentieth century thought cannot be ignored.

In contrast to the nature of animals, Marx starts with a concept of human nature but makes a distinction between human nature in general and human nature as modified in each historical epoch. He employs the categories of 'power' and 'need' to express it. He further subdivides them into natural—those powers and needs which man shares with every living entity, and species powers and needs which man alone possesses. Though natural powers serve as the basis for species powers, they can become species powers themselves as the evolution of human sexual relationships shows. Three inter-connected processes, viz., perception, orientation and appropriation work to relate man's powers to the world of objects in Marx's system. The modification of powers and needs occurs primarily due to the influence of forces and relations of production of that historical era. To satisfy his basic needs, man experiences himself as a member of a class under definite social conditions, which produce class characteristics in him through their direct effect on the individual's powers and needs and indirect creation of interests, which he then tries to satisfy. Thus, without lapsing into relativism, Marx provides a dynamic historical concept of human nature, though he does not develop systematic theory of it. One can identify three basic components of his concept of man. First, as a part of nature, man is an object. Second, as a part of society man's opinions and attitudes are functions of social relations. And finally, man is the result of his practical activity, a being of praxis, as a maker of history along with other man. Marx's key concept of 'self-activity' forms the basis of his definition of man as a 'being of praxis'.

The ultimate destiny of man, according Marx, is the realization of full creative potential of man, of man becoming whole in place of alienated man of capitalist society. By his deep analysis of alienated labour, *Marx brings out man's four-fold alienation*. Man is alienated from the product of his labour from the activity of production from himself as a member of human species and from his fellowmen. The cause is private ownership of means of production. Alienation can be transcended only by ushering in a communist society through revolution, which throws off ruling capitalist class and transforms private ownership into public ownership. Our contention is that any controversy about 'younger' and 'mature' Marx, as suggested by Althusser and others is of little value because Marx's concern for alienation and its transcendence runs through whole of his work. However, the two strains, critical and deterministic, visible in his thought, can be attributed to the intellectual evolution of Marx from earlier influence of Hegel to more objective understanding of socio-historical change.

For earlier Sartre, there are two modes of reality. Being-in-self. Being-for-itself and characterizes entities other than man and its characteristics are passivity, immobility and complete lack of consciousness. Being-for-itself is human reality and its characteristics are pure consciousness and absolute freedom. Knowing and being known is the fundamental relation between the For-itself and In-itself. Sartre argues that this is possible because of the 'nothingness' at the centre of the For-itself, which signifies the distance on object from the consciousness. The capacity to fill this gap is identical with freedom. Thus, freedom is the very nature of human reality. Things behave as they were made to behave where as a conscious being is aware of his own possibilities. Man, in Sartre's opinion, is not what he is, he is what he is not. Man has undetermined future to be decided by the choices he makes. Man is a plan; he is what he will be.

Though, Sartre argues, conscious being in isolation is nothing but emptiness, he encounters other conscious beings through their glances, which make him Being-for others. It is accompanied by fear or shame for it reduces For-itself into an object of another's consciousness. This *reduction of man into a thing is the very negation* of human freedom. Thus, every human being is the natural and primary enemy of the other. Conflict is unavoidable to human relationships because it is impossible for the other to be subject and object simultaneously for as soon as one becomes object of other's subjectivity, he is devoid of that freedom which other wants to possess.

Sartre in his earlier writings posits the view that there is no human nature, no God to look after man. Man simply is, his existence is the result of an accident. There is no inherent purpose in his existence apart from which he himself creates. So man is the sole creator of values. Since man's destiny is within himself, he can always realize it by choosing and acting as free and responsible man. Yet it is an endless quest. Apart from certain *a priori* constraints such as, the fact that man is born and will die, he has a past and live in a world with other men, man experiences anguish while deciding among various possibilities and, therefore, tries to escape from his freedom by an act of 'bad faith', either by thinking oneself as a thing or regarding oneself as bound by some given social purpose. Thus freedom assumes profound responsibility. In choosing for himself, man chooses for the whole mankind. Whether good or bad, man carries the burden of the result of his choice. Every man is free and responsible for his action. The exercise of this freedom can be considered authentic or inauthentic according to the choices made in the situation. Sartre defines authentic choice as having a 'clear and lucid consciousness of the situation', and authentic existence as 'self recovery of being', but fails to provide a criteria for prescribing as well as identifying authentic act.

At the end of 'Being and Nothingness', Sartre promises to give an account of his ethics. But he faces the dilemma of preserving this radical concept of freedom and account for unending conflict among human beings, which makes mockery of absolute freedom. To resolve this contradiction, Sartre in his later writings is compelled to consider man, not as an isolated individual but member of a group with similar approach to the world. He tries to accommodate his concept of absolute freedom within the Marxist framework of history and society. For this purpose, he frees orthodox Marxism from philosophical materialism and incorporates human agent as its basis. This he achieves by importing his own theory of consciousness into Marxism *via* interpretation of praxis. Sartre advocates the study of mediations, the way in which men interiorise their situation and totalize their actions, as the key of understanding the relationship of men with history. Since human praxis is dialectical in form, Sartre claims the necessity of dialectical reason to describe man's place in world history. In his 'Critique of Dialectical Reason', Sartre charts out the dialectical course of human praxis in several groups of which man is necessarily a member and in which his choices are made.

The notion of 'scarcity' and the concept of 'practico-inert' play important roles in later Sartre's understanding of human destiny. It is because of scarcity men oppose each other and regard each other as obstacles to their ends instead of ends in themselves. Human praxis struggling against scarcity produces worked matter, which dominates man in such a way, that man becomes a product of his product. Thus, the basis of alienation lies, not in various modes of human relationships, but in the profound penetration of human relationships by scarce, processed matter. Individual alone cannot abolish alienation. It can be done only through group action. The group is formed on the basis of common needs and common dangers and is defined by Common praxis. It happens in two stages, the grouped in fusion and the organized group. By pledge the group in fusion is transformed into organized group. It is bound by the fraternity of fear. Yet the destruction of the group is inevitable. Thus for later Sartre recovery of freedom is possible only in-group action directed against the structures that atomize man. Unlike his earlier views, this is socially qualified freedom. Facing a concrete situation one's choices are tragically narrow, yet one can always do something of what has been done for him. Therefore, one cannot support the contention of Marry Warnock and others that there is a radical break in earlier and later Sartre. What we find is the shifts in the meanings of same concepts put in different contexts. This is ascribed to his intellectual evolution. His concern and belief in man's freedom to shape his destiny is constant throughout his whole work.

Comparing the views of Marx and Sartre, we find many similarities and differences. The role of philosophy for both is to guide human praxis. Both rule out any supernatural origin and destiny of man was they do not believe in the existence of God. Instead they consider delinking of man from God as a necessary step of liberation of man. Both are not much concerned with metaphysical questions. Their primary interest is in man and destiny here and in this world. Both reject idealism and traditional materialism, but differ on the nature of consciousness. Sartre considers it fully autonomous, to which Marx disagrees.

They agree that history and thought are dialectical movements, which can be understood only by dialectical reason but differ on the meaning of contradiction. Their differing views regarding subjectivity of individual consciousness put them on different paths. Whereas Marx starts from history and reaches the individual in the end, Sartre begins with the individual and develops his theory of history afterwards. Thus man for Marx is not an isolated individual, but member of a class and human history is mainly the history of class struggle. But Sartre tries to understand historical development on the basis of totalization of multiplicity of individual praxis. This dichotomy serves as the basis of their differing views of human nature praxis, alienation and dealienation of man.

Any fixed concept of human nature is not acceptable to Marx and Sartre. Marx do accept a universal core, but Sartre talks only about common human condition. Both give primacy to praxis to bring about changes in social situation but the relation between individual praxis and class praxis is more clear in Sartre than in Marx. Alienation is the main concern of both, but whereas Marx locates it in the relations of production, for Sartre, it plagues man only through the mediation of matter. The road to dealienation of man for both, lies through revolution but they differ in causes and means to it. What strikes most in Marx as well as in Sartre is the recognition that man can be master of his own destiny. For Marx's, freedom consists in possibility of dealienated labour in a communist society brought in by social revolution. Sartrean man is essentially free but is fearful of his own freedom and avoids the responsibility of authentic living.

When one focuses on the critical evaluation of the standpoints of Marx and Sartre for ascertaining their contribution to our understanding the problem of man and his destiny, one finds that both the thinkers fail to provide a valid proof for their disbelief in the existence of God. Their treatment of man's urge for transcendence and belief in religion is one sided and, therefore, cannot account for the revival of religion in modern times. Paying little attention to metaphysical questions, Marx as well as Sartre lack a valid criterion of truth and a systematic theory of knowledge. Marx's materialism is too vague and fails to provide a materialist theory of consciousness. Sartre's assumption of a division between For-itself and In-itself is without any adequate proof. The attitude of both the thinkers to put man against nature is questionable because it has led to dwindling of nature's resources in the present era.

Our probe further reveals that Marx's concept of human nature is too rationalist, normative and over-optimistic. It fails to see any inherent, negative tendencies in human nature. Sartre even does not recognize any such common human nature. Both views neglect the role of irrational passion in human behaviour. Though both the thinkers add to our understanding of alienation of man, Marx's theory cannot account for all forms of alienation. The abolition of private property has not ended workers alienation even in socialist countries. Sartre's contention that alienation is a function of *practico-inert* qualified by the fact of scarcity can explain, up to some degree the abiding alienation in socialist states. But scarcity remains inherent condition of man. Therefore, Sartre's hope of ending alienation in post-scarcity society seems hope in vain.

Marx's concept of man as a being of praxis, reformulated by Sartre to include the subjectivity of the individual can serve as a model for analysis of social relations. Marx's contention that in existing class societies, there are real conflicts of interest leading to class-war, is an important contribution though it does not cover all types of conflicts. For a better understanding, Sartre's concept of scarcity and *practico-inert* are very helpful. Marx's concept of revolution and inevitability of his law of historical changes may not be considered valid yet the idea that one cannot understand history without taking into account the role of class-struggle and of technological level of society cannot be ignored.

Marx's concept of *fetishism* of commodities helps us to understand how the relations between individuals in a capitalist society appear as relations between commodities. His concept of love provides us a criterion to judge how far natural relations between man and woman have been humanized. Yet focusing mainly on group relations, Marx pays little attention to relations between individuals. Sartre's brilliant exposition of sexual love fills the vacuum only up to some extent as he also lacks a theory of relations.

Both, Marx and Sartre recognize the possibility and exercise of genuine freedom to shape one's destiny. For Marx, it is always limited and lies beyond socially necessary about time. Thus Marx clarifies the material basis of human freedom. Sartre's concept of 'bad faith' opens our eyes to our own acts of self-delusion to run away from the responsibility of exercising our limited freedom. The idea of whole man in a classless society as the ultimate destiny of man remains undeveloped in Marx's writings. Similar is the case of Sartre's idea of authentic living. Both lack a systematic theory of ethics. For them, it is useless to talk about it till alienating conditions *persists*. The important thing is that they do not accept alienated man for natural man. We are indebted to them for pointing out that mere intellectual understanding of human alienation will not abolish it. It is only through group action, historically effective changes can be brought about. Thus, a true synthesis of the views of Marx and Sartre may give us a coherent social philosophy to guide our actions in realizing human destiny.

Chapter – 10

A Critique of Some Contemporary Utilitarian Theories

Pradeep Prasad

Ethics, apart from other things, considers evaluation of voluntary actions of human beings. The question is, "what is the ultimate goal of the voluntary actions ?" In reply to this question, we find two kinds of first principles or ethical norms under "normative ethics", namely, *ethical teleology* and *ethical deontology*. Teleological ethical principle is the one according to which the *summum bonum* or the highest end of human life is to act according to a definite purpose (teleos), so that the state is arrived in which good produced is over and above evil produced. It may be said that ethical teleology speaks of a purpose in life whereby the good attained is as much valuable than any comparable things in life. This is true for both individuals and collectives, and, therefore, universal in nature. However, ethical deontology speaks of no definite purpose, such as having pleasure or happiness, rather, it says that to perform duty is by itself so valuable that it becomes the end of life. We can say that any action through conception of rightness and goodness which is intrinsically valuable and not done for the purpose of anything else, is the highest goal in life. Naturally the deontologist asserts that no action is valuable because it is an end towards a means rather, it is an end in itself. The deontologist, therefore, holds that good and right actions are better than evil no doubt but good and right are not evaluated in terms of means, and, therefore, acts ought to be done for their inherent end value.

Contemporary utilitarianism as a teleological theory is causing effective ripples in the ethical circle. The contention of this chapter is to find out that the teleological principle in its latest form is worth discussing for some of its positive contributions. Utilitarianism is a teleological theory according to which the highest purpose in human life is to do some such actions so that maximization of pleasure or happiness in human society is made possible. In one sense we can say that utilitarianism speaks of "utility" as the highest purpose of human life, meaning thereby, usefulness of actions such as production of good over evil in the world which is best exemplified in pleasure maximization. Therefore, utilitarianism in some sense supports hedonism of the altruistic type. It speaks of the importance of moral agent's pleasure maximization as well as that of the collective. Some of the utilitarians emphasize that psychologically, human nature is such that we are compelled to maximize our pleasure, and as social beings that of others. Being an altruistic theory, utilitarianism has to answer an important question, that is, how do we come to know that at a given epoch an action done has in reality maximize pleasure or good ? The answer lies in computation of the consequences of our action, which is empirical, and, therefore, not intuitive and *a priori*. Naturally the utilitarians are consequentialists, and for that matter, they have to wait for the future epoch to come to know whether or not an action done has turned out to be really useful. Contemporary utilitarians do not differ because almost all of them accept the basic presuppositions of utilitarianism as found in the writings of Hume, James and John Stuart Mill, Jeremy Bentham, Henery Sidgwick and G.E. Moore.

The rise of contemporary utilitarianism is not only due to the sharp criticism of pleasures of life as only valuable thing rather, due to the deep interest shown by many thinkers who should be best classified as non-philosophers because they do not belong to any school of philosophy or official philosophy. Hence, the growth of contemporary utilitarianism is owing to some writings beyond the field of traditional ethics, mainly the scholars of economics. This does not mean that contemporary utilitarianism is nothing but an economic point of view rather, it is a special way in which the economists interpret "teleos" of life, that is, maximization of good over evil. The readers of contemporary ethics are careful not to speak in traditional language to say utilitarianism is a pleasure-theory or ideal-theory rather, it is the theory of the good for man or it is the theory of maximization of good. Many thinkers thus come to realize that interpretation of utilitarianism should not be restricted to maximization of pleasure rather it covers many more useful and beneficial things for humans so that in the world good weighs over evil in many ways. According to contemporary utilitarianism, therefore, the interpretation of the use of notions of "benefit" and "good" has to expand, just as for the economists, welfare of people living in the world is good. However "economic welfare" is not all, some other contemporary utilitarians speak of the expansion of the meaning of good in different terms.

I would like to concentrate mainly in the analysis of *the general, negative* and *cooperative utilitarianism* because these three types of utilitarianism are less known to us and, therefore, needs some clarification for their meaning. General Utilitarianism, following the basic tenets of utilitarianism, is a consequentialist theory, which speaks of the maximization of happiness in human society as a greatest ideal. Being a consequentialist theory it speaks of the rightness and goodness of actions on the basis of the consequences of those action, which, however, amounts to the maximization principle. Hence the most desirable consequences are maximization of happiness for the *humanity at large*. Nevertheless, general utilitarianism, like rule utilitarianism, does not lay stress on the rules of actions which produces best consequences. Similarly like act utilitarianism it is not concerned with the nature of actions in each changing situations that produces best consequences, rather, general utilitarianism is concerned with the question of the *situations* in which *generally people* prefer to do some such actions which will amount to the best consequences. Hence, general utilitarianism is not worried about what a person should do in a particular case or what rule should moral agents follow. Rather, it conceives of some such actions, which, when performed generally by the people, would amount to, for instance, general good. Such utilitarianism would ask, what will be the case if *every other person* in the world would start helping the poor in case to prevent poverty in a society? It would try to find out whether or not everybody in the society by helping poor in case of poverty alleviation will end up in the maximization of benefit of people. General utilitarianism thus brings up a very important truth inherent in general moral thinking because in our society, if some people start giving alms to the poor to eradicate poverty, we often ask, "what will happen if the general public starts giving alms to the poor ?" Inherent in the question is whether or not giving alms to the poor by us will be in any sense producing a desirable consequence, i.e., maximization of happiness ? This amounts to say that if giving alms in case of poverty alleviation produces general good for people, then myself as a moral agent should be so good to give alms, and equally true is that every other person should be so good that they give alms to the poor. Interestingly, general utilitarianism holds that if certain actions are found to do no good or rather does bad generally, then every person should retrain from that action. Hence, general utilitarianism is not interested in knowing what a particular moral agent thinks in a particular situation about the consequences of actions, rather takes interest in what consequence would follow if everyone does some actions. Donald H. Regan in his work, "Utilitarianism and cooperation" nicely brings out the gist of general utilitarianism by saying, "General utilitarianism speaks an act is right if and only if the consequences of it being performed by the agent and all other agents similarly situated are at least as good as the consequences of any other available acts being performed by the agent and all other agent similarly situated."[1] Similarly the view has been stated by M.G. Singer. "The idea behind general utilitarianism is that if something is right for one person to do in a certain situation, then it is also right for anyone else who is similarly situated to do and, hence, that one cannot ask simply what effects one's proposed action will have in a particular case, rather, one must ask, what the consequences would be if everyone were to act likewise in such cases"[2].

General utilitarianism has a distinct advantage over act and rule utilitarianism insofar as it sidesteps both the problems of isolating particular moral agent in utilitarian decision making as only important factor and the consideration of some arbitrary rules of actions about which there is no common agreement. Hence, it appeals to transcend agent-focusedness and fixity of rules. However, general utilitarianism is not completely free from problems though it appears that it is another form of universalizable principle of utilitarianism. The main reason is that general utilitarianism does not clarify the sense of "general" . What does it really mean when we ask, what would happen of everyone was in the same situation? Really speaking, everyone cannot be conceived as artificial group covering the whole population which exist now or whenever because it is very difficult and absurd to skip the importance of particular moral agent or a section of people or class of people for the best consequences.

From the above discussion about general utilitarianism one important point emerges, general utilitarians is about participation of different sections and interests in our society to churn good consequences of actions for our benefit. This does not assume the participation of all people but more and more people so that we come to know which actions are best for a particular group of people and society at large. This clearly demonstrates that evaluation of consequences of actions does not amount to (as general utilitarianism holds), "what would happen if everyone were alike" rather, when everyone starts thinking alike about courses of actions and about what would be their likely consequences. This clearly hints the need of cooperation among more and more people regarding evaluation of actions for best consequences. This is no imagination or thought experiment rather to come together to decide a course of action about which though there are likely disagreements, agreements supercedes disagreements at particular time to draw a desirable course of action. Clearly, according to

Donald Regan and Roy Harrod, "Cooperative utilitarianism is one theory which emphasizes that those agents who are prepared to behave morally are engaged in a common undertaking which requires a shared recognition of the need for co-ordination and a shared willingness to go beyond ideal rules and counterfactual assumptions. In short, cooperative utilitarianism is one theory which recognize that co-operation is the heart of matter"[3]. Whereas cooperative utilitarianism because supported by Donald holds that, what each agent ought to do is to cooperate with whosoever "co-operating in the production of the best consequences possible given the behaviour of non-cooperators"[4].

This form of utilitarianism clearly avoids the basic problem faced by the act, rule and the general utilitarianism in mentioning that while thinking about the best consequences of action for the public in general, it is narrow and even unpragmatic to ask about what actions a particular agent should do in a situation or what rule should moral agents follow or what should he imagine if many people were in his situation. Cooperative utilitarianism rather directs the moral agents to present himself readily to any co-operative venture in society that produces the best consequences, to identify the number of co-operating people who would strive for best consequences. For this it is an important to ascertain the behaviour of the non-cooperators, to find out what are the best patterns of behaviour for the cooperators and to guarantee that cooperator is doing his desirable part in best pattern. But there are questions; first is that a cooperative venture to find out the best consequences does not and should not disregard and avoid the non-cooperators because the non-cooperators are not harmful for people and are not unethical. We all know that any venture which is beneficial for the people as such must keep in mind the important opinion and disagreement of non-cooperative groups otherwise a group of cooperative people will be so unethical who do not care and dare to face the non-cooperators. Hence, a utilitarian decision-making should bring every other non-cooperators close for a moral debate so that in the long run through a consensus, there remains no non-cooperators.

Coming to Negative utilitarianism proposed by Karl Popper in a small note in volume 1, chapter 5 of *The Open Society and Its Enemies*, we find that we should be concerned not much with the maximization of happiness rather *minimization of suffering*. This amounts to say that though maximization of happiness is desirable utilitarian goal, it is closely associated to an essentially negative effort on the part of the moral agent, which is nothing but trying to abolish those adverse factors which prevent us from realizing the highest ideal. Though these adverse factors may be many. We can put them as factors contributing to human suffering. This is how the more and more is human suffering, and the least is our negative effort to abolish suffering, the least is the maximization of happiness. Hence, if one wants that in human society there should be more and more happiness, there should be less and less suffering. Naturally Karl Popper stresses on a negative point which is in fact pragmatic, and it does seem to be theoretically possible but if we follow it seriously, we have many curious things to accept. R.N. Smart in his essay on Negative Utilitarianism in *'Mind'* (16, 1958, p. 542-543) points out that the Negative Utilitarianism may not be commended to the common people in our society because it would be rather absurd to call upon them to minimize suffering and not strive to maximize happiness. It is understandable that one should fix an ethical goal in life which is positive rather than negative because it is pointless that if we are not serious about happiness, we cannot minimize our suffering. If poverty, for instance, is undesirable human suffering then, it is not important to minimize poverty rather to eradicate it completely through positive measures so that maximization of happiness is possible. J.J.C. Smart thinks that Popper's derivation of the principles of 'toleration' and 'resistance of tyranny' cannot be derived from negative efforts. Hence, tyranny will be proved rather than abolished and for that reason there will be no minimization of suffering rather than maximization of it. Yet, J.J.C. Smart thinks that "Even though we may not be attracted to negative utilitarianism as an ultimate principle, we may concede that the injunction 'worry about removing misery rather than about promoting happiness' has a good deal to recommend it as a subordinate rule of thumb".[5] It is good idea sometimes that when policy maker are not agreeing on which goods to be promoted, they may better try to agree on which measure to be avoided. This is particularly useful when our cooperative effort sometimes fail under the pressure of disagreement.

On the basis of discussion we may say that the contemporary utilitarian theories have many attractive points which remarkably improve on the traditional act and rule utilitarianism, but taking in isolation, not one theory is foolproof. However, we may conclude saying that we should make a policy by taking care of the idea that if something is far good for moral agent, it should be good for others as well. Further, if good has to be produced, people should cooperate on theoretical practical bases and that ethical disagreements must be replaced by agreement through cooperation towards eradicating the evil factors preventing the good for man.

REFERENCES

1. Regan, D.H., *Utilitarianism and Cooperation,* Clarendon Press, Oxford University Press, 1981, p. 95.
2. Frankena, W.K. *Ethics*, Prentice-Hall, New Delhi, pp. 37-38.
3. Regan, D.H., *op.cit.* p. 145.
4. Regan, D.H., *op.cit.* p. 124.
5. Bernard, William & J.J.C. Smart, *Utilitarianism : For and Against*, Cambridge University Press, 1985, pp. 29-30.

Chapter – 11

John Rawls's Sense of Justice

L.G. Chincholkar

John Rawls in this chapter on 'The Sense of Justice'[1] refers to the sense of justice as a natural sentiment in human beings. He has approvingly quoted Rousseau that "it is no more moral conception formed by the understanding alone, but a true sentiment of the heart enlightened by reason, the natural outcome of our primitive affections".[2] Rawls justifies Rousseau's this view through — what he calls — psychological construction and analytic construction. This chapter intends to formulate and evaluate his concept of the sense of justice.

The psychological construction consists of three layers of natural human psychological development. These refer to the emergence of moral feeling of guilt and its corresponding relation with natural attitudes as he calls them. According to him sense of justice is a natural development of the human moral personality. Any human action not based upon sense of justice cannot have moral worth. The three types of psychological development are as under —

1. Authority guilt;
2. Association guilt; and
3. Principle guilt[3].

Authority guilt emerges when a person subject to certain precepts or obligations to some authority violates them. This is apparent even in child-parent relationship where a child has no sufficient understanding. This relation implies "love, trust and faith in authority". If there is no feeling of guilt, it implies that there is no relationship of love, truth with authority. If there is a feeling of guilt it is expressed in an inclination "to confess and ask for forgiveness".[4]

The second, the association guilt is a result of any violation if the rules agreed to while participating "in a joint activity of those who regard themselves as associates" [5] are not adhered to. This may be expressed either in reparation (to make good loss to others), apology, acceptance of penalty or reproofs and "diminished ability to be angry with others".[6] The relation of mutual trust and friendship are the results of certain "psychological principle in human nature"[7] in such a cooperative system.

While the two previous guilts were concerned with "actual natural attitudes"[8] and with certain person or persons, the principle guilt refers to the principle rather than person. Rawls asserts the third psychological law thus : "given that the attitudes of love and trust, friendly feeling and mutual respect, have been generated in accordance with the two psychological laws, then, if a person (and his associates) are the beneficiaries of a successful and enduring institution or scheme of cooperation known to satisfy the two principles of justice, he will acquire a sense of justice".[9] This will be expressible in the "acceptance of those particular institutions as just (as defined by the two principles and from which he and his associates have benefited)".[10] It may also manifest in "willingness to work for (or at least not to oppose) the setting up of just institutions or for the reform of existing ones where justice requires it"[11]. Rawls further points out that "Guilt feelings associated with the sense of justice are characterized as principle guilt feelings since in their explanation reference is made to principles of justice."[12] The principle guilt feeling arise from the violations of institutional norms accepted as "satisfying the principles of justice".[13]

In brief, Rawls means that the sense of justice is the result of the development of the human being. It is also co-extensive with the psychological attitudes which are generally characterized by love, friendship, trust, etc., in the sense that in the absence of these attitudes there is no guilt feeling which is a moral feeling, and moral feeling has worth only when based on the sense of justice. If the feeling of guilt does not arise it betrays absence of friendship, love, mutual trust, cooperative attitude, etc. Since this is the case, if everyone in the given system has a sense of justice, the more stable such a system becomes. Such an inherent stability of any institution, therefore, is a result of reciprocal cooperative relationship amongst the members of such a system. Such a psychological construction is a cumulative, cooperative and consistent whole and is most stable. The authority guilt, the association guilt and the principle guilt express the successive developments of moral personality based on a sense of justice which is natural and is believed to be present in all rational beings. For Rawls, guilt feeling is a moral feeling. If it were not so, he argues, we could not explain the feelings of such guilts which arise from the relevant violations. Absence of guilt would, therefore, mean, for Rawls, absence of such basic attitudes like love, trust, etc. A society bound by moral codes respected by its members cannot but have guilt feelings upon its violations. Therefore, the question with which the psychological construction mainly concerned is this: "if a person, given his circumstances, fails to have a certain moral feeling, is there a natural attitude which would thereby be shown to be absent ?"[14]

Elaborating the relation between the moral feeling and the natural attitudes, he points out that a "natural attitude and a moral feeling are both orderings of certain characteristic dispositions"[15] and that such dispositions are interrelated in such a way that "absence of certain moral feeling implies the absence of certain moral attitudes; or alternatively, that the presence of certain moral attitudes implies a liability to certain moral feelings: These propositions are necessary truths".[16] Thus if there is no love there would be "absence of disposition to feel guilty".[17] Therefore, feeling guilty is a defining feature of the natural attitude love.

Thus Rawls's psychological construction is designed to "show how the sense of justice may be viewed as a result of a certain natural development"[18] and "why the capacity for the sense of justice is the fundamental aspect of moral personality in the theory of justice".[19] Accordingly he has tried to justify the sense of justice as a natural corollary of human development.

Now it is worthwhile to be acquainted with the basic questions involved in his analytic construction of the sense of justice. His analysis of the concept of justice raises two such questions. They are (i) "to whom is the obligation of justice owed?, that is, in regard to whom must one regulate one's conduct as the principles of justice require?; and (ii) what accounts for men's doing what justice requires?"[20] His answers to these questions are (1) "the duty of justice is owed to those who are capable of a sense of justice; and (2) "if men did not do what justice requires, not only would they not regard themselves as bound by the principles of justice, but they would be incapable of feeling resentment and indignation, and they would be without ties of friendship and mutual trust. They would lack certain essential elements of humanity".[21] Having now been acquainted with Rawls's justification of the sense of justice we may proceed to evaluate the same on the basis of our understanding of it.

Rawls's sense of justice is an elaborately thought out concept trying to explain the nature of the concept of justice. What is justice? How do we come to acquire it? Is it a universal, unfaltering moral feeling? How are we guided in our quest of justice? These are some of the important questions regarding which we may also seek enlightenment from Rawls's sense of justice.

He has emphasized guilt feeling in his psychological elaborations and distinguished between authority guilt, association guilt and the principle guilt. While the authority guilt and association guilt refer to persons, he says, the third principle guilt refers to principles. His distinction amongst three types of guilt is avoidable because (1) even the principle guilt ultimately refers to persons since principles are always meant for guiding the conduct of persons. Therefore, all the three guilts could be found to be referable to persons whether directly or indirectly. There is no principle in any moral theory which has no reference to human conduct at all; and (2) All the three guilts arise from certain commitment by a person. Thus if there is no commitment or acceptance of any principle of conduct there is no feeling of guilt. This is true in case of authority guilt and child-parent relationship also. The only possible difference is that child's commitment is implicit, of others it is explicit. Therefore there does not appear any difference of principles upon which the guilts could be separaely categorized as Rawls has done.

Rawls also appears to argue in a circle when he claims that the sense of justice manifests in "willingness to work for (at least not to oppose) the setting up of just institutions or for the reform of the existing ones where justice requires it". Thus sense of justice prompts establishment of just institutions. And what are the just institutions? They are as prompted by the sense of justice. Again if the sense of justice manifests also in the reform of the existing moral fabric "where justice requires it" then it would mean that moral reform prompted by moral sense is possible only when justice requires it. How this sense of justice is to be distinguished from the requirements of justice we do not know. It may mean that there is a category of "justice" distinct from sense of justice. While the sense of justice is a natural development "justice" appears to be some other distinguishing feature. If sense of justice manifests in the willingness for moral reform or establishment of just institutions it is not clear how requirement of justice could again be made precondition for such a reform.

Besides, if moral reformation were a result of natural development of the sense of justice and if moral pattern of a society were reflective of the sense of justice, there could possibly be no resistance to moral reformation in a society since it would come off as a natural consequence of the sense of justice. The situation, however, is otherwise. This also becomes clear when we know how *Sati* custom is justified even by highly educated men and also women in some parts of India. Almost every attempt at moral reformation evokes resistance. Therefore, it may have to be accepted that either the sense of justice is not 'natural development' as Rawls stresses or that a vast majority of persons are bereft of the gift of this natural development or that it is relative to and formed or influenced by respective social situations. In either case then it is neither natural nor intuitive. Nor does it explain how could such a sense be a base of rationality or any such other principle as claimed by Rawls.

Besides, his distinction between resentment and indignation — which are moral feelings — is too vague. His description of resentment as a reaction or response to the wrongs of others causing injuries to us and of indignation as being a response to the wrongs of others causing injuries to others is rather artificial. If violation of any moral principle elicits any unfavourable response from us it stems from our acceptance thereof as a moral principle and there appears at least no theoretical significance in distinguishing them in a way he has done. Besides, he also asserts that anger and annoyance are distinct from resentment and indignation. If "in order to experience resentment and indignation one must accept principles which specify these rights and wrongs", there appears no reason to exclude anger and annoyance as being basically distinct since they are also indistinguishable responses to the violation of certain accepted norms of behaviour. The distinction, therefore, appears to be more verbal than factual. Rawls also accepts that they are sometimes indistinguishable. The fact is that resentment and indignation too are behavioural patterns as are anger and annoyance and there is practically no yardstick to measure the responses separately as being either moral feelings or only behavioural patterns as Rawls has chosen to do. Possibly moral disapproval would be a better illustrative term to characterize response to violations of moral norms because such a disapproval is neither resentment nor indignation. It is also not necessarily expressed through them. It would also do away with the possible confusion between various terms used by Rawls, i.e., resentment, indignation, anger, annoyance. Similarly it can be said that a person without a sense of justice and acting only on self-interest and expediency may be incapable of moral disapproval but not incapable of experiencing resentment and indignation, though such a person may be without ties of mutual trust and friendship.

Again, the sense of justice does not appear to be a natural product but a product of social understanding. If humanity were one, if the natural attitudes and dispositions were same its 'sense of justice' should have evoked at least similar evaluations under similar situations. But as has been pointed out this is not so. Also, there does not appear any reason — as Rawls appears to have believed — why a sense of justice should always be in contrast to self interest. Self interest need not always be opposed to trust, friendship or love. The concept of enlightened self-interest is involved in Rawls's association of guilt also.

For Rawls capacity for a sense of justice is both sufficient[22] and necessary.[23] Sufficiency involves two principles of justice. The first requires that the special benefits gained by natural superiority should simultaneously benefit the less fortunate also; and (2) that the duty of justice is "owed to those who could participate in the contractual situation of the original position and act on it."[24] According to Rawls possession of sense of justice is possible only when there is natural capacity therefor. This natural original capacity is necessary for the emergence of a sense of justice.[25] This capacity may be less developed in a child or may be impaired either by illness or accident. Rawls points out that even if a person is not "owed to duty of justice" he cannot act arbitrarily. Capacity of sense of justice is necessary even to avoid cruelty to animals. He is right when he says that even if nobody complains about unjust treatment like children or persons in certain types of situation, conduct corresponding to sense of justice is necessary. His view that justice is a "necessary condition of the worthiness to be happy indicates that happy"[26] moral life is possible only when it is based on justice. He rightly upholds the dignity of a person as a moral being. Here he echoes Kant in this respect. Because of this dignity, he avers, every person is "sovereign"[27] and all are at an "initial position of equal liberty".[28] Since such 'sovereignty' of a person as a moral being is essential for his moral worth as an individual Rawls's recognition thereof is an important hallmark of his theory of justice.

Is Rawls an intuitionist like Butler or does his sense of justice correspond to moral sense of Moore? The answer would be that his sense of justice is neither Butler's conscience nor is it Moore's moral sense. The reason is that the sense of justice requires a capacity therefor. Not all may have this sense. Besides the 'conscience' of Butler or the 'moral sense' of Moore are said to be intuitive and universal. Such is not the case with the sense of justice. It is a product of human evolution and subject to the processes of evolution.

He is a utilitarian and also a rationalist provided these theories are based on the sense of justice. Contrasting his position with classical utilitarianism and aristocratic ethics he explains that classical utilitarianism "holds that a capacity for pleasure and pain, for joy and sorrow is sufficient for being a full subject of rights"[29] while aristocratic ethic takes as certain attributes and capacities such as "strength, beauty and superior intelligence and which would impose the requirement of initial equality only within the same rank and allow original inequalities between superior and lower ranks".[30] He further points out that analytic construction does not start from such initial inequalities. It allows only those contrasts which a moral principle inheres and only those circumstances which betray "conflict of claims".[31] Such conflicting claims raise question of justice which is fairness in action. It follows from this construction, Rawls points out, that "capacity for the sense of justice is the fundamental aspect of moral personality in the theory of justice".[32] He appears to argue in a circle here. What is moral life? That which is based on justice, he would say. And what is the sense of justice? It is the fundamental aspect of moral life would be his reply.

Rawls's correlation between violation of a moral principle and corresponding resentment or indignation may not hold in all cases. Resentment and indignation may not always result from such violations. A person may be equidistant from them. The concept of *niskama karmayoga* (desireless action) — in which all actions including moral duties are sought to be done with a detached outlook — would not admit of such a relation. Because even if a moral principle is violated the response of *niskama karmayogi* — i.e. a person who follows the principle of desireless moral action — would not result in either resentment or indignation. Both the responses are the results of attachment and where detachment to the results of an action is the only right perspective, cool equanimity and consequential corrective measures may be the only response and not either resentment or indignation as believed by Rawls. Both are the disturbed states of mind which a *niskama karmayogi* would not entertain. Rawl's Corelation may not apply in such a case and would be restrictive to that extent.

It should have now been clear that Rawls analytic construction is based on two basic principles, i.e., (1) all persons are basically equal originally, and (2) capacity for a sense of justice is the fundamental aspect of the theory of justice. In the light of this if we now recapitulate the two basic questions raised by Rawls initially our answer thereto would be (1) that the obligation of justice is owed even to those who are and also those who are not capable of sense of justice; and (2) if men do not fulfil the requirements of justice, they would not regard themselves, bound by the principles of justice but still they would be capable of feeling resentment and indignation because resentment and indignation may not always be the natural results of the violation of moral principles. Detached equanimity could also be a response thereto.

It is, however, difficult to substantiate categorically and fully his views that a person not fulfilling requirements of justice would be bereft of 'essential elements of humanity'. What are the 'essential elements of humanity'? If love, friendship or mutual trust express such elements then avarice, wars, slavery, treachery for patriotic cause and human massacre therefor are equally deemed essential elements of humanity and are justified accordingly. Would sense of justice of Rawls ever militate against the inhuman butchery of lakhs of animals and also of humans resorted to ensure survival of "humanity" through countless medical and non-medical experiments throughout the world? Rawls has taken, it appears, a very restrictive view of the essential elements of humanity. Actually, unlike what he deems, a person fulfilling the requirements of justice could still be bereft of the essential elements of humanity as indicated above.

From the above considerations it may be pointed out that the sense of justice of Rawls — as indicated earlier — is neither natural nor universal. It is a result of social influences in a given society and is relative thereto. If it were natural and available to all, then possibly the moral problems would become less complex and more amenable to easy solutions than what they have been. Also his triple distinctions between the guilt feelings is avoidable and all of them can be placed under the principle guilt since all guilts ultimately follow from the violation of commitment which is a common feature for them all. His necessarily true propositions that presence or absence of moral feelings connote corresponding presence or absence of natural attitudes is at times unrealistic. For example, he says that if there is no love, there would be absence of disposition to feel guilty. This is not always so because one may love and yet feel guilty if the love, though a natural attitude is not permissible under the given social situation as happened in case of the Arabian Princess. Love does not seek permission of the sense of justice to love.

However, Rawls presents a remarkable exposition of his sense of justice. His psychological and analytical constructions have been elaborate and illuminating. He rightly says that the concept of justice has a family of principles. His insistence on basic equality and dignity of human beings and simultaneous distribution of benefits achieved by naturally superior humans amongst those not having such superiority as principles of justice are as noble as they are important. Their influence extends far beyond purely moral field and have a bearing on socio-economic-political ramifications for any welfare society. The sense of justice is the base of rational life, for when it is absent, rational life is not possible. He is a rationalist, utilitarian and a hedonist too if they all are based on the sense of justice. Though one may not always find oneself in consonance with his views, it is apparent that his theory constitutes one of the latest and original expositions dealing with some of the basic problems in moral philosophy.

REFERENCES

1. From *Moral Concepts* edited by Joel Feinberg, Oxford University Press, 1982.
2. From *Philosophical Review* Vol.72 (1963), pp. 281-305. Quoted from Ref. No.1 p.120.
3. From the paper "The Sense of Justice" from the work *Moral Concepts* edited by Joel Feinberg. Oxford University Press, 1982, p.124.
4. *Ibid.*, p.125
5. *Ibid.*, p.126
6. *Ibid.*, p.127
7. *Ibid.*, p.129
8. *Ibid.*
9. *Ibid.*
10. *Ibid.*
11. *Ibid.*
12. *Ibid.*, pp.129-130.
13. *Ibid.*, p.130.
14. *Ibid.*, p.133.
15. *Ibid.*,
16. *Ibid.*, p.134.
17. *Ibid.*,
18. *Ibid.*, pp.120-121.
19. *Ibid.*, p.121.
20. *Ibid.*, p.120.
21. *Ibid.*,
22. *Ibid.*, p.136.
23. *Ibid.*, p.137.
24. *Ibid.*,
25. *Ibid.*, p.138.
26. *Ibid.*, p.139.
27. *Ibid.*,
28. *Ibid.*,
29. *Ibid.*, p.140.
30. *Ibid.*,
31. *Ibid.*,
32. *Ibid.*,

Chapter – 12

A Note on Sartre's Ethics

S.A. Shaida

The way Sartre tries to reflect on man within his philosophical project, he comes closest to one of his well known statements he makes about being-for-itself, i.e., it is what it is not and it is not what it is. In other words, at the present moment whatever a man is, he is not a fully realized and true being the way he projects himself to be and whatever he is as an authentic being, he is not at the moment of his present reflection. As a perpetually growing and self-creating being, one is never identical with oneself.

It is accepted by many a critic that in his magnum opus *Being and Nothingness* (*BN*) as well as in his plays like *No Exit* we find an extremely morbid and disparaging view of man. This morbidity glares at us piercingly when Sartre describes the nature of inter-personal relations and explains how personal conflict underlines all modes of human relation. Surprisingly, the freedom of for itself which is the *sine qua non* of authentic existence sinks into inauthentic mode of being in the process of defending it against the ouslaught of other subjects. Such an impression is strengthened on account of Sartre's oft-quoted statement like '*man is a useless passion*' or '*hell is the other people*'. Such characterizations of man are supported by what Sartre has to say with regard to the misconstrued subject-object paradigm of human relations. It appears that the Hegelian account of the master-slave relation has been lifted in its essence from the Phenomenology of Mind and grafted in the soil of *BN*. It is only when one reaches the later part of *BN* or one takes Existentialism and Humanism more seriously that a different perspective appears, prompting us to change our understanding of Sartre's concept of man (and of his ethics as well) as reflected in *BN*.

It seems highly probable that the understanding of most of us and specially various descriptions and criticisms of the so-called ethics of *Being and Nothingness* are seriously flawed. What is generally said about Sartre's views on inter-personal relations boils down to one simple observation that he advocates a theory of '*man against every man*'. The moment a *for-itself* enters into the orbit of another *for-itself* there is an inevitable conflict or confrontation. One seeks to destroy the other out of the fear of being destroyed by the other. Sadism, masochism, hate or shame are the phenomena which dictate human behaviour but provide a fragile foundation of sociality. The ontology of being, as expressed in *Being and Nothingness,* suggests that man is engaged in perpetual antagonism to save his own subjectivity and freedom. What accrues from such a situation is mutual and reciprocal, though unsuccessful, attempts at enslavement and objectification of each other. The apparent hopeless situation, painted in his major work, has generated unpleasant responses from various quarters. Lukacs characterises Sartre's existentialism as a kind of 'bourgeois nihilism' and Roger Garaudy calls it 'literature of graveyard'[1]. There is a general feeling that not only the various characters in his literary works but men at large are psycho-pathological cases and his analyses of human condition sometimes resort to a sort of existential psycho-analysis to help them in their understanding of themselves. But, in our view, there is a need for a radically different approach toward understanding Sartre's ethics, specially in the context of *BN*.

There seems to be a contradiction between *Being and Nothingness* and some other smaller works like *Existentialism and Humanism, What is Literature?* or his essay on Baudelaire. But if we try to move with Sartre from his early ontology to later anthropology, and try to (arrive at a holistic and integrated concept of man, his freedom, responsibility and commitment toward oneself as well as others as developed in *Being and Nothingness* (specially toward the end of this work) it dawns on the readers that all that he has said earlier is a grim reminder that how difficult it is for a person to be authentic which in all cases she ought to be if she is to be true to herself. Honesty and sincerity are the practical mode of the authenticity of the for-itself. We will briefly look into some features of *Being and Nothingness* which belie the popular impression it creates in many minds.

It is a common practice to talk of ethics of *BN* and in this context to feel completely baffled at the description of human relations which he provides. But the key to a judicious appreciation of his thought lies in the concept of Bad Faith and man's deliverance and salvation from it through, what he calls, 'a radical conversion'.

In fact, it would be more appropriate to talk of 'unethics' of *BN* rather than ethics. All that he says in this context amounts to a negative approach. It is not an expression of what one ought to do or what one ought to be but what one ought not to do and what one ought not to be. All that men mostly do to salvage his freedom and subjectivity is to negate the attempts by others at destroying his subjectivity and this he does by objectifying other so that he escapes being objectified. This life-and-death struggle manifests itself in various forms of behaviours which can be labelled as sadism, masochism or hate.

Men often sink, into *bad faith by* way of escape not only from other's onslaught on his being but also from his own inauthentic being. Basically, bad faith is making one's facticity into transcendence and his transcendence into facticity. He tries to become what he is not and he is not what he becomes. The underlying emphasis in the entire work is on self-recovery—an ideal which he shares with Nietzsche. Hence, his analyses of human behaviour and inter-personal relation are nothing but an indictment of all that men do in the state of *bad faith.* The very term *bad faith* has an overt moral commitment— a commitment to be authentic and to be free from self-deception. What he thinks in *BN* is that in our relations with others we cannot recognise each other's freedom since we are in a state of perpetual conflict and, therefore, communality and togetherness are far cry within the arena of being-with-others. But it is neither inevitable nor desirable. Toward the end of *BN* he holds that man's proper self-understanding and his authentic awareness of the ontological structure of his existence, which is the aim of what he calls existential psycho-analysis, would arise when man repudiate the 'spirit of seriousness'.[2] Sartre's aim in this work is to work out 'a means of deliverance and salvation'[3] by overcoming the state of *bad faith* in order to live at the level of authentic existence. In a footnote in the chapter on concrete human relations he writes:

> These considerations not exclude the possibility of an ethics of deliverance and salvation. But this can be achieved only after a radical conversion which we cannot discuss here.[4]

In his later works he has kept on expressing how can we attain deliverance and salvation and what does it mean.

From the point of view of Sartre's ethics, the most important work after *BN* is *Existentialism and Humanism* (hereafter *EH)*. The pivotal theme in this book is human freedom in its moral-social dimension unlike the ontological aspect of *BN*. Freedom is the ground of moral action, decisions and projects but it is not freedom in isolation. It is linked with freedom of others with whom we live and with whom we enter into mutual relation as inevitable feature of human situation. There is a Kantian tone in his statement when he says:

> I cannot make my own freedom my aim unless
> I make the freedom of others equally my aim.[5]

The apparently strange combination of objectivism/ universalism and subjectivism in Sartre's ethics should be viewed with respect to his approach and commitment on the one hand and the content and choice of action on the other. As Kant says, one ought to do one's duty for the sake of duty and refuses to lay down any specific duty except the very general imperative concerning respect for humanity. In Kant's words:

> Act in such a way that you always treat humanity, whether in your own person or in the person of any other, never simply as a means, but always at the same time as an end.[6]

For Sartre, freedom of others is as important as one's own and since freedom is the foundation of all values, we cannot deny it to others who, as subjects, are as free as we are. Once he leaves behind what and how men in bad faith act, he assets the significance as well as the possibility of recognising others' freedom and the treatment of others as ends. His assertion that in chosing for himself, he is choosing for entire humanity shows the movement from the individual to the group and the community which provides the appropriate moral space within, which man's projects are undertaken and choices are made. Freedom and engagement or commitment are interdependent. Sartre admits that once there is commitment I am obliged to will the liberty of others at the same time as my own. Acceptance of freedom for the sake of freedom as well as the recognition of, and commitment to, other's freedom find its fulfilment not in isolation and alienation of the individual but in living-together and 'being-with-others'—Mitsein. In order to remain free one need not destroy other's freedom. It can be done through the project of reciprocity and mutuality. In group, morality is not only 'with-others' but also 'for-others'.[7] It is significant to note that :

> The actions of men in good faith have, as their ultimate significance, the quest of freedom itself as such ..... we will freedom for freedom's sake in and through particular circumstances. And in thus willing freedom, we discover that it depends entirely upon the freedom of others, and that the freedom of others depend upon our freedom.[8]

Freedom, manifest in engagement, is a serious challenge to man because he is not only accountable to himself but he has to universally justify the image of man he is projecting through his choices, decision and actions. These are intact underwritten by the Kantian consideration that what would happen if everyone did the same and this question must be asked by every person in good faith lest he may sink in self-deception.[9]

The emphasis in all human project is to choose what a man is or wants to be and even in *BN* such a choice is made not in isolation but realizing his situation with others. He says:

> I can neither abstain in relation to what I am (for the other)..... nor can I submit to it passively..... whether in fury, hate, pride, shame, disheartened refusal or joyous demand, it is necessary for me to choose to be what I am.[10]

For Sartre, even if man is haunted by his own contingency and the feeling of being de trop, he has to create a meaning for his existence in and through commitment to some self-created project. Like Neitzsche's self-recovery through art, Sartre also sometimes thinks of salvation through literary creation as a desirable way of leading a meaningful life. He makes the hero of Nausea Roquentin arrive at such a decision and approvingly describes in his essay on Baudelaire how the latter too finds redemption in and through literary project. The point, however, is to choose what one wants to be in full realization of what one's condition or situation is and to which one must be disposed freely in the light of one's understanding of oneself. In other words, consciousness acts within the condition which operates at that time (facticity) but at the same time man can and does change his condition through his own acts and choices (transcendence/value). This is the existential version of Engel's dictum that man is the product of history which he himself makes.

The difference between *BN* and his later writings is marked by the difference between individual morality and social morality.

BN is an indictment of individual behaviour grounded in *bad faith* and an invitation to unfold the demands of living in good faith though it involves a 'radical conversation' which can be brought about by commitment to socialist ideology. In his work *Baudelaire* he criticises him not only for evading commitment (as in case of Roquentin) but mainly for resisting socialist commitment. In *What is Literature,* which states the theoretical basis for what he called 'committed literature; the emphasis on writer's freedom is aimed at bringing about an intellectual freedom in the public to bring about a change in society.[11]

And this change must be to bring about a free and classless society without exploitation and dictatorship. Its explicit formulation is found in *Critique of Dialectical Reason* where existentialism becomes subservient to Marxism. The formal ontological freedom *of BN* has by now turned into material freedom of action or praxis rooted in sociological and political demands.

To conclude, the search for authenticity prompts Sartre first to relentlessly analyse human condition in the state of inauthenticity which is the lack of one's own freedom and the denial of freedom of others.

For Sartre, freedom is the all-encompassing mode of existence whereby one not only acts in freedom but lives one's freedom. Even though we live in certain situations (facticity), we can always move beyond it (transcendence). His project against the inauthentic mode of life in *BN* is the negative dimension of his project. It precedes the positive and the optimist sequel of explicating what is authentic mode of life. As Sartre says:

> Authenticity consists in having a true and lucid consciousness of the situation, in assuming the responsibilities and risks that it involves, accepting it in pride or humiliation, sometimes in horror and hate.[12]

REFERENCES

1. See Richard Garudy, *Literature of the Graveyard,* International Publishers, New York, 1948.

2. Satre, J.P., *Being and Nothingness*, tr. Hazel E. Barnes, N.Y. 1956, Pocket Books, 1966. Hereafter *BN*, p.796
3. *Ibid.*, p.797.
4. *Ibid.*, p.534.
5. Sartre, J.P., *Existent4ialism and Humanism*, tr. Philip Mairet, London, Methuen, 1948, (hereafter *EH*), p. 52.
6. Paton, H.J., *The Moral Law*, Hutchinson & Co., 1948, p. 91.
7. *EH*, p. 52,
8. *EH*, pp. 51-52,
9. *EH*, pp. 30-31,
10. *EH*, p. 529,
11. Sartre, J.P., *What is Literature*, tr. Bernard Frechtman, Methuen, 1951, p.119
12. Sartre, J.P., *Anti Semite and Jew*, tr. Becker, N.Y., 1965, p. 90.

Chapter – 13

Existentialist Ethics

With Special Reference to Sartre

S. A. Shaida

When we talk of existentialist ethics we are not in a position to refer to any text, which can give us a systematic and consistent account of any or several thinkers, which may help us to understand their ethics. There are a number of thinkers who come under the rubric of existentialism like Kierkegaard, Heidegger, Jaspers, Sartre, Marcel or Camus, but none of them wrote any treatise on ethic. One towering figure who is often left out of the generally accepted list of existentialists is Freidrick Nietzsche whose ideas are not only very close to existentialism, but who also influenced men like Albert Camus and others. In the absence of any reliable document on ethics, our discussion of the existentialist ethics has to be tentative and liable, at times, to different interpretations. Nevertheless, there are certain tendencies, modes of emphasis, protests, and denials, which create a harmonious note within the philosophical symphony of the twentieth century Continental ethics. But a more convenient way to initiate our discussion of existentialist ethics is to note what it is not. Till the age of Neitzsche and Kierkegaard (and in some quarters even today) there were three significant trends in ethical thought namely, utilitarianism of Mill, the formalistic deontological theory of Kant and the essentialistic theory of Aristotle. What is common in these three is the use of reason — whether instrumental or formal. The existentialist distrust of such reason-based. straightforward 'rule-book' morality is rooted in their revolt against the established Hegelian epitomization of Reason according to which the individual becomes the dispensable cog in the Cosmic machine. In different ways this protest or revolt is spearheaded by Marx, Nietzsche and Kierkegaard. The universally applicable maxims of morality are considered inadequate and even misconstrual of the nature of values, which are meaningless without subjective and personal involvement of the person who accepts it and adopts it as a way of life.

The overall philosophical commitment of the existentialists, despite varying emphasis and differences in the mode of presentation, is to the ground of his reflective choice and freedom. It is asserted that man chooses himself to become whatever he wants to become through his acts and projects. He may not have absolute total freedom because, as Sartre admits, man moves within the poles of fact facticity/situatedness and transcendence, but man surely has total responsibility within the realm of possibilities. In various thinkers, such a concept of responsibility, which is also beset with uncertainty, often causes anguish, anxiety or angst, which becomes one of the modes of being of man. So, if we apply the principle of economy we may hazard a view as per which there are two important concepts — subjectivity and authenticity — around which the entire corpus of their writings — both philosophical and literary — moves.

As we have pointed above, even though there is no proper ethical work and even if most of them, except Sartre, did not see its necessity, all that they have written is a 'prolegomena' to an ethical theory — provided we want to construct one.

Let us briefly consider in our introductory discussion, how some of the important writers have formulated the issues and problems, which directly lead to ethics.

Kierkegaard addresses himself to the Socratic dictum '*know thyself*'. Such knowledge brings oneself to the question how to become what one is because one is not necessarily what one is in terms of one's choice, one's projections, one's acceptance of a possible self-created image of himself. To be true to oneself is the real pre-condition of being moral. The emphasis of Kierkegaard is *not on what is morality but how to become moral.* This is also the existentialist's first step towards authenticity. In his book '*The Present Age*', Kierkegaard laments that 'Our age is essentially one of understanding and reflection, without passion'.[1] Similarly, Nietzsche in *The Birth of Tragedy*[2] observes, 'Knowledge kills action, action requires the veils of illusion'. For Kierkegaard, the passionate commitment of man manifests itself in his realization that in order to be authentic he must grapple with himself in the inwardness of his self. Almost all the thinkers agree that one cannot go beyond oneself in creating his own image but often we are seduced by the bewitchment of language or traditions. As Kierkegaard saw, the institutionalized religion is the negation of real religion. One stands before God in faith and the prevalent academic and political culture was against such subjective and individualistic attitude. Since Hegel advocated all-pervasive logocentric mode of thinking, most of the nineteenth century revolt was against reason as the objective nomos as embedded in Hegeliam thought. Kierkegaard's levelling process, Nietzsche's 'herd morality' or 'slave morality' (with its related concepts). Marx's alienation and dehumanization or Heidegger's fallenness/ everydayness all repent the loss of the subject and individuality, man's anonymity and total externalization of man's inwardness. For the existentialist, the so-called moral objectivity and the talk of universal norms are ethically irrelevant. The authenticity and integrity of man is lost and Kants' call for treating man as an end disappeared in the maize of capitalistic society. Hence, return to man's own self as Neitzsche says, by creating himself freely. Kierkegaard or Marx also express similar view though in different idioms. Nietzsche seeks to transcend the determinants of both nature and culture and such a self-overcoming individual is, what he means by, the *ubermensche* (the superman) with a strong will-to-power. In his concept of man's development towards authenticity, he adopts the model of creative art where the artist creates his own images and symbols — unmasking the veils of self-deception. This image is echoed in Camus' treatment of the myth of Sisyphus — the absurd and the tragic hero. In short, authenticity in Neitzsche and all the existentialists connotes a state of harmony and integrity between the inner self and its external manifestations. Such a self can be known by us through the Buberian I-Thou model or, as Marcel says, it is to be confronted as a mystery.

In Nietzsche's thought the search for authenticity begins with the admission of the distinction between 'truth' and 'truthfulness'. Truth implies objectivity and corresponds to facts while truthfulness is a subjective state of consciousness expressed through motive, intention or purpose. In this works *Day Break*[3] and the *Gay Science*[4] he makes it clear that rational self-knowledge can come through adherence and commitment to truthfulness which makes someone authentic.

Nietzsche distinguishes between two modes of authenticity (Schopenhaeur as Educator)[5]. One is derived from biological metaphor of a plant actualizing the potential of the seed in unique ways. As he says, "everyone is a unique miracle" — a unique aggregate of drives and wishes. Authenticity implies the ability and the decision to manifest this complex phenomenon fully in his life. The other uses the metaphor of art and artistic creation. Man's wish and attempt to attain authenticity lead him to reflect his own indeterminacy by spontaneous choice of one of the many alternatives and possible ways of life. Nietzsche expects an authentic person to live and act like an artist who freely shapes his life as a work of art. Nietzsche unmistakably expresses his preference for the latter model.

Nietzsche rejects crude naturalism and determinism and denies the view that the innateness of one's nature completely determines oneself. Nietzsche is more concerned with cultural conditioning and formative influences, which shape our character. To become what we are is to create ourselves freely. To this end, we must know ourselves as against nature and culture. His well-known adherence to the concept of *amor fati* (love of fate) is a willing and heroic acceptance of what is inevitable. What constitutes the facticity and situatedness of man must be drawn into man's horizon of being— to be transcended if possible and if desired. This brings Nietzsche to the assertion of his concept of self-overcoming which is central to his philosophy. It is indeed key to his most crucial idea of will-to-power. In his work *Thus Spake Zartushtra*[6] he calls it an 'unending will to overcome oneself'. This self-overcoming is directed towards attainment of maturity, authenticity and power (obviously not in common-sense meaning). Nietzsche's will-to-power is in fact the quest for authenticity, the will to become a free creator of oneself. The acme of will-to-power lies in his idea of ubermensch (over-man or superman). He upholds the state of self-consciousness which is devoid of veils of ignorance and rationalizations which involves the process of unmasking. Stripped of veils and self-deception, a man can move towards authenticity. Like Sartre, he believes that authenticity is essentially a state of integrity between art's self and its external manifestation, i.e., his acts and projects.

Sartre's authentic man, who is truly conscious of his freedom and responsibility, accepts his facticity or situations on the one hand and his ability to transcend, what Jaspers calls, his 'limit situations on the other. In his 'every-dayness' he is involved in bad faith but has the power and ability to go beyond it into the stage of 'good faith' — if he so chooses.

In Kierkegaardian vein, Sartre asserts that authenticity does not denote "objective qualities" since the notion of authenticity is beyond objective language.

In *Being and Nothingness*[7], Sartre describes human reality as 'being which is *what it is not and which is not what it is.* Authenticity is something we are aware of when 'we flee it'. In Sartre's discussions a negative as well as a positive meaning of authenticity is manifestly present. Negatively, its presence is discussed in its absence, in the passionate search for it, in inauthenticity or `bad faith'. Positively authenticity appears as negation and critique of inauthenticity or inauthentic mode of life. The latter implies not only self-deception but also denial of commitment, of one's freedom and responsibility. Bad faith emerges when one denies one's facticity and transcendence on the one hand and seeks to become the impossible conjunction of being-in-itself and being-for-itself on the other. Like Kierkegaard and Nietzsche, Sartre seeks to bring about the transition from objective sincerity to personal authenticity. Authenticity requires an incessant movement of becoming a movement towards self-transcendence and self-creation. One can say that Sartre seeks to bring into focus the emotional-existential commitment of men in good faith.

REFERENCES

1. Kierkegaard, S., (1940), *The Present Age,* O.U.P., London.
2. Nietzsche, Friedrich (1967), *The Birth of Tragedy,* tr. W. Kaufmann, N.Y., Vintage
3. Nietzsche, F., (1982), *Daybreak*, tr. R.J. Hollingdale, Cambridge University Press, Sec.73.
4. Nietzsche, F., (1974), *The Gay Science*, tr. W. Kaufmann, N.Y., Vintage.
5. Nietzsche, F., (1983) – 'Schopendaeur as Educator' in *Untimely Meditations*. Tr. R.J. Hollingdale, Cambridge University Press.
6. Nietzsche, F., (1954), 'Thus Spake Zartushtra' in *The Portable Nietzsche*, tr. W. Kaufmann N.Y.,Viking.
7. Sartre, Jean-Paul (1957), *Being and Nothingness*, tr. H.E. Barnes, London, Methken.

Chapter –14

Idealistic Ethics of J.G. Fichte

M.N. Sinha

In the history of western thoughts, ethics is generally treated as the science of morals. It elaborates a moral code of behaviour of the human person and show with utmost concern what is worth striving for, what behaviour is good and, above all, what gives meaning to life. It is also understood in the sense that it deals with the essence of morality, its origin and development, the laws which determine moral standards and their historical character. The ethics enunciated by J.G. Fichte can also be analyzed on some such lines. It will be quite discernible in course of this study that Fichte is an adherent of the idealistic understanding of morality in the history of human thought.

Fichte's ethics has its background and this background can rightly be termed as Kantian. As a conscientious Kantian, Fichte led idealism concealed in Kant's conchshell of formalism too far to infuse in it vigorous life through criticism so that one can have a glimpse of verifying kernel. His system of morality, therefore, presents his brilliant record of life full of action. One can be visibly moved with its demand for action, a nobler morality underlying it and the possibility of duty and virtue with a heart in human freedom environing it. It reminds of originality founded in the great system of thought propounded by Plato, Aristotle, Haraclitus, Spinoza and Kant.

The ethics of Fichte forms the central core of his entire system. His explanations on this point contained in his writings, such as 'The science of Rights, 'The Science of knowledge,' 'The Vocation of Man, Religion, Characteristics of Present Age, and Address to the German Nation', amply prove that his ethics permeates his entire system of thought. To name his one of the pioneering books as 'The Science of Rights' confirms the above noted assertion. Here he deduces the conception of Rights, their applicability and application through social institutions and organizations. For him, the science of rights is the real philosophical science[1] which should not be confined within the realm of formal philosophy in which "a rational being . . . . acts in a determined manner".[2] This has an obvious reference to Kant's formal ethics on which Fichte's ethics is an advancement.

Kant in his ethics, rooted morality in the absolute imperative of duty. It has no reference to any external ends to which the Kantian will is directed. It is simply to the right direction of the will itself. "There is nothing good but the good will", says Kant. This assertion of Kant entirely confines ethics to the chain of Moral Reason only to reach his key, the categorical imperative : Act only on the maxim which thou canst at the same time will to become a universal law. The ethics propounded in the above maxim of Kant, was subjected to various criticisms, such as drifting heavily towards formalism and also for its stringency.[3] Fichte tried to overcome formalism and stringency of Kantian ethics and filled it with concrete contents. He advised, therefore, to surpass the abstractness of Kant's Moral philosophy and bring it on concrete footings. Such ethics can only base itself on contents emanating from purified ego who acts for reflection and is the object of intellectual intuition. The purified ego combines within himself the elements of rationality on the one hand and freedom on the other. "I posit myself as rational that is, as free. In doing so I have the representation of freedom."[4]

For Fichte, "a national being acts in a determined manner."[5] Here the word "determined manner" does not smack the note of determinism but indicates that the rational being acts according to the rule of law. It is the job of the philosopher to express and expand this rule of law, a necessary condition of self-consciousness.[6] The act in a determined manner is, in fact, the manner of acting in it."[7] It is reflected in the act itself. Fichte, therefore, takes into account the nature, determinants and application of the rules of law at the same time. These three are inseparably related.

In Fichte's moral philosophy, the conception of rights assumes the form of an original conception of Reason. This conception satisfies the necessary condition of self-consciousness, the manner of acting in it and origination in this act of the reflection. The condition of self-consciousness shows that a rational being first of all, posits itself as an individual and then, posits itself self-consciously, Thus, self-consciousness of individual definitely refers to the rational individual being. Such rational being is one among many rational beings.

The manner of acting in self-consciousness necessarily refers to an individual having freedom. The individual action of a free being is also one among many beings. The conception of Rights receives real meaning only in relation of one rational and free being to the others. They are, therefore, Co-determinants as one determinant is the freedom of others. The relation of free being to each other can be distinguished here clearly.

The origination in the act for reflection is indicative of the content of the conception of Rights. It involves the conception of freedom, the power which rational beings necessarily gives vent to each other. Fichte writes, "The conception of freedom involves originally only the power, though absolute spontaneity to form conception of our possible causality, it is only this power which rational beings necessarily ascribe to each other, But that a rational individual, or a person should find himself to be free requires something's more, namely, that a result in the external world should follow the thinking of his activity, or that he should perceive the effect of his free causality."[8] It is apparent, therefore, that the rational being's freedom receives expression in the external world only when free causality is seen producing its effect..

Fichte also states "the object of the conception of Rights and, for him the whole object of it lies in a community between free beings as such."[9] There is necessity for relation of freedom of others by a free being here. It indicates that one member of the community by restricting his external freedom through his internal freedom should pave the way for other's freedom also. Such community, for Fichte, should he based on the conception of Rights which has as its essence the conception of reason and also the appropriating freedom. This conception of Right is essentially deducible from 'the Moral Law'[10] according to Fichte. The restriction of individual freedom for promotion of universal freedom in Fichte's thought, therefore, acts as the rule of law and provides "a new sanction for conscience, through the Moral Law".[11] Here Fichte's moral philosophy transcends the realm of the science of Rights to form an essential part of the Science of Morality.

Fichte draws a very subtle distinction between the two, i.e., between the Science of Rights and the Science of Morality. The question of morality crops up only because thinking and acting do not come in complete correspondence. One is bound in consciences through his knowledge of what shall be morally bound to respect the conception of Rights. This moral aspect is the core of the science of Morality. In the Science of Rights, we can see that men are bound only by their arbitrary relation to live in community with others.

All these clearly show that Fichte's ethics transcends abstractness of Kant's moral philosophy and replace abstractness with concrete contents. The purified ego is the root of all his moral principle and ideas. It is an object of intellectual intuition. It is a rational and free individual engaged in promotion of universal freedom always ready to provide a new sanction for conscience through the Moral Law. Thus, Fichte's ethics is out and out a representative of idealistic ethics in the history of human thought.

REFERENCES

1. *The Science of Right*, p. 16.

2. *Ibid.*, p. 17.
3. Mackenzie's: *A Manual of Ethics,* p. 194 -204.
4. *The Science of Rights,* p. 17.
5. *Ibid.*
6. *Ibid.*
7. *Ibid.*
8. *Ibid.*, p. 18.
9. *Ibid.*, p. 19.
10. *Ibid.*, p. 20.
11. *Ibid.*

SECTION – II

VIRTUE ETHICS

Chapter – 15

Ethics of Virtue – Is it applicable ?

Dipasikha Chakrabarty

A standard criticism against virtue ethics is that it cannot be applied to real value-laden moral issues such as abortion or euthanasia, in contrast to rule-based ethical systems, which are applicable. In this chapter, I want to explore this criticism to see how virtue ethics fares in comparison with ethics of rules and try to unravel the basic disagreements between virtue ethics and deontic ethics.

It is true that there are hardly very few books and articles discussing real moral issues or "applied" ethics in the terms of virtue ethics. And the philosophers usually associated with virtue ethics, for instance, Foot, McDowell, MacIntyre, Anscombe have been particularly concerned with theory; not with applying it to gain conclusions about actions. Some critics are struck by the fact that "persons of good moral character" often do not know what should be done in order to resolve the value-laden problems of the society. Hence, a discussion on the morality of acts remains important in deciding what morally good people should do.

It is true that Philippa Foot has tried to offer a solution to euthanasia but her paper was rejected on the grounds that her conclusions are not codifiable, i.e., not eligible to be formed into rules that legislators want to come up with. Foot began with a set of intuitions, about the seriousness of taking human life, and 'the value of death with dignity', about the fact that euthanasia is done for the sake of one who dies, about the relevance of whether or not the person wants to die and the special duty of doctors and so on — all of these counting as "conventional wisdom". Then we turn to Foot's ethical theory expecting that it would enable us to answer the question, "What I do in such and such case of euthanasia?" Foot's article does not even profess to do this. Foot's article does not give us any simple rule or rules about the permissibility of euthanasia; it leaves the problem in the same difficult state. All it states is that, the above factors are relevant and make the problem more complicated.

Michael Tooley and James Rachel, however, have come up with some kind of right sort of answers. Tooley tells us that if the patients are not persons any more, we can kill them off and do not have to worry about all those other considerations. Rachels said that there is no distinction between the active and passive, so we can forget about that distinction. They impose some order in the chaos of our intuitions, and thereby come up with solid, concrete guidance. An ethical theory that cannot do this is considered as useless. In the words of Onora Oneill, an ethical theory should give us clear guidance about what is right and what is wrong, in the form of rules and principles or in other words, to "provide an algorithm not just for some situations but for life."[1] And virtue ethics does aim to produce such an algorithm. Echoing this view, Louden has said, "Due to the nature of the moral virtues, there is a very limited advice on moral quandaries, that one can expect from virtue-oriented approach. We ought to do, what the virtuous person would do but it is not always easy to fathom what the moral exemplar would do were he in our shoes. Furthermore, somebody asks him, why he did what he did, the answer might not be very enlightening. We would not necessarily expect him to appeal to any rules or principles, which might be of some use to others."[2]

In answer we can say that, if all our judgements within some area are perfectly clear and consistent, then we can sum them up in a rule –but then we do not need the guidance of a theory. If, on the other hand we are not clear, as for example in cases of euthanasia and abortion, and find it all very difficult, why do we think a theory is going to help us and resolve our dilemmas? Why should it be a condition of a moral theory that it should provide an algorithm for life? It is quite natural and possible that so many people should find particular decisions about abortion or euthanasia so very difficult because *they are actually very difficult*. Here we should point out very clearly that virtue ethics, far from being a failure to resolve the dilemmas, is very well positioned, perhaps uniquely so, to admit the *undecidability* of such value laden problems. Virtue ethics puts the virtuous agents at the centre of its theory and "persons of good moral character are often the first ones to recognize that they *do not know,* —what ought to be done."

The critics of virtue ethics, however, interpret this to mean that the morally wise are the first to recognize the need for a moral theory, which settles every issue. Perhaps they are thinking of the virtuous as saying, "there must be a clear answer to the question of what we ought to do about abortion or to what I ought to do about my mother's staying on the life support system, but I cannot see what it is."[3] On the contrary, I think of the virtuous as saying, "well, this is a complex issue; let us consider some particular cases." Thus the virtuous people may make moral decisions without believing that, what they are doing, *is the* right one and the only thing to do in that situation. The problem is with the 'tragic dilemmas". In the latter case also the virtuous persons may differ as to the question — "what should be the right thing to do in these circumstances?" For the right question is, "what would a virtuous agent do ?" and not "which is the right act?" Thus, for example, they can very well say, that, this one had an abortion and this one did not, but went ahead with pregnancy; or this one asked the doctor to switch off the life support machine while the other one asked the doctor to continue the treatment.

This undecidability is a characteristic feature of virtue ethics. Now is virtue ethics, by its appeal to virtuous agents, uniquely positioned to build in this sort of undecidability, or can deontic ethics too? Sophisticated deontologist like Onora O' Neill points out that "principles under-determine decisions and may claim, along with the Aristotelians that, what enables a person to apply them correctly, is a virtuous disposition, engendered by habituation. But it is not clear that under-determination implies undecidability."[4] We can legitimately say that, virtue ethics provides a formidable account of action in undecidable cases too, enabling one to say, "she did well in so far as she did, what was *honest*".

But there are complicated cases where it is difficult to solve them so easily. A virtuous agent is one who has the character traits of justice, compassion, honesty and charity; but there may be cases where the virtuous agent is forced to act unjustly, and dishonestly, and this is indeed a problem of virtue ethics. There may be cases from which no one, even the most virtuous can escape without being untouched by immorality. These are indeed 'tragic dilemmas' from which it is impossible to emerge with 'clean hands'.

We can try to resolve this issue by *adjusting our virtue concepts* in such a way that the virtuous agent is allowed to emerge from extremely difficult situations, with 'clean hands'. For example, when an honest moral agent is forced to tell a lie, we may interpret it such a way so as to justify his telling a lie. But it is not possible to tailor all such virtues.

Rosalind Hursthouse has shown, in her article on Applied Virtue Ethics, how virtue ethics stresses the important virtues along with rules and principles of their application, e.g., honesty as a virtue and cruelty as a vice certainly seems to entail settling on 'Act honestly' and 'Don't act cruelly' as rules and principles. So we can legitimately say that virtue ethics is concerned with 'being' as well as 'doing'.

Some act-centred virtue –ethicists are opposed to accept such rules of guidance about the rights and wrongs of *types of acts,* such as abortion, euthanasia or foetal experimentation or eating meat or not telling the truth. And that is what is called for. In reply we may say that the level of act-description in virtue ethics is already *morally-laden* — being in terms of the virtues and vices. Then there are two different lines of thought that may be developed. One is that whether a particular character trait is a virtue or a vice or neither is culturally or socially determined. Hence, the virtue ethicist's 'rules' determine only what is right or wrong in their particular culture or society. But the *concept of virtue* has no reference to culture — it is only a character trait that human beings need to do or fare well — in this world and not in the particular culture or society we happen to find ourselves.

The second line of argument is as follows : we all know that we should not act dishonestly ; but that is no help when I am trying to decide, for example, whether or not to tell a patient the truth about the act that he has cancer. Some may say that I ought to tell him while some others will say the opposite, and then I am stuck. This shows the uselessness of starting with rules that are already morally laden, as the virtue theorist's rules inevitably are. So the trouble with the latter is that they are too difficult to apply. Virtue theorists tell us that the fully virtuous agent knows when an act is dishonest and when it is not ; but we may still ask, "of what use is that to the rest of us ?"

To answer this let us quote Rosalind Hursthouse— "Are you suggesting that a condition of a moral theory is that it would make life easy ? Should the wisdom be something that any clever adolescent could acquire just by being taught the right rules? Surely a constraint on any moral theory is that it should have built into it an explanation of a truth expressed by Aristotle; that moral knowledge cannot be acquired merely by attending lectures . There are mathematical geniuses, but rarely, moral geniuses. Virtue ethics builds this, by couching its rules in terms, whose application may indeed call for the most delicate and sensitive observation ."[5]

This defence of virtue ethics falls short in another objection. It is said that the act descriptions used in virtue ethics cannot be similarly applied in case of classifying people by character traits. Thus for example, cruel people inflict pain on others and we have the concept of cruel acts. Honest people avoid lying and thus we have the concept of honest acts. In these two cases virtue ethics provides 'rules' of acts. But there are other types of acts such as abortion, euthanasia or animal experimentation, where an act's being of that type is morally significant. And virtue ethics cannot be 'the algorithm-for-life' in these cases because these act-descriptions are entirely independent of classification of people. There is not a particular type of character who typically goes in for, abortion, or euthanasia or animal experimentation. So it is not possible to apply the rules of virtue ethics in these cases.

But still, granted that abortion is sometimes permissible and sometimes wrong, one must be able to say why it is permissible or wrong. And giving the reason somewhat leads to some sort of generalization that any case of abortion in similar circumstances would be permissible or wrong. And that would naturally be a statement of a rule or principle. So in a way, *virtue ethics can produce 'rules governing abortion'*. So we can rightly say that virtue ethics can produce "rules governing abortion, not of course the sort which the deontic theorist expected, but rules which rebut the claim, that virtue ethics cannot say anything about the right and wrongs of acts such as abortion, euthanasia, etc."[6]

But here too the objection may be, "You are just helping yourself to non-virtue based concepts. What account can you give about taking of human life, except that it is a concern for only the virtuous? In answer we can say that this objection is based on a misunderstanding of what virtue ethics involves. It is often thought that, virtue ethics, in being agent-centred rather than act-centred, in starting with virtues and vices rather than right or wrong acts, is committed to a sort of reductionism. Accordingly, it considers that the concept of virtuous agent is the only concept relevant to morality and that all other moral concepts should be reduced to the concept of virtuous or vicious agent. "We should remember that virtue ethics also claims that part of virtuous person's practical wisdom is her knowledge, her correct appreciation of what is truly good, truly worth, truly important and truly serious."[7] So the virtue ethicist does not say that 'taking life is a serious matter because the *virtuous take it seriously*, —on the other hand the virtuous think that taking life is a serious matter because *taking life is in fact a very serious matter*.

There is, however, a slightly different version of the problem: that here are cases in which applying the virtue and vice terms does not yield an answer to "what should I do?" Suppose someone 'youthful in character'[8] as Aristotle puts it, finds herself in an apparently conflicting situation, after applying those terms ; then she will not be able to decide what to do unless she knows of a virtuous agent who can guide her. But her quandary is the result of her lack of wisdom and this is what virtue theory expects .

Christine Strawson, in his book, Virtue ethics, insists that the inability of virtue ethics to be useful in applied ethics is due to the *disagreement* among virtuous agents, whose virtues do not follow the same course of action. "Any virtue theorist who writes about real moral issues, must rely on her audience's agreeing with her application of all these concepts . But some other virtue theorist might take different premises about these matters and come up with different conclusions—there is no way to distinguish between the two."[9]

Though a standard reply to the objection is, the appeal to the standards of practical wisdom possessed by the virtuous —on a case by case basis . R .J. Wallace draws our attention to the problem of disagreement : "If there were lack of convergence among connoisseurs of wine as to which wines are good and which wines are bad, then it would be correspondingly implausible to suppose that their judgements are rationally well-supported, or that they represented a normative ideal of correct discrimination?"[10] Wallace suggests that the virtuous are precisely in the position of "extensive lack of convergence". He continues, — "other connoisseurs of the moral life are apt to be moved by case-specific reasons, for acting in quite different and incompatible ways, and this will undermine the normative dimension of practical reason : the idea that the exercise of judgement enables its possessor to discern the uniquely *correct or right* thing to do, in particular cases of actions."[11]

It can be replied, that the search for the *uniquely correct* thing to do, is misguided. Why should uniqueness be required? The real problem, however, is not the need of *uniquely correct solutions* to moral problems; but the fact that there is too much disagreement even between virtuous agents applying virtues of practice. Even if a virtuous agent adopts a good course of action for one set of good reasons, there may exist good reasons for adopting other courses of action also. So they may naturally disagree as to which course of action is best or right? So Susan Wolf charges virtue ethics of, *indeterminacy*. "There will be cases in which there are good reasons for one position and good reasons for an incompatible position and no farther overarching principle and perspective from which these can be put into any further objective balance. In such cases one might say that both positions are equally right . Or one might say that there is no right answer, no fact of the matter about what is right."[12]

Rosalind Hursthouse supports this view by saying that different virtues may tempt us in different directions. Thus, for example, in a value-laden problem, self-protection points towards finishing it over, perseverance points towards continuing; tolerance and openness point towards involving more affected parties, efficiency points towards neglecting some of them; caring points to giving her further chances, benevolence points towards sacking her. So it is no wonder that different virtuous agents may recommend different courses of action. This claim can be understood in two different ways, (i) virtues may contain in-built—rules or precise instructions to perform certain actions; and (ii) virtues are not constituted by set of rules but are rather, *prototypes.* On this understanding of virtue, individual virtues, though providing good reason for conflicting actions, may not require those actions. According to the notion of virtue as *prototype* one might think of a virtue as a framework of broad constraints,which is then made more specific according the specific situations.[13]

But, does this solve the problem of disagreement among the virtuous? Strawson has offered three replies to this solution, First, the most important part of the solution is that it requires richer and exhaustive understanding of the particulars. The difficulty of the value-laden problems is that, enough details are never supplied. Secondly, we must be clear about the nature of the differences Are the virtuous agents disagreeing about *the* thing to do ? It need not be the case that each is saying that the other is wrong. The understanding of a virtue as *a prototype* shows that why this is so : a virtue is not a collection of rules guiding actions in hard cases. More likely, they permit different actions. Finally and most importantly, we should appreciate that virtuous agents having different roles, perspectives, forms of life and expertise, need to exercise the virtues of practice The analogy between wine connoisseurs and virtuous agents is not appropriate. For wine connoisseurs in wine tasting, taste wine with their own preference for flavours and brands, without consulting the view of others . But in case of solving or taking decisions in value-laden problems, moral agents can never be in isolation—he must take into account other virtuous agent's views and opinions.[14]

The whole confusion regarding the application of ethics of virtue in solving the value-laden problems is due to the fact that the skeptics have very wrong idea about the models of applying normative ethics preferably by the so-called moral engineers, as such. It is not true that Virtue ethics, in order to be applicable, must be interpreted in the form of engineering models, i.e., to apply virtues or a set of virtues artificially by an agent or by persuasion to resolve an ethical impasse. On the contrary we can justify the applications of the different virtues of ethical corroborators in solving the value-laden moral problems, when we take recourse to the method of *"ethical corroboration"*. "*Intersubjective corroboration* implies a close corroboration of moral viewpoints in considering value-laden problems, i.e., (i) arguing and debating about decisions needed to resolve a moral problem, and (ii) arranging and encouraging moral discussions in order to resolve moral problems."[15] Thus applying virtues to resolve the value-laden problems is not equivalent to applying any theory of normative ethics; on the contrary, it involves the application of some of our basic virtues and our common ethical knowledge along with a close participation and interaction with other interested parties. Ethical corroboration thus can be said to be a valuable model 'I' applying virtue ethics, in so far it does not become a handmaid of a group of people. The skeptics, however, still contend that the prospect of people's participation in intersubjective corroboration is not very bright since it really amounts to the application of our knowledge of social mores, customs, norms or personal and social virtues, and these are not eligible to be called 'applying virtue ethics'. We can refute this charge of the skeptics by saying that a collective resolution of moral problems does not presuppose moral dogmas and there is surely some difference between common-sense morality and applying common ethical knowledge through intersubjective discourse. Normally we hardly distinguish between the two because we believe that one may easily replace the other, but to do it actually may be a great mistake. We have to accept that as a responsible member of the Indian society, we may naturally possess diverse moral opinions and consequently they may reflect in our individual behaviour. Thus in cases of moral decision-making we are sort of bound to transcend the so-called dogmas and apply our common moral knowledge comprising of rightness, oughtness and dutifulness. An ethical discourse is bound to move from 'what is usually done' to 'what is ought to be done'. Sensibly speaking, the most important virtue of virtue ethics with regard to the resolution of value-laden practical problems is that the corroborating parties need to be *virtuous*. They should realize that they have some rights as well as 'obligations' towards this community .The urge 'to do' for the sake of existence is the basic virtue to be expected from us and in the absence of which no corroboration can take place. It is stressed in Indian philosophy that unless our intentions (or "*abhisandhi*') are pure, our efforts in practical life hardly make any sense.

REFERENCES

1. Oneill, Onora. "Kant After Virtue", *"Inquiry"*, Volume XXVI, December 1983, pp. 387-401.
2. Louden,Robert. B. *American Philosophical Quarterly,* 21 [1984], pp. 227-236.
3. Hursthouse, Rosalind . *Virtue and Reasons*, Oxford University Press, England, p. 63.
4. Oneill, Onora. *Kant After Virtue, op., cit.,* p. 407.
5. Hursthouse, Rosalind. *Virtue and Reasons, op. cit.,* p. 68.
6. *Ibid.,* p. 72.

7. *Ibid.*, p. 76.
8. Aristotle, *Nicomachean Ethics*, trans by Terence Irwin, Hacket Publishing Company, Indianapolis, 1985, pp. 160-161.
9. Strawson, Christine. *Virtue Ethics*, Oxford University Press, England, 1987, p. 223.
10. Wallace, R.J. Virtue Reason and Principle, *Canadian Journal of Philosophy* 21, 1991, pp. 465-490.
11. *Ibid.*, p. 491.
12. Wolf, Susan. "Two Levels of Pluralism", in *Ethics*, 102, 1992, pp. 785-798.
13. Hursthouse, Rosalind, *Virtue and Reasons*, *op. cit*, p. 80.
14. Strawson, Christine. *Virtue Ethics*, *op. cit.*, p. 288.
15. Guha, Debashish . "Intersubjective Corroboration", *JICPR*, Vol. XIX, No. II, 2002, p. 54.

Chapter – 16

Ethics of Virtue –The Western View and the Classical Eastern View

Dipasikha Chakrabarty

Ethics of virtue was initially introduced to distinguish an approach in normative ethics, which emphasizes the virtues or moral character in contrast to an approach which emphasizes duties or rules [deontology] or one which emphasizes the consequences of actions [utilitarianism]. Until thirty years ago, normative ethics was dominated by just two theories : deontology, which was inspired by Immanuel Kant and utilitarianism, which derives its modern formulations from eighteenth and nineteenth century philosophers, such as David Hume, Jeremy Bentham, James Stuart Mill and John Stuart Mill. Gradually a change was noticeable; the emphasis started shifting from "norms" to character and traits of moral agents. Virtue ethicists started asking, how we should "be" rather than what we should "do". The reasons for the revival of virtue ethics may be traced to several factors. Part of the answer lies in the fact that the prevailing literature ignored or sidelined a number of topics that any adequate moral philosophy should deal with. Two most important features are 'motives' and 'moral character', while others are, moral education, moral wisdom, friendship and family relationship and the most important question of what sort a person should I be and how I should live. Let me now throw some light on the important Western views regarding ethics of virtue.

Western view of ethics of virtue is essentially monistic in nature and stresses *character* at the core of morality. The Western thinkers define virtue as a character trait that a human being needs for his eudemonia. They profess that the central moral question is not, "what ought I to do ?" but what sort of a person am I to be ?" The virtuous person is someone "for whom proper conduct emanates characteristically from a fixed disposition ."[1] Though there is not much of agreement as to the exact nature of virtue, still we can claim the following common ground : the virtuous dispositions lead the moral agents to be sensitive to the goods and ills to which people are exposed in particular situations and to respond positively. On the epistemological side, the monists hold that the perception of the virtuous agent is the original and central source of knowledge of how much good to pursue, for whom, in what circumstances and how vigorously. The Western Ethicists further assert that the virtues are natural to humans, i.e., they are implanted in us naturally, in such a way that the virtuous agents benefit from virtue, both individually and socially. Living alone and living without virtue are both harmful to us.

The greatest exponent of Western virtue ethics is Aristotle. Aristotle in his Nicomachean Ethics focuses more on the inner traits and character of the virtuous individual, than he does on the rightness and goodness of actions. He further stresses that the rightness of an action does not depend on motives or habits of the person. Rather a virtuous individual is someone, who, without relying on rules, is sensitive and intelligent enough to perceive what is right and noble, through his or her practical wisdom, which is trained by philosophical wisdom. The imperatives of the practical wisdom is the origin of a habitual state of mind or what is right intention. This empowers the person to choose the right,at the right moment, for the right reason, towards the right person, at a right degree. When Aristotle makes the virtuous man a standard of what is virtuous, he primarily means that, it is his conduct, his choices, not just dispositions, which is the standard.

In contemporary times, Michael Slote's *agent-based virtue ethics* stresses that moral status of acts is entirely derivative from independent aretaic characterizations of motives, character, traits or individuals. This clearly implies that the virtuous individual does what is noble or virtuous because *it is noble thing to do,* rather than the statement that whatever a virtuous person does, is virtuous. According to Slote, a virtue is an admirable trait of character of the agent and its admirability need not be based on its tendencies to promote further value or good of the agent.[2] Gary Watson, in his writing, "On the primacy of character "has also stressed a similar monistic view of ethics of virtue. He said, "in an ethics of virtue, how it is best or right or proper to conduct oneself, is explained in terms of how it is best for a human being to be."[3] In other words, he claimed that the basic moral facts are facts about quality of character and moral facts about actions are secondary to these. James Martineau's agent based conception of morality treats "compassion" or "benevolence" as the highest motive . Some others, such as Hume, Hutchenson and now, Jorge Garcia have placed a special emphasis on compassion or 'benevolence'. All these can be said to be 'monistic'in their approach to ethics of virtue, in so far as it focuses on this or that part of character of a moral agent or moral agents and believes that keeping agent at the helm of virtue-talk would be necessary and sufficient.

However some thinkers are critical about the above view. The most common charge is that the Western view of ethics of virtue does not provide us with exact and detailed guide for action . But this thesis is difficult to evaluate since codifiability seems to be a matter of degree. The radicalists, however, attacked the attempt of formulating any 'agent-based' theory of virtue. First of all, they argue that, these theories appear to vitiate the common distinction between 'doing the right thing, and 'doing the right thing for the right reasons'. If rightness of an action is made to depend upon the rightness of motives and wrongness, in terms of bad motives, then there will be every chance of misjudging an action, e.g., the prosecutor who does his duty by trying to convict a defendant, but if he is motivated by malice rather than by a sense of duty, will that not mean that the prosecutor does the wrong thing in prosecuting someone out of malice? Is this not very unfortunate ?

It does not follow from the agent-based assumption that, he acts wrongly if he acts from malice.

The critics argue further that, if the evaluation of actions is dependent on the virtuous agents then, we can legitimately deduce that, if one is virtuous person, it cannot morally matter what one actually does, i.e., a virtuous person or his actions are not subject to moral constraints In this light, monistic approach to ethics of virtue seems to be highly 'autistic' and 'antinomian' approach to ethics —an approach that seems to go against the notion that the moral life involves 'living up to 'certain standards of behaviour.'

The theory of virtue built on universal benevolence is also not without charges. The main problem of this approach is that, this form of morality is over-demanding and calls for too-much of self sacrifice. We can try to answer this, by citing several versions of morality based on universal benevolence, which are surely not over-demanding. A satisfying version of it may be interpreted as follows, i.e., acts are right if they come from a motive that is "close-enough" to universal benevolence, rather than insisting that only acts exemplifying the highest motive is acceptable. But such a view does not entail that the virtuous individual can choose any action he or she pleases without the goodness of her actions or behaviour being compromised. For a benevolent agent is capable of choosing many actions that 'do not' reflect his benevolence . Or, we may say in other words that it is presumably within one's power to refuse to help and if so, then his actions will not show benevolence. So benevolence cannot be made the 'touchstone' of moral evaluation. However, as Slote has said, "benevolence involves not only the desire to do what is good or best overall for the people one is concerned about, but also the desire that no one of those people should be hurt or suffer, morality as universal benevolence can explain why we might be horrified at killing one to save many, even if in the end it holds that, that is what we morally ought to do."[4]

Classical Eastern ethics of virtue, on the other hand, goes one step further and claims that ethics of virtue is not only monistic in nature but it is necessarily *transcendental* . It should be pointed out at the outset that it is very difficult to find out an exact counterpart of the word 'virtue' in Indian ethics. It is sometimes identified with *dharma* in the latter whereas in other instances it is called *sadguṇa* (good qualities) or *kalyanaguṇa* (beneficial qualities). The word *dharma* formed from the root *dh*, to hold, means that which holds a thing and maintains it in being . Every form of life, every group of men has its *dharma*, which is the law of its being . Interpreted in this way, *dharma* or virtue is conformity with the truth of things; *adharma* or vice is opposition to it.[5] Sometimes the *Upaniṣads* make a distinction between *satya* or truth and *dharma,* the latter representing the practice of virtue and the former, the principle underlying it. But later it is also stressed that, both together constitute *dharma*, in the *complete sense of the term.* The ancient Vedic view of virtue referred to the good result following from the performance of vedic rituals and sacrifices. But at the same time, it also emphasized *inner purity.* Thus, truth, godliness, honour to parents, kindness to animals love for man, abstinence from theft, murder and adultery were inculcated as the essentials of good life. Thus in course of time, the sphere of *dharma* or virtue widened to include *both internal traits of character as well as duties* of a moral agent or moral agents and of the members of the society or state as well. Thus arose the threefold classification of virtues : (i) those described as 'general' *sādhārana-dharma* which comprise acts, indicative of virtues like kindness and truth-speaking and are equally obligatory to all; and (ii) those termed 'special' *varnāshrama dharma* which are relative to one's social class and (iii) those virtues attached to the particular stage one has reached in life's discipline *âsrama* Faithful adherence to *dharma* would naturally lead to *moksa* or liberation, after a series of incarnations. '*Moksa*' or liberation means 'perfection', not in the theoretical sense but in the practical sense of rising above pleasure and pain, praise and blame, heat and cold, loss and gain and becoming one with the Absolute or Transcendental Reality, which is Pure Consciousness, Pure Knowledge and Pure Bliss. ("*Satchidānanda*"). Thus '*moksa*' is not an intellectual achievement but a possible state of 'transcendental' existence attainable by humans, through the practice of the virtues. The virtues are thus primarily instrumental and indispensable for the well-being of man. From ancient times, Indian thinkers were attracted by the quest of the inner self or the '*ātman*'. Spiritually advanced sages realized after deep meditation that, this self or '*ātman*' is '*Brahman*' or Absolute. This fact enhances the dignity of man and makes him the centre of attraction. So, whatever may be the mode of empowering the spiritual potentiality of man, it is emphasized by almost all the schools of Indian philosophy that the virtues are very important for the ultimate realization of man. Yet we have to understand that Indian ethics of virtue is not called 'transcendental' merely for the reason that the ultimate end of human life is transcendental; rather it neither considers the traits of a moral agent to *be most important* but because the transcendental ethics of virtue speaks of the inculcation of the virtue of oneness or *abheda*, within this world of plurality and within the appearances of different values and virtues. It is within *ta* that the realization of *satya* is taken to be the crux of virtue and this is the spirit of the ethics of virtue. Here a natural feeling is that if the realization of *ābheda* is the crux of virtue, whose virtue is it anyway? Is it not the virtue of a moral agent and for that reason, it is the monistic idea put in a different form? Further if this realization of the ultimate virtue be most crucial then what is meant by liberation or *moksa*? (i) Is Indian ethics of virtue egocentric? and (ii) Whose liberation do we need? It appears that the liberation is of a person but not of persons or the entire existence. Does Indian Ethics of virtue constrict liberation to that of an individual/individuals? And does it call for such virtue inculcation in an individual? Now if it calls for the liberation of the entire existence, one may jump to the conclusion that at best we have pluralistic virtue ethics, as in the case of the realization of *satya* or selfhood in man, monism has been ascribed to the Indian ethics of virtue. There may be a serious category confusion here which has to be noticed first. We speak of both epistemological monism and metaphysical monism. But equally true is that we speak of *ethical monism* which is not exactly the same as any one of the two mentioned above, but they are all interrelated in the context of Indian ethics of virtue. Thus to say that, *moksa* is the only *summum bonum* or the only ethical ideal of life "is not equal to saying merely that *moksa* is the ultimate essence in existence. (metaphysical monism), or *moksa* is merely a case of unity or oneness of the knower and the known" (epistemological monism). In the broad context of Indian ethics of virtue, when we use 'monism', we may find Indian thinkers supporting the notion of 'well-being of the moral agent' we may find Indian ethical thinkers supporting the notion of 'well-being of sentient and non-sentient beings or the 'well-being of the whole existence'. But more pertinently, the Indian thinkers speak of unique cosmic evolution from many to one.[6] It is not merely 'well-being' of 'one' or 'all.' or both. Neither is it both . It is little confusing to say that moksa is 'well-being' in any of these senses. *Moksa* may be looked upon as transcendental ethical virtue within a corporeal being who realizes or attempts at realizing "oneness,"among plural existence. It is also a kind of divinisation of the entire existence and a conception of unique evolution. A moral agent is virtuous also in so far as he realizes that ultimately even the corporeal *bhuta* [matter] evolves to the ultimate reality or *satchidānanda* because it is the latter which has *involuted* in the forms of the *bhutas* and thûs the reality is in essence, 'one'. This transcendental ethical virtue thus leads a *consciousness renaissance in man*, so much so that he or she intends, decides and acts with the basic spirit of oneness and inevitably this leads to the removal of bondage not for the one or many but for entire existence. Thus one conceives *moksa*-urge even in the *bhutas* when it evolves to *manas, praṇa*, *atimānasa*, and *satchidānanda.* It is a cosmic urge which is all-pervading.[7] This urge, the ultimate ethical one is the virtue or *dharma*, that is the intrinsic property of existence . We may recall that this all-pervading intrinsic ethical virtue is the Ṛta, the cosmic manifestation of *satya*— the ultimate or Absolute Reality. This consciousness renaissance in moral agents and an urge to liberate makes sense in the Indian ethics of virtue, which understood properly would provide a cue to *relative* truth inherent in monism as well.

REFERENCES

1. Kosman, L.A. *Essays on Aristotle's Ethics*, University of California, Berkeley, 1980, p. 103.
2. Slote, Michael. *Virtue Ethics*, Oxford University Press, New York, p. 241
3. Watson, Gary . *On The Primacy of Character* by Stephan Darwall, Blackwell Publishers, Malden, MA, USA, p. 237.
4. Slote, Michael . *Virtue Ethics*, Oxford University Press, New York, p. 244.
5. Radhakrishnan, S. *Hindu View of Life*, The Macmillan Company, 1927, New York, p. 78.
6. Ghosh, Aurobindo, *Life Divine*, Aurobindo Asram Publications, Calcutta, p. 101.
7. Ghosh, Aurobindo, *ibid.*, p. 102.

Chapter – 17

Purushartha

D.K. Chakravarty

Thinkers of the world are despondent about the staggering headlines of newspapers. Disintegration and disruption have gripped our society. A belief has gained ground that spiritual truths are almost of no use in a practical world. As a consequence, emphasis is laid on the materialistic and mechanistic aspects of life, on narrow racial, communal and sectarian interest and there is an ever increasing confusion of aims and ideas in people's minds. Indians now are exposed to the sinister influences of a predominantly materialistic society. Intellectual spoon-feeding has stunted their initiative and capacity to ponder and seek and ask meaningful questions about life. Alienation from religious tradition has deprived them of the power of primordial images necessary for a rich life; modern education has created a materialistic bias and deprived on youth of the support of a religious vocabulary without which it is difficult to frame spiritual ideas. The realization of the spiritual nature of man and of the ultimate reality underlying the universe made religion the foundation-stone of Indian culture and civilization. In the passionate words of Radhakrishnan, "From the beginning of recorded history, Hinduism has borne witness to the sacred flame of the spirit which must remain forever, even while dynasties crash and empires tumble into ruins. It alone can give our civilization a soul and men and women a principle to live by", (S. Radhakrishnan,

Religion and Society, George Allen and Unwin, London, 1959, p. 3). The secret of the extraordinary vitality of Indian culture lies in its conception of values or *purusarthas—dharma*, *artha*, *kama* and *moksa*. The four-fold scheme of values is not a gift from heaven but an emergence from human nature. *It is the criterion of being man.*

The Indian frame of reference has at its centre the concept of a multi-dimensional autonomous man. It must be noted at the very outset that the concept of man in the Indian tradition is radically different from the Western concept. The scriptural literature of the West, particularly the Judeo-Christian, tells us that the very life of man is the result of the original fall, which in turn is the result of original sin. On this view every man is considered to be a born sinner who should be ashamed of his very being, his very existence. On the other hand in the Indian tradition, men are supposed to be *amṛtasya putrah*, children of immortal bliss. The *Aitareya Aranyaka* declares that man is the abode of Brahman *ayam puruso brahma-loka* (II.13). In the Indian tradition a person is constituted of three bodies, each inside the other. The outermost is the *sthula sarira*, the gross body, subject to growth, ageing, death and decay. Inside the *sthula sarira* is the *linga sarira* or *suksma sarira*, the subtle body which constitutes almost the entire content of a man's personality and is with him till he attains liberation. It is the focal point of the theory of *karma* and reincarnation. Inside the subtle body is the *karana sarira*. There is nothing corresponding to it in the Western thought. These three are referred to as bodies because they are the products of matter in its gross and subtle forms. They constitute the non-spiritual aspect of the truly spiritual part of man, *atman*.

In Indian tradition there is no dichotomy between the spiritual and the social life, between religious and secular activities. As life is a unity, it cannot be divided into watertight compartments. The spiritual values express themselves through ordinary ways of life. Man is more than matter, he is not a brute or a body. He is a vibrant living spirit, a spark of the divine fire. The mystery of the universe stirs in man as the mystery of the self, The *atman*. Through the discovery of the centre of the universe in the centre of man, man is revealed in his infinite dimension as a self-transcending being. The modern age is witness to a crisis in ethics, a breakdown of traditional values. Most of the problems in individual and social life can be traced to the failure to recognize the divinity lying at the heart of all beings.

Samkara says in his Introduction to the commentary on the *Gita* that religion of the Vedas is two-fold! *pravṛttilaksana* – with a tendency towards the world, and *nivṛttilaksana* – with a tendency away from the world, that is, towards the ultimate truth. The former is for *abhyudaya* of men and the latter for *nihsreyasa*. Both these types of religion are necessary in this world for men of different temperaments. It is needless to say that the enormous majority of mankind is inclined towards the *pravṛtti* type and only a very few have inclination for *nivṛtti*. There is no antagonism between *pravṛtti* and *mukti*. In *sattvika* form of *bhoga*, both the *bhokta* and the *bhogya* are moulded by some elements of transcendence. Here *bhoga* turns out to be *yoga* and thereby a unity is established between the *prakṛtika* and *atmika* or transcendent existence. So in such instances *bhukti is not opposed to mukti*. The first three of the four-fold values (*tri-varga*) have been prescribed for the *bhakti*-type of persons. The fourth, *moksa* is meant for the *nivṛtti*-margins. So the worldly attachment is never "eternally condemned".

The first-three *dharma*, *artha* and *kama* are treated as the universal warp and woof of all ordered human society. But *moksa* is regarded as a trans-social pursuit meant for those few who dare to go deeper into the spiritual dimension of life. For others, this experience of transcendental freedom comes within the limitations of social context, as *dharma* which is the confluence of social and trans-social ends of life. Literally, *Purusartha* admits all that is worth of being sought for in human life in its varied and wide dimensions including the physical, psychological, moral and spiritual. *Purusartha* is not a mere recognition of the factually desired but is ideally worthy of being sought for. It is not simply four sets of cardinal values but a four-fold system properly organized in our value culture. *Dharma*, *artha* and *kama* are all relative ends and lack absolute significance. *Moksa* is not on a par with these subsidiary ends. As liberation from all that is perishable, it is the highest of the ends that men desire, i.e., the *summum bonum*.

That pleasure is a natural object of desire is an obvious fact. Indian thinkers give due recognition to *kama* as the worthy object of pursuit. This does not mean that it endorses the principle of pleasure for pleasure's sake. *Kama* will have to work in harmony with other values and not in complete separation from *dharma*. *Artha* in the form of power and wealth is the means of subsistence for a man. Ranging from sensual pleasure to artistic delight, *kama* enriches *artha* with qualitative experience. But *artha* and *kama* are subservient to *dharma*. In the metaphysical sense, *dharma* means the essential nature of a thing, but in the ethical sense, it means those duties and obligations which one appropriate to one's station in society as well as those action and duties which are intrinsic to the moral nature of man. So *dharma* is all-comprehensive and secures the material spiritual substance and growth of the individual and society.

Indian tradition does not look down upon material prosperity or organic satisfaction but treats them as valid pursuits. It considers *lobha* or greed and *moha* or delusion, arising from unchecked cravings, as unethical, because they are anti-social. The function of *dharma* is to restrain these pursuits from becoming anti-social. Bereft of *dharma* a man becomes reduced to a beast. Duty determined by one's natural bent in accord with the law of one's own being (*svabhava*) as well as competence (*adhikara*) and environmental conditioning (*sanskara*) is *svadharma*—one's own way of life. *Svadharma* is conducive to spiritual growth. The way of prosperity (*abhyudaya*) and the way of supreme felicity (*nihsreyasa*) are not contradictory but complementary. The concept of *moksa* gives a new dimension to the problems of morality. *Moksa* does not devalue earthly values but transmutes them into proper instruments of spiritual life. Though *moksa* implies eventual renunciation of all finite interest and ends and such are ideal may be impossible for the majority of people, yet renunciation in the sense of detachment (*anasakti*) and service is recommended for all. Renunciation has a two-fold character; negatively, it moves away from the impermanent and positively it gets anchored in the permanent. It is sheer misunderstanding to say that renunciation consists in sacrifice of the world, not enjoyment of the world. Good life is a happy life, not only here and now but also hereafter. True renunciation is a natural development and fulfilment of good life. But renunciation in the sense of abandoning all duties is never advocated. The four *purusarthas* together constitute one goal—*moksa* which perfects and is perfected by *dharma*, and *dharma* which disciplines our pursuit of *artha* and *kama*.

The charge that is very often laid by critics against *moksa* that it is a selfish individual salvation having no regard for the good of others is based entirely on ignorance of its real meaning in the Indian tradition; man: has a two fold journey: one, on the secular temporal plane as an individual and a part of society fulfilling his duties in life, and the other, as a seeker of his true spiritual nature which is ever integrated with the cosmic reality. As a sensory being man is a member of the empirical world; or a rational spiritual being he goes beyond nature, beyond the domination of natural cause and effect, submitting to the norms he sets up and emancipating himself from all objectifying influences (including cord). That is why Kant says, ". . . . the will of a rational being can be a will of his own only under the idea of freedom." (*Ground work of the Metaphysics of Morals*, Hutchinson's, London, 1948, p.116).

Self-realization is not self-seeking in the narrow sense. The recognition of the spiritual essence in oneself enables one to go beyond the limitations of the ego. Through the realization of unity of one's own self with the spiritual essence in everything, one achieves boundless expansion and harmony with all beings. The strangle hold of egotism is destroyed and the inner floodgates of love and compassion in the human heart are opened. Altruism is in-built in us. If we consider the holistic nature of human reality, it becomes intelligible why the disequilibrium produced by man's alienation is remedied in his search for better equilibrium, a state of complete identity which is described beautifully in the *Gita*:

"His own self dwelling within all beings, all beings within his own self." (6.29). There is the "I" everywhere and everything in "me." (6.30)

In Indian tradition every man is born with debts and his whole life is a process of repaying them—the debts to the ancestors, the debt to the seers and sages and the debt to gods. In the Western tradition man is born *with rights* but in the Indian tradition man is born with *obligations*. There is a sound basis for a stable social order in our traditional image of man. If the ideal citizenship is the spirit of service, the spring of the spirit must be sought in the philosophy of renunciation. It has now become a fashion to consider all national problems in terms of power. So we are engaged in a kind of competitive social work. The ideal of service is vitiated by politics. Indian tradition does *not define politics as a struggle for power*. It visualizes a new kind of politics, not a politics based on the power but a *politics elevated by the spirit of renunciation*. The spirit of detachment and service pervades the outlook of ancient thinkers. But it was gradually lost among the majority of Indians and the term 'renunciation' was applied to *moksa* alone. The lack of the spirit of detachment and service has brought about great unsettlement in Indian social life. Service is not an act of charity. It is an obligatory social act based on ontological fact. Every man is born with certain natural dispositions and limitations which he cannot overcome. This law determines the duties of a person. One need not be bewildered at the pluralism of social existence of man, for the goal is consummation in the unitive experience of self-realization. A great desideratum of the present age is the unity of humanity despite all diversities. The only way to love and harmony among men is to find a common ground of human relationship that transcends all distinctions. The recognition of the spiritual essence of man provides such a ground. This ancient wisdom has to be propagated in a modern voice, not just an echo of an old word but the authentic expression of a new realization.

Chapter – 18

Concept of *Dharma*

The Metaphysical Foundation of Indian Ethics

V. T. Sebastian

One of the key notions that have come to occupy an evermore visible place in the discussion of Indian ethics is the concept of *dharma*. This concept is said to be the object of theoretical and practical reflections while dealing with the problematic of ethical theories and practices as it has paved way for the sanctioning authority of ethical considerations in Indian societies. This chapter intends to argue that the concept of *dharma* is the bedrock of Indian ethics and have situated its applicability in the social, political and economic domains of Indian societies. My analysis of this concept considers *dharma* in relation to its metaphysical and ethical presuppositions as the *summum bonum* of Indian ethics. That is to say that, on the conceptual dimensions, there is a determined philosophy of ethics in the concept of *dharma*, which shapes the meaning of human life as the leading principle of Indian life.

Concept of *Dharma*: Preliminaries

In the Indian social, political and philosophical thought, the concept of *dharma* is predicated with multiple shades of meaning. *Dharma* is said to be the nature of things and the law of their being and relationships, a cosmic order permeating the universe, rules of social and individual conduct, moral righteousness and religious duty. There are diverse ways in which this term has been used both in the Indian Philosophical systems and day-to-day life experiences. It stood for religious observance, justice in the societal living, righteousness in one's conception and perception of things and ideals, conformity to law, obedience to the present social order, sense of duty in human beings, etc., and hence, this concept has not only a religious and moral standing in the average Indians but it has an ethical and legal significance in the cultural sensitivity of this country. Accordingly, all human values, norms, duties and rights— individual and social— were explained by referring them back to this concept. The concept of *dharma*, the central concept of this culture, is not that of something commanded by a God, but that of an order in the very nature of things, the nature of things being an expression of ultimate reality, rather than the arbitrary creation of an all powerful will of a God. To appreciate and appropriate the wider meaning of this concept with regard to its ethical and metaphysical implications, let us try to understand its origin and development, which is rooted in the Vedic concept of Ṛta.

Ṛta and Dharma

As understood earlier, *dharma* is a very complex concept in the religio-philosophic literature of India. In fact, the authentic name of Hinduism is *Sanatana-dharma* or Eternal Law. The word *dharma* is derived from the Sanskrit root *dhri—dharati* = to hold fast, uphold, bear, support, keep in due order. The etymology suggests the real notion of *dharma* as that which sustains and maintains the universe in due order. Expressions such as *dharma-putra*, *sahadharmini*, *dharmikam*, *dharmistha*, *dana-dharma*, *dharma-pada*, *dharmasya giani*, *dharmacara*, *dharmam saranam gacchami*, *dharmo raksati*, etc. are quite familiar words to all Indians.[1] Accordingly, this concept stands for ethics, religion, morality, virtue, spirituality, truth, good conduct and so on:[2] it also stands for natural and positive laws, the moral code, and the various distinct duties of the individual. The whole religio-philosophical and didactic literature of India lays great emphasis on the necessity of maintaining *dharma* for spiritual realization. Various systems of Indian thought emphasize the observance of *dharma* as a *conditio sine qua non* of internal purification leading to eternal bliss. The *Advaita* system too presupposes in the aspirant a great degree of mental purity and good dispositions obtained through the observance of *dharma* even before the aspirant actually enters the path of *jnana*.[3] But in Vedic literature, instead of *dharma*, we have the concept of *Ṛta*.

Ṛta and its Importance

The Vedic Indians, like their Hellenist brothers, were struck by the law and order, rhythm and harmony, prevailing in the universe.[4] Behind the rhythmic occurrences of natural phenomena such as day and night, full moon and new moon, high tide and low tide, heat and cold, sunshine and rain, summer and winter, spring and autumn, the Vedic Indians detected the eternal law or perennial order which they called *Ṛta*.[5] The universe itself is said to be founded on *Ṛta*, and moving according to it.The concept of *Ṛta* as cosmic order was later extended to the field of sacrifice (*yajna*), and to the sphere of human conduct. The Vedic concept of *Ṛta* is thus applicable to the course of 'macrocosms' (universe) as well as to the microcosms' that is man;[6] it is applicable also to the sacrifice that mirrors the 'macrocosms in parvo.' *Ṛta* can, therefore be rendered as 'cosmic order', 'moral law', 'sacrificial law', 'truth', 'righteousness', etc. The eternal Law, *Ṛta*, according to the ancient Indians, is eternally established by God '*Varuna*' and is zealously guarded by him. Hence, any irregularity in the field of sacrifice or in the sphere of human conduct was deemed to be a breach of *Ṛta*, the universal law; such breach of *Ṛta* was counted as a sin (*enas, agas*); and sin is an offence against *Varuna-deva*, the promulgator and guardian of eternal *Ṛta*. Thus we see in the *Vedas* the idea that the violation of moral law is a sin and that sin is a fetter.

Knowledge of *Dharma*

What is the ultimate norm of *dharma*? The usual answer is that 'tradition' (as embodied in the *dharma-sastra* and other *smṛti*-texts), the practices (*sadacara*) of the *dharma* knowing people, wholesome customs of people at large, etc., form the norm of one's action: they tell us what *dharma* is. For all practical purposes, the *dharma-sastra* prescribed the *dharma* for each and every individual of various *varnas*/castes and *asramas*.[7] To say that "*dharma-sastras* and practices of holy men constitute the *dharma* or norms of human conduct" does not answer the questions ultimately; it is of little use to say that one should act this way "because the holy texts say so, or holy men did so". The question can again be asked: "Why should we obey the *dharma-sastras* or why should we follow the holy 'men?" The radical question, therefore, is: "what is the ultimate basis or criterion of such and such as *dharma*? How did the knower of *dharma* themselves know that such and such acts are *dharma*, and such and such acts are *adharma*? The traditional answer has been more or less as follows: "The *Ṛsis* had a deep insight into the highest Reality that directs the course of these manifold phenomena." But the question still remains unanswered: "What is the ultimate reason for holding definite actions as constituents of *dharma*? The ultimate justification of *dharma* cannot be human authority." Some scholars hold the view that the resulting harmony of the doer with the Highest Reality was implied as the ultimate justification of *dharma*. Creel points out that the ideal of *moksa* as *summum bonum* or Supreme Value could be the ultimate norm in relation to which *dharma* could be recognized; but this is not clearly argued.[8] The reason for this attitude is based on the fact that the common folk are content to follow *dharma* as prescribed by authority and tradition. The view that something is right merely because scripture says so makes the distinction between good and evil purely arbitrary; the distinction would not, then, be based on a difference in the nature of good and evil. Moreover, if scriptures arbitrarily saying something makes it right, we would have to acknowledge that it could just as reasonably have said the opposite of what it said. In that case, one needs to ponder over certain criteria on the basis of which we could reasonably argue for the validity of scripture's saying so. *Advaita-Vedanta* judges the value of the *dharmic* character of an action in its relation to the Supreme Value, the *Nishsreyasa* that is Brahman or *moksa*.

The Triad of *Dharma: Dharma-trimurti*

Hindu tradition recognizes three distinct categories of *dharma*, viz. *sadharana* - or *samanya-dharma* (*dharma* for all people irrespective of caste or asrama), *varnasrama-dharma* (*dharma* for distinct castes and *asramas)* and *moksadharma (dharma* to be practiced in direct view of *moksa* or perfect liberation).

1. *Sadharana-dharma* or *Samanya-dharma.* Manu enumerates the following virtues as belonging to the *sadharana*-or *samanya-dharma*: steadfastness, forgiveness, calmness, wisdom, learning, truth and restraint of anger. A more simplified list is: non-violence (*ahimsa*), truth *(satya),* non-stealing (*asatya*), purity (*Brahmacharya* or *Sauca*) and non-possession (*aparigraha).*[9]
2. *Varnasrama-dharma.* The basis of the 'the Hindu way of Life' used to consider *Varna-asrama-dharma*, "as a practice in one's daily life.[10] Hindu scriptures in general regard *varna* which later metamorphosed into caste as a divine institution. Thus the *Bhagavad Gita* says: *catur-varnyam maya sṛstam, guna-karma-vibhagasah."*[11] The first distinct mention of the four *varnas* is found in the *Purusa-sukta* of the *Ṛgveda* where it is said: *Brahmano'sya mukham asid, bahu rajanyah dṛtah Uru tad asya yad vasyah, padhyam sudro ajayata.* When the Primeval Person was sacrificed by God, "His face became the Brahmin; his arms were made into the *Ksatriya*, the warrior; his thighs became the *Vaisya,* the merchant; from his feet the *Sudra,* the servant, was made."[12]

3. The *Moksadharma.* The third category of *dharma* is *Moksadharma,* i.e., *dharma* directly leading to *moksa* or perfect liberation (*sasvata-mukti) Moksadharma is* also called the *nivṛtti-dharma*; and all the rest of the *dharma* is then called *pravṛtti-dharma*; *pravṛtti-dharma* thus includes the *sadharana-dharma* together with *varnasrama-dharma* (i.e. all the *dharmas* in the field of the first-three *purusarthas*). Hence, the *pravṛtti-dharma* is in the field of activity whereas *nivṛtti-dharma* entails the total abstaining from the rejection of all *pravṛtti-dharma*. A *moksadharmin* rejects all actions or *dharmas* (*sadharanadharma* + *varnasaramadharma*) and engages him in contemplation leading to perfect rapture or ecstasy (*nirvikalpa-samadhi or asamprjnata-samadhi).* Quite naturally, such a *yogin* practicing *moksa-dharma* has to abandon all *karmas* and *dharmas.*

Relations of *Dharma* with Society

What is the essential and universal character of *dharma*? The *Chandogya Upanishad* clearly states that along with the creation of diverse orders of man, — who are broadly classified as *Brahmins, Kshatriyā, Vaishyas* and *Sudras* — *dharma* was created for the purpose of binding them together into one whole living organism and levelling up their differences — in order that peace, harmony and unity might be established among the diverse classes endowed with diverse characteristics and varying degrees of intellectual, physical, political and economic powers, which sustains, unifies, develops and strengthens the human society as one organic system. The need, was, and then felt to formulate *dharma* in accordance with the requirement of the common man in different spheres of his activity. *Kautilya's Artha Shastra* was an attempt to take *dharma* into the sphere of polity. *Manusmriti* is an attempt to bring out the application of *dharma* in the ethical and religious spheres. The various *Dharma-Sutras* concern themselves both with secular and religious laws. In most cases they study man in relation to his society. We shall illustrate this by reference to the attempt made by Manu.

The entire society as envisaged by Manu is classed under four groups, each with distinct spheres of duties and obligations. The basis of this classification is the "division of labour" or what is sometimes called "specialization of functions". The aim behind this classification was better service to the society as a whole. This is what is erroneously, and often contemptuously called 'caste system'. The four classes in which society came to be divided are – *Brahmins, Kshatriyas, Vaishayas* and *Shudras.* Each class was expected to devote itself to the performance of duties peculiar to it – Brahmins to intellectual and spiritual pursuits, *Kshatriyas* to soldiering and maintenance of law and order, and protection of the society from external threats and aggressions, *Vaishyas* to agriculture, commerce, trade, industry, animal husbandry and so on, and *Shudras* to the service of all others. All these classes could ensure perfect coherence, justice and harmony only if they worked in close liaison with one another. Plato, viz., rulers, soldiers and producers of goods of common consumption who roughly correspond to the *Brahmins, Kshatriyas* and the *Shudras*, envisaged a similar scheme of division of the society. It was thought that such a division of labour would invariably result in greater degrees of specialization and acquisition of skill. But in course of time the entire scheme became so rigidly followed that it gave rise to castes and sub-castes, group's birth, not worth, became the right to continue in one's ancestral group. A Brahmin's son, for instance, would become a Brahmin and would be so respected. There was no corrective to this growing and governing rigidity. That is why emphasis was laid not on merit *(guna)* but on birth *(janma).*[13]

Another classification is also mentioned which is based on the concept of *ashrama.* Humanity is divided roughly into four stages– *brahmacharya, grahastha, vanaprastha,* and *samnyasa. A brahmacharin* was a student who was supposed to live and study under the guidance of a qualified teacher and observe the various norms. *Grahastha* was a householder who was enjoined to lead a married life. A *vanaprastha* was the one who sought to develop strong spiritual motivation and lastly *samnyasin* was one who sought renunciation of all that was worldly and strives for spiritual enlightenment by undergoing various austerities.

It seems that presence of *dharma* in the universe, underpinning the right functioning of things, sometimes thought of as their norm, sometimes simply as their nature, was taken for granted in ancient India, and this was so not only for the Hindus but also for the Buddhists and Jains, even if they interpreted *dharma* in different terms. Radhakrishnan says that *dharma* is the stable condition, capable of giving perfect satisfaction to man and of helping him in the attainment of happiness and salvation. Its end, according to him, is the welfare of all creation. Mahoney summarizes the whole content of *dharma* in the following way: "The aggregate connation here suggests that in the South Asian cultures *dharma* represents 'correctness', both in a descriptive sense (the way things are) and in a prescriptive one (the way things should be), and reflects the inextricable connection in the religious thought of India between ontology, ritual ideology, social philosophy, ethics and canon law."[14] With the explicit aim of preparing the individual for effectively discharging the various obligations, both towards him and the society, the early Hindus thus devised a four-fold scheme of life. These are – *brahmacharya*, which enjoins study of religious texts, performance of *Yajnas,* and abstinence from sense-enjoyment, faithfully serving the teacher and observing certain vows. *Grahastha,* which included the sincere observance of all the duties of a householder, leading a happy and contented married life, extending charity and hospitality to all. *Vanaprastha,* which required performance of five great *Yajnas* as a token of love and affection towards the gods, of gratitude to the saints and the seers of the past and the present for showing others the path of peace and progress, of respect and remembrance towards the deceased ancestors, of seeking the welfare of all human beings, and, lastly, of all beings.

The four *Asramas* indicated above *(Brahmacharya, Grahastha, Vanaprastha, Samnyasa)* signifies a stoppage or stage in one's life in order to prepare for the further journey to attain final liberation. The first is the student stage, the period of education in the theory of *dharma*. The second (*Grahastasrama*) is the time for the practical application of *dharma* in the pursuit of *moksa*. Each stage, therefore, goes with a dominant theme of social and individual duties with scripturally ordained "do's" and "don'ts". Therefore, it may be said that the system of *Ashrama* is not merely theoretical and for that matter, the duties mentioned against the four orders of life are not merely hollow precepts too.

Dharma and Religion

It is paradoxical that *dharma* is regarded by some as a source of conflict and acrimonious to the feeling of fraternity among the citizens. Such an impression has been created because of the misinterpretation given to this concept, as meaning religion and religiosity. According to Dr. Bhagwan Das, it is an ethico-religious conception which includes "religion, rites, piety, specific property, functions, etc., but overall the duty incumbent on man in the situation he may be in."[15] There is a vast difference between 'Dharma' and 'Religion', especially as the latter term is used in the west. Religion is defined in the west as recognition of a supernatural power and a body of rites and obligations ranging from prayer to propitiation. Revealed religions in the west advocate that man reaches his ultimate end by God's grace. If religion connotes one's specific values and relationship towards the Transcendent, *dharma* refers to the sum total of relationship to one's being as well as to all other beings. In the Indian thought, man attains his 'goal' through *dharma*. Sri Aurobindo has correctly pointed out the implications of *dharma* in the following way:

> "The *dharma*, at once religious law of action and deepest law of our nature, is not, as in the western idea, a creed, cult or ideal inspiring an ethical and social rule; it is the right law of functioning of our life in all parts. The tendency of man to seek after a just and perfect law of

> his living finds its truth and its justification in the *dharma*. Everything indeed has its *dharma*, its law of life imposed on it by its nature . . ."[16]

The meaning of the Sanskrit term *dharma* is open textured. It is not indicative of any religion. In fact, there is no term, which corresponds to *dharma* in any language of the world. All the rules of righteous conduct for human beings in every sphere of human activity fall within the meaning of *dharma*. Religion means a mode of worship of God by all believers, even if they call Him by different names. There are many religions and there are instances when religious fanaticism creates conflicts. But there is only one *dharma*. It applies to all human beings. It sustains life. It does not create conflict and hence described as not to be defined at all.

Dharma as rules of right conduct was evolved as a solution to the manifold problems arising out of the natural instincts of man. The great thinkers of ancient India asserted that unless the desire (*kama*) to have all earthly pleasures and wealth (*artha*) and the desires emanating from anger, greed, passion, infatuation and enmity, the six fold enemies of every individual, are controlled by rules, incessant conflict, fight and consequential loss of happiness, peace, as also the loss of material pleasure itself, would be inevitable.

It is for this purpose that rules of *dharma* were expanded to cover all aspects of life. While the word *dharma* has a wide meaning, fundamental rules of *dharma* common to all human beings are laid down thus: *ahimsa* (non-violence); *satya* (truthfulness); *asteya* (not acquiring illegitimate wealth or coveting the property of others); *shoucham* (purity of mind and action); *Indriyanigraha* (Control of Senses) are common *dharma* for all. Having laid down the rules of *dharma*, the doctrines of *trivarga,* i.e., *dharma*, *artha* and *kama*, were laid down. The injunction to every individual following from the doctrine of *trivarga* was that desires and material wealth must be rejected if they were contrary to *dharma*. In the words of J.S. McKenzie "the term *dharma* covers not only conduct but the whole conglomeration of conduct that we settled or established". *Dharma* protects those who protect it. Those who destroy *dharma* get destroyed. Therefore, *dharma* should not be destroyed so that we may not be destroyed as a consequence thereof. The meaning it conveys is that an orderly society would be in existence if individuals act according to *dharma* and thereby protect it, and such an orderly society, which would be an incarnation of *dharma*, in turn, protects the rights of individuals through the instrumentality of the state (*rajya*). A rule in conformity with *dharma* was, therefore, called *dharmarajya* (rule of law). Professor S. Radhakrishnan, in the course of his speech on the adoption of the Constitution in the constituent assembly quoted that *dharma* has become the basic structure of our civilization, culture and of *rajadharma* — the constitutional law of ancient India to be obeyed by the kings. The mandate of *rajadharma* was "just as the mother earth gives equal support for all living beings, the king should protect all his subjects without discrimination". Radhakrishnan opines that *dharma* is the stable condition, capable of giving perfect satisfaction to man and of helping him in the attainment of happiness of salvation. Its end, according to him, "is the welfare of all creation".[17] These considerations suggest that *dharma* in the Indian context, is said to be the law of human progress and human rights *via* the doctrine of *dharma*. The basis of human rights and human progress is based on the metaphysics of the human person whose value considerations have the basis on the doctrine of *dharma*. Such metaphysics of *dharma* operates as the meaning-giving source regarding the rationality of a discourse on human rights and its praxis. Manu's prescription that "*dharma*" is the way which has been followed and lived with perfect purity of heart may be understood in this way.

Dharma and Human Dignity

The concept of *dharma* as understood in its collective aspect is the foundation of all Hindu ideas of progress and social order, which have to be construed in the light of higher ends of man, so to say, in the light of the spiritual goal of life. Understood in this way, *dharma* and society are closely related to each other and society is a product of man. So, we may say that society, man and *dharma* are interlinked. A healthy society is that which can sustain equilibrium between the forces that make for change on the one hand and ordered progress and stability on the other. A living society ought to have both the power of continuity and the ability to change. As Professor Radhakrishnan writes, "In the history of every community a time comes when radical changes in the social order becomes obligatory, if the community is to exist as a living force and continue to progress."[18] Accordingly, *dharma* from the root "*dhr*" which means 'to hold together', 'to sustain', concerns not only the moral but social and cosmic orders. That is why such concepts as *kartavya – karma* (duty) *niti* (customary moral code) *sadachara* (good conduct), etc., are implications of *dharma*. The ideal society is the *dharma* society, which embodies innocence and assures the individual of innocent existence while striving for liberation. Covertly, the ethical strength of *dharma* as the ethics of human rights lies in the ideal that the life and personal dignity (worth) of individuals in a society has its proper value, which can neither be dissolved in nor derived from anything else but from the doctrine of *dharma*. In other words, human dignity and the quality of life always and necessarily refers to man's everyday life. Human dignity and the quality of human life is not an achievement but is precisely an ability to live humanly, which the doctrine of *dharma* teaches. From this standpoint, *dharma* as human rights consists in enlarging the general conditions of life in order for the existence of human beings to be ever more full and improved and for the possibilities of human life to develop in as many ways as possible for individuals, communities and cultures. Thus *dharma* not only relates to the relationship between man and supernatural but also to all relationships between the individual and society. If, by it, for instance one means the family or *jati,* then *dharma* holds these limited institutions together. But on the other hand if by human society is meant the whole nation, then *jati dharma* does not hold. It is obvious that only *sadharana dharma* binds together the whole nation and humanity. It is *svadharma*, in the sense of each man doing his duty, that suits his *svabhava*, talents and temperament, and for which he is trained (without any limitation on the basis of ancestral occupation) that is conducive to the development of society.

The basic meaning of *dharma* is the moral law, which sustains the world, human society and the individual. Thus it replaced the Vedic concept — Ṛta — the principle of cosmic ethical interdependence. Ṛta stands for the cosmic order including natural, religious and social phenomena. It is said to be the cosmic course and all natural phenomena are subject to its laws. In the social field, it applies to a moral order that sustains both individuals and societies. Accordingly, the concept of *Ṛta* denotes both harmony and order not only in the cosmos but also in society. When Upanisadic mysticism and 'quietism' came to be included in the religio-ethical ideal, *dharma* was differentiated between activity (*pravṛtti*) and retirement from life (*nivṛtti*). *Nivṛtti* itself then became a separate end of man called *moksc* or spiritual liberation. *Dharma* thus refers not to the whole of relig.on but to the rightful activities and such ethical duties and ideals as right, righteousness, virtue, justice, morality, beneficence and non-violence. *Dharma* as Customary Morality "The moral system under which moral standards are based on customs, which in turn are accepted without reflection, is called customary morality or group morality"[19]. In a customary society, social cohesion and continuity is based on the imposition of customs. In such a society customs are the approved ways of doing things. These customs are handed down from generation to generation. And such customs are enforced by public opinion. One who does not follow these customs is condemned and may be punished by excommunications. Thus customary morality is based on love for the family members, respect for elders, etc. Customary morality asserts a foundation through rituals, and beliefs, which are ordered with an aura of the sacred. Customary morality is one of the primary ways whereby a social group distinguishes between its members, distinguishes its members from others, and classifies persons and patterns of life. It is typical of customary morality to affirm a source of authority beyond human experience and to tie the authority on scriptures, beliefs, and values to this grounding. Although customary morality entails human knowledge and will, yet it does not formulate a rational content. Customary morality invokes a specific sense of the transcendent according to the particular religious traditions. Understood from this perspective, we may say that morality based on customs, beliefs, rituals and authority are called customary morality. Some customs are definitely anti-human and thereby meant that they have no relation with the upliftment of human beings. By reason of their own beliefs and values, they are often alert to what is arrogance and to what belittles the claims of the holy, the scriptures, the authority and the claims of the 'excluded`. The customs like untouchability, disfigurement of the widow, offering of animal sacrifices to appease the gods, etc., were not only antihuman but were practiced with a claimed moral authority which was claimed to be based on *dharma*.

The main difficulty arises when conforming to a custom is declared as *dharma* and the opposite is declared as *adharma*. Such an identification of *dharma* narrows down this concept. This is the main social problem standing in the way of fulfilling obligations based on ethical as well as legal considerations. There are two significant statements by Manu regarding the sanctity of customs. 'The customs handed down in regular succession among the *varnas* and the mixed (races) of that country is called the conduct of the virtuous men" *Achara paramo dharma*. Consequently, Manu declared that *achara* is the highest *dharma*.

Dharma as Reflective Morality

Dharma, we have noted, is coextensive with morality. Customary morality, as noted above, is one side of morality and the other is reflective morality. Under customary morality, where custom and habit plays a great role, the margin of freedom is comparatively little. The average man may be held in line, but the exceptional man, who might forge ahead into new and better ways, is kept behind. This is not so in reflective morality.

By reflective morality is meant that stage of moral development in which men formulate moral judgements on the basis of a reflective evaluation of principles and a careful examination of facts in their relation to human life. With the growth of law as distinct from custom, conflicts inevitably arise. The precepts of the past are too rigid to apply to the guidance of conduct under new situations. As exceptional circumstances and new difficulties arise, men are stimulated to reflect upon the principles underlying custom, law and conscience in general. Reflection is thus inevitable. Eventually, man questions at times the content and worth of what was done in the past and think about the suitability of the present demands. *Dharma*, as it is not said to be static, thus, is not merely based on tradition or custom but is based on truth and reason. When tradition is in conflict with truth and reason, then it can hardly be called *dharma*. This shows the importance of reason as a factor in the proper ordering of human affairs. However, it was recognized that reason must be firmly associated with the demands of truth and social well-being.

Dharma as Justice

Dispensing justice in Hindu thought means arranging matters so as to ensure the victory of *dharma* or *satya* over *adharma* or *asatya*. *Dharma* is always considered as a power, which preserves so that if a king or any person helps in the victory of *dharma* over *adharma,* he will surely gain well-being. And if he does not take the side of truth, he would be destroyed by his own *adharma*. Manu declared that, "*Dharma* when violated, destroys; *dharma* when preserved, preserves. Therefore, it should not be violated".[20]

In a very broad sense justice is the virtue by which everybody and everything receives its due. Justice has to do with external actions in relation to others. It regulates the duties that man is strictly bound to discharge towards God and his fellow men. The fundamental notion of justice is equality, which is concerned with equality of persons. And by equality is meant, giving each his due so that each person may possess which is due and which enables him to be a self-acting, independent and self-ordering person.

There are several ways in which the ethical question of *dharma* as justice confronts us. As slavery, considering the lower castes as inhuman, ethnic cleansing and many like episodes have shown that injustice toward the other is closely correlated with what might be termed the violation of human spirit— the notion that moral claims to just and equal treatment are bounded by the confines of an in-group, say for instance, a particular section of people. Injustice is premised on, first, the exclusion; and secondly, the subordination of those who do not belong to the in-group. Discrimination and inequality work together to constrain and incapacitate certain castes in the society, which necessarily help others.

Clearly in the history of humankind there have been periods of violence, even of systematic violence against individuals, peoples and sometimes the entire culture of a division of people. And the pity is that the state, which is supposed to be the guarantor of people's rights and enables the free development of life in society in all its modes, becomes a mute spectator. Seeing the state as a source of violence of human rights, especially of the people who belong to the lower castes, is based on the objective actions it either carries out or avoids with regard to guaranteeing life as well as the citizen's political, economic, civil, social and cultural rights which is detrimental to the doctrine of *dharma*. In the Indian context, the state had been in the past a mute spectator with regard to the safeguarding of the rightful claims of the oppressed.

Although justice was regarded as the second most important duty of the king, yet he was not able to dispense justice as per the doctrine of *dharma*. The first duty was supposed to protect the masses from external enemies. *Dharma vyavahara* (law suits) and *danda* (punishment) are used to express the idea of justice according to the particular context. That is why these are called the best instruments for rendering justice.

Dharmasastras and Epics hail *danda* as the chief means of preserving *dharma* and the king as the protector thereof. The king was expected to protect *dharma*, which was understood as the just social order. But unfortunately, such a conception of just order was taken in terms of class hierarchy or *varnasrama dharma*. "The king was expected to preserve the caste order. He was further expected to use his power of punishment not only against criminals, but also against anyone who dared to overstep the limitations of his class (caste) profession and thereby threatened the stability of the society".[21]

Theoretically, all were equal before law and that included the kings, and his relatives. "Manu even opines that a king should be fined a thousand times more than the common man for the same offence". But practically, all were definitely not equal before the law. Brahmins were notably above the law and Sudras were given a very prejudicial treatment by the same law.

It amounts to saying that the Hindu social morality was meant to be an ideal of justice, but is vitiated by the inherent flow of social discrimination against the 'lower' classes. Inter-personal morality was determined by class (caste) distinctions and hierarchy, resulting in grave injustice to the lower castes and an overall undermining of a healthy social or inter-personal morality. What the Hindu tradition could not develop was the concept of social justice based on the idea of social equality of men.[22] It is not because of the fact that the idea of justice is absent in the Indian thought or in the Hindu society. It was considered as the duty of the state to administer justice when the social cohesion and mutuality of communities are vying with each other for the dispensation of social justice. But the state could not do it either because of the social pressures it received from the upper castes or because of the lack of will as a Brahmin who was otherwise the advisor to the king exhorted the king.

Dharma as Law

Law as understood by the Hindus till the years 1956, is a branch of *dharma* enunciated in the *Dharmasastras*. *Dharma* includes not only the religious, moral and social duties but also the legal ones. According to ancient Indian tradition, law did not derive its sanction from any temporal power, but the sanction was contained in *dharma* itself. *Satapatha Brahmana* thus declared, "since *dharma* is the king of kings, more powerful and rigid than they, nothing can be higher than *dharma* (law) by whole aid as by that of highest monarch, even the weak may prevail over the strong".[23]

The *dharma shastras* laid down the minutest rules for the guidance of the king himself. It was his duty to uphold the law and he was as much subject to it as any other citizen. The king was not only the lawmaker, but also had to enforce law. It may be said that *dharma* was fully conversant with the law of reasoning but in actual practice it got tainted. In other words, *dharma* does not consist in blind conformity to customs. One should rely upon intelligent understanding of the situation in order to determine what is *dharma* and what is *adharma*. Understood thus, we can say that reasoning, compassion and conscience are considered as the three chief ingredients of *dharma*.

Dharma and the Consideration of the Other

So far, we have been examining the concept of *dharma* with its various dimensions, viz., as duty, conscience, customary morality, reflective morality, justice, etc. It was our endeavour to show that the analysis of this concept is plausible for the re-examination of *dharma* as the basis of Indian ethical thought and social life. Here arise two important questions, (1) How is it possible that the individual accomplishes *dharma* by meaningful acts, that he is guided by a norm — *dharma* itself — and motivated by *dharma*? (2) What is the structure of *dharma* to which the concept of realization, of meaning, of ends, of acts of rights refers? We shall answer these questions in our next phase of inquiry with particular emphasis on the relevance of this concept to the present Indian society.

Our discussion thus far on the concept of *dharma* has attempted to offer some of the characteristics of this concept by emphasizing its wider connotations and vivid dimensions. Some of the issues, which appeared, are seemingly profound irritants to any methodology of which such a concept is, when exemplified for a philosophical scrutiny. However, our interest in understanding this concept is focused on *Dharma* as the basis of Indian ethical thought and, more specifically, on the problems entailed by the question "who is the other? It does not refer to the other simply as an isolated and absolute self — providing that such a self were even possible. On the contrary, the question presupposes and refers to the whole field of inter-subjectivity for which reason *dharma* is always and par excellence social and ethical in character. The issue is this. How are we to understand the placement of the individual in *dharma* – *dharma* as lived/practiced by individuals in their everyday lives? In other words, how do I relate myself with the other?

We have already touched upon the beginning of an answer to this query by exemplifying this concept in its varied aspects. We understand that the laws, which regulate the relationship between individuals and individuals and the cosmos and the individuals, define, in some ways, the nature of things themselves. This idea of an eternal cosmic order that pervades all of existence is found in the concept of '*rta*' that occurs in Vedas and later in the concept of *dharma*.

Thus in terms of its own valuation, the Hindu tradition must be considered as a tradition, which emphasized *dharma* in man's various spheres of existence. Two points may be particularly noted here :

(i) The domain of *dharma* is one of several sphere of mundane involvement. Access to such an understanding is initiated by our awareness of one's life situations in its varied aspects, which implies our rights, duties, perceptions and convictions.

(ii) There is continuity of Indian life, which is made possible by individual memory, traditions, and also reinforced and enlivened by collective understanding, which got developed over time. It is the context, which endows us with a capacity to interpret our value norms with our traditions. It requires a new hermeneutic understanding of

> how these manifest and reinforce our cultural traditions and value conceptions. But the individual who chooses to fix upon, utilize or celebrate his interpretation should appropriate the relevance, which governs his existence, and give an edge to his situation.

We have stated earlier that, it is in having *dharma* that man differs. He is not just a cause but also a consequence of *dharma*; thus *dharma* circumscribes the individual and social life of men. It conditions his past, present and future in terms of the ways he orients himself to it. Man's birth, his future course of birth or freedom from it, his socialization, his role and status in the family, caste and society, the meaning and aims of his life and his relation with the physical and the supernatural are defined by and dependent on *dharma*. Individuals come and go but *dharma (manava-dharma)* goes on. *Dharma,* therefore, transcends man and accompanies him in the world thereafter. It is said to be accumulated through the process of rebirth. It is a force, a power but not a supernatural power in the religious sense of the term.

Dharma : Two Conceptions

In the Hindu tradition, the moral use of the term *dharma* is a derivative of its natural use and ultimately something ought to be such and such because that will be the fulfilment of its nature. But in the Hindu tradition, the moral use of the term *dharma* got intertwined with its natural use, so to say, that something, which ought to be moral, is but natural to it. But what is special about Hindu tradition is the wide acceptance of the idea of *dharma* as the basis of all functioning in the universe without the support of any philosophical reflection in the course of time got ambiguous of this concept and hindered the development of a critical tradition in the sphere of social thinking. Whatever order happened to develop in the society through the natural process of interaction between various forces present therein was accepted as the working out of *dharma*.

Resultantly, the four ends or goals commonly known as *purusarthas* underlie the Hindu attitude towards life and daily conduct. The first of these, *dharma*, if characterized by righteousness, duty and virtue, there are other activities through which one seeks to gain something for oneself or to pursue one's own pleasure. When the object of this activity is some material gain, it is called *artha*; when it is love or pleasure, it is called *kama*. Finally, there is renunciation of all these activities with the aim of attaining *moksa.*

Want of philosophical reflection and critical attitude that engineered the Hindu society owing to its political, religious and cultural factors made the Indian society hierarchical in character and confused two different conceptions of *dharma*, one corresponding to the nature of a thing as it is, relevant to the idea of physical laws, and the other — the norm things are required to achieve — relevant to the idea of social, political and religious laws. *Dharma* when it functions as a natural or descriptive concept (the way things are) is quite different from *dharma* when it functions as a moral or prescriptive concept (the way things ought to be). But both may be referred to as the nature of things particularly when it means the essential nature, not accidental properties, so that the distinction between nature and norm disappears. Accordingly, there was a calculated and intentional confusion between the two uses of the term *dharma* and took the purely descriptive as the prescriptive, that believes that something is *dharma* (morally commendable) because it is *dharma* (happens to be the way and hence its nature in the sense of what it is). It paved way for the justification of caste system and untouchability on the ground that it is part of *dharma*, the implication being that the irregularities of the system ought to be there as lawful, right and virtuous, because it is the nature of it. Since a religious and lawful sanction has been volitionally attached to it, the initial ideal was lost sight and the system developed fissiparous tendencies and evolved the code of inequities, which have given it a bad name outside as well as inside India. Unfortunately, the cultural and religious supremacy of the Brahmins who were supposed to uphold the meaning and worth of the doctrine of *dharma* could not do the same and identified it with *varna* and *jati* with privileges based on birth and which prevented the concept of Human Rights in this country. The essential basis of the *varna* system metamorphosed later as the caste system was the development of groups of individuals in consonance with their qualifications in virtue and justice; the keystone of the structure was not detachment but union. The element of exclusiveness and untouchability was otherwise repugnant to the social philosophy and tradition of not only the Aryan race but also of their philosophy, which was rooted in the doctrine of *dharma*.

The picture of the Indian society that one gets from the political treatises and the law books is that of a full-fledged caste society where all kinds of functions — intellectual, religious, political, military, commercial and manual — were being carried on by hereditary groups each functioning according to the traditional rights as laws, according to rights/laws specially made by the group itself, such as a guild, or according to local customs and organizations such as caste and village councils in inter-dependence with one another but without much interference from outside agencies including the political authority itself. The various groups of the society thus enjoyed a large measure of internal autonomy, within of course of their own limitations, and the main functions of the society were carried on in a decentralized manner according to the customary laws of caste over which the king had no authority.

Such an idea of unity and plurality-relativity implied in India's social philosophy viewed the society as an organism. Accordingly, the Indian conception of a society was not a collection of individuals loosely joined by self-interest but an integral unit like an organism made up of many different but interrelated and mutually dependent parts. Thus if *sudras* were required by 'sacred law' to be the servants of higher castes, the higher castes were ordained by the same law to look after *sudras* and their families as a matter of duty, infringement of which according to *Kautilya*, was a punishable offence. The interests of different groups were ameliorative and not antagonistic because they have basic needs and goals in common interdependence and harmony were, therefore, natural.

Each part or group contributed to and received from the whole. The good of an individual was tied up with the good of all.

The world-view, which this culture fostered and developed, was the universal unity and harmony of all beings. Resultantly, the issue of individual rights among men or *varna* or *jati* did not take the shape of a problem, nor did any form of struggling for individual rights become recognized as a legitimate moral activity. The philosophy of ideal unity, which this culture fostered, has its beginnings from *Ṛg Veda's purusasukta* onwards and generated the desire for cooperation rather than rebellion and the desire for individual rights has never been a problem. This world-view has never accorded the common man that his individual needs/rights to be protected. Even the philosophical trend did not encourage struggling for power, dominance or self-advancement. Given the philosophical background and the conception of man as a part of the cosmic *Purusa* and also because of the ideal of harmony and unity, the issue of Human Rights could not detain the status of a genuine and independent problem. The individual grievances as well as the group grievances were sacrificed in relation to the value of universal unity. Hence, conceptually, not only were the actual experiences of human relations ignored but also the issue of Human Rights never aroused as a problem. As for example, the idea of justice had never been regarded in this culture as the central idea while dealing with human relations. The harmony and the consequent equality of men were to be arrived at through compassion and the mutual conscious striving for harmony.

Such a line of thinking and philosophy in this culture sprouted the distinctive idea of social harmony and social democracy, which is rooted in the concept of *dharma* and *varnasrama. Dharma* and *varnasrama* was meant to realize the individual that the performance of one's own good leads to the good of the society. Such a societal order, along with its required social, economic and political aspects, has to follow from *dharma* itself. Thus the presence of *dharma* in the universe, underpinning the right functioning of things, sometimes thought of as their norm and sometimes simply as their nature, was taken for granted in India, not only by the Hindus but even by the Jains and Buddhists too. Hence, the Indian social and religious philosophy recognized an organic vision of society where all functions were recognized as essential parts of one order.

The Indian world-view and philosophy has never accorded that the individual rights is absolute or that his reality must be recognized unconditionally and necessarily. What is relevant with regard to the doctrine of *dharma* is that it provides the necessary tools for the realization of an ethics of human rights as it necessarily implies one's relation with the other. It is not simply theoretical or matters of preference. The doctrine of *dharma* is meant to make life ever more possible at exemplary levels with criteria and standards of quality, that is, with universally desirable value. Hence, the Indian conception of *dharma* doctrine has validity and meaning for the basis of an ethical thought in this culture as it has provided a norm for accepting and appreciating persons in community, their realities and possibilities.

***Dharma*: The Metaphysical Foundation of Indian Ethics**

In view of the above considerations, we understand that from a strictly Indian philosophical perspective, the requirements of morality — individual and social — has an absolute and categorical status in the concept of *dharma*. Categorical, in that morality depends on no further ends, least of the moral agent's desires which they may serve; absolute in that for their sake man will give up any other end or desire which conflicts with *dharma*. Accordingly, a discussion on the concept of *dharma* imposes the idea that Indian conception of ethics and morality has an absolute and categorical imperative in the concept of *dharma*, independent of the moral agent's desires, and the moral claims that such requirements are binding even on the man who has no regard for them.

The concept has been considered as one of the most significant concepts in Indian thought and society. It is said to be the force of the "ought". This term has been denoted as law, virtue, justice, proper and specific duties, moral precepts and righteous course of conduct. Accordingly, it is said to be the force that circumscribes the individual and social life of man. It conditions his past, present and future in terms of the way he orients himself to it. Resultantly, man's birth, his socialization, role and status of the family, caste and society, the meaning and aims of his life and his relation with the supernatural are defined and dependent on *dharma*. *Dharma*, therefore, in the Indian context, transcends man's worldly life and accompanies him to the world hereafter. That is why *dharma* is considered to be the fundamental ideal of human life. All other ideals, i.e., *kama, artha* and *moksa* are based upon it.

Ethics as understood by the Indian sages needs an explanation. It is not merely a science of conduct for them. It is a science, which seeks to define the conditions for the possibility of happiness based on duties and rights rather than mere righteousness. It is the science of the good and the art of realizing it. The requirements of this art — *dharma* — must be justified by relating the action enjoined to the attainments of these ends entailed by *dharma*. But the requirements of *dharma* bind us whatever our ends or desires might be; they are not to be justified by reference to anything beyond *dharma*. Other values— *kama* and *artha*—may be determined, given their status as values by our own purposes and desires but those of *dharma* determine which purposes or desires we may or may not pursue. Therefore, the presence of *dharma* in the universe, underpinning the right functioning of things, sometimes thought of as their norm, sometimes simply as their nature, was taken for granted in ancient India and this was so not only for the Hindus, but also for the Buddhists and Jains, even if they interpreted *dharma* in different terms. The *Chandogya Upanishad* clearly states that along with the creation of diverse orders of man who are broadly classified as *Brahmins, Kshatriyas, Vaishyas* and *Sudras*, *dharma* was created for the purpose of binding them together into one whole living organism and levelling up their differences, in order that peace, harmony and unity might be established among the diverse classes endowed with diverse characteristics and varying degrees of intellectual, physical, political and economic powers which sustains, unifies, develops and strengthens the human society as one organic system.

Accordingly, the need was then felt to formulate *dharma* in accordance with the requirement of the common man in different spheres of his activity. Thus *Kautilya's Arthashastra* was an attempt to take *dharma* into the sphere of polity. *Manusmriti* is an attempt to bring out the application of *dharma* in the ethical and religious spheres. The various *Dharma-Sutras* concern themselves both with secular and religious laws. In most cases, they study man in relation to his society. We have already illustrated this by reference to the attempt made by Manu.

The idea behind all such organizational schemes must, indeed, have been quite mature and imaginative. In every aspect of the social life, certain definite laws of behaviour were formulated, and no room was, therefore, left for arbitrary choices and decisions. One could not in any sense claim impurity from the duties that related to one's station of life. Only then could the society function in a stable and progressive atmosphere. Nothing can then be farther negating or other worldly. It is true that the goal of life is admitted to be *moksha*, yet such an ideal is not realizable in a vacuum. The performance of *dharma* relative to one's station or stage in life is the prerequisite to one's happiness and perfection. The idea was to make the individual realize that the performance of one's own good leads to the good of the society. In other words, we may say that the attainment of *uttamapurusa* state of life is possible in the Indian ethical and social thought, only when there is order in society and the individual is directed to follow the pursuit of the *purusarathas* and *varnasrama dharma*. Such order, along with its required social, economic and political aspects, has to follow from *dharma* itself. The kind of life that concerns and constitutes *dharma* is by no means the hypostasis of an ideal, on the contrary, preoccupation for human life is defined in immediate and direct relations with persons in the society in their concrete situations. What interest us here, therefore, are the possibilities of human existence and the way they ground human rights. Looked at from this perspective, the above elucidation obviates the necessity to consider *dharma* as that abides by the principle of the association of morality will and action.

Our enquiry into the metaphysical foundations of ethics *vis-à-vis* the *dharma* doctrine, suggests by analogy that ethics is some sort of a superstructure to be constructed only once the philosophical bearings of its metaphysical foundations are laid out. The Indian philosophies in general and the *dharmasastras* in particular have, in a variety of ways, insisted that ethics should not, or ought to be an autonomous enterprise largely independent of the descriptive and explanatory aspects of the sciences or metaphysics. As branches of philosophy, ethics and metaphysics are parts of a common critical and constructive enterprise that aims ultimately to be at once existentially adequate, analytically clear and rigorous, categorically general and speculatively comprehensive. But ethics and metaphysics diverge in the central themes and the leading questions that they pursue. Ethics is the philosophical attempt to articulate and evaluate human conduct, whereas, metaphysics is the systematic philosophical enquiry into the question of what there is and how the different categories of things are related to one another. It may be understood that the Hindu ethical doctrines are implicit in Hindu metaphysics *via* the doctrines of *ṛta and dharma.* Accordingly, Indian philosophers have discussed ethical questions both from the subjective and objective standpoints.

Objective ethics deals with social welfare. It is based on the Hindu conception of duties (*dharma*) determined by a man's position in society and his stage of life (*varnashramadharma*) and also upon certain universal duties *(sadharanadharma)* common to all human beings. But objective ethics is not an end in itself.

All through Hindu ethics, both its original formulations and in its later developments, the subjective value of action has been emphasized. In the scheme of objective ethics as mentioned earlier, each stage of man's life (*brahmacharya, grahastha, vanaprashta, sanyasa*) has its corresponding duties and responsibilities. It is the duty of a student to acquire knowledge, the duty of the householder to serve society according to his capabilities, the duty of the recluse to lead a life of contemplation and the duty of the *sannyasin* to lead a life of purity, freedom and fearlessness. A *sannyasin* is free from all worldly duties. He relinquishes them when he takes the vow of monasticism. He cultivates the knowledge of Reality and constantly radiates that knowledge. He is beyond all categorical imperative and no unethical action is possible for him. He is regarded as the very embodiment of truthfulness, goodness and fearlessness. He no longer strives for ethical perfection; virtue embellishes all his actions. He devotes himself to the welfare of others without preparing himself for the highest consummation of human life.

Besides the objective duties based on the caste and stages of life there are laid down the common duties of man, the *sadharanadharma*, which are the foundations of moral life. Manu, the lawgiver, enumerates these common duties as follows: steadfastness *(dhairya)*, forgiveness (*kshama*), good conduct (*dama*), non-appropriation or the avoidance of theft (*chouryabhava)*, control of the senses (*indriya-nigraha*), wisdom *(dhi)*, and learning (*akrodha)*. It may be emphasized that purpose of objective morality in Hindu ethics is to create an ideal society, facilitating its members to develop their highest potentialities. Such a society enables men to cultivate the subjective morality. Philosophers, regardless of their conceptions of the supreme end of man, admit the empirical reality of the individual, endowed with volition, desire, will, conscientious duty, emotions, etc. The goal of Hindu ethics is to train them and transform man's faculties in such a way that they shall lead the individual to the realization of *moksha* or liberation. In other words, ethics is based upon metaphysics and determined by it.

The concept of *varnashrama dharma* constitutes the ideational nexus of a cultural continuum of Indians through the ages. Thus, throughout the ages, the Indians have believed that when actions are determined and controlled by *dharma*, it promotes the development of a healthy society. It suggests that the good- *summum bonum*— is to be understood in terms of the realization of the potential. Realization of potential is inevitable and universal, if we understand the same from the *dharma* point of view. The governing potential of a living organism includes the capacities to do a variety of things. It is the task of normative ethics — *dharma* as objective morality— to elaborate and justify the value categories of fullness of these potentials.

The ultimate justification of a philosophical theory must appeal to its power to solve theoretical problems and to illuminate a range of concepts, theories, and phenomena in a suitably intelligible, coherent, and adequate way. Obviously such a justification must await the explication of the theory with sufficient definiteness that denials can be formulated and compared. Thus there arises a fundamental question: How are we to understand the relevance of *dharma* for the individual in the present day society? The question may be formulated in a nearly philosophical manner thus: Given a human career, what are the most general conditions necessary for accounting its coherence in the present day society?

The *varna* system, although enabled the Hindu society to survive, instead of completely disappearing as many other societies had disappeared under similar conditions yet could not uphold the spirit in which it was formed. As Pratima Bowes argues, "it happened because a society functioning on caste rules and regulations could somehow carry on under its own steam, so to say albeit in a state of frozenness and without any visible institutions, like churches monasteries and so on, and it thus proved to be virtually indestructible. Besides this, there was the belief in a timeless being which through changes of progress and degeneration remains essentially the same. And this made the Hindus believe that the Hindu religion, called *Santana Dharma* had always existed and would always exist whatever the ups and downs brought about by time, and this enabled them to accept the reverse in their fortunes with a certain degree of philosophical calm, resulting in their capacity to wait patiently for the next phase of change when time would inevitably alter the picture."[24]

The frank acceptance of inequalities of various sorts in a society – status, need, function, material wealth—where the Brahmin would serve the Sudra, despite their status and capabilities, was relevant to India's cultural traditions than the doctrine of equality developed in the west. This doctrine, by extension, retains its importance in the ethical sphere too. Ethically, then each individual is entitled to a fundamental consideration as a person who fulfils his purposes and not the purposes of other human beings, however, excellent they may be. Thus each individual becomes a *purusa* whose identities have achieved self-expression. It can happen if the society and its interdependence of privileges and responsibilities in a hierarchy of values are accepted in the present day society in place of the individualistic idea of sheer competition and its political component, the reservation for jobs on caste basis.

We have seen in a general way, how through the institutions of caste, in a less marked way perhaps, through the institution of *ashramas,* the course of the individual is defined for him. In all this, the idea of authority was fundamental. The individual is required to attain the most inner aspect of him, so to say, realization of self. The term realization means the awareness, the awakening and consciousness of *atman*, attainment of which are the goal of ethics, the adoption of values and their adherence to duty. Such an attainment is not merely an ideal but an actual state of existence, experiential, real and attainable in empirical life.

If the goal of ethics is self-realization, in the sense, which is expressed above, the *dharma* (law, righteousness, duty) is not something authoritarian or imposed from above. If the performance of duty is motivated by the commandments forced on individuals either by society or by an organized institution or even by an external God, it would be reduced to an external constraint on the human mind. Since every man is a *purusa* in the Indian context, a code of conduct imposed by an external authority is bound to be resented by him sooner or later for two reasons. First, such an imposition conflicts with individual freedom and the *atman* (self) of man. Secondly, man's reason would lead him to ask: "Why should I be moral and conform to an external, authoritarian code of conduct"? In the west, the very inquiry about the utility of ethics has led to the controversy between rationalism and materialism or intuitionism and utilitarianism and has ultimately brought about an annihilation of ethics. The controversy over the nature of an ethical judgement has been responsible for the confusion in contemporary western ethics. Like contemporary theology it is in a state of confusion. The eternal and anthropomorphic notion of God has given birth to radical theology, which declares the death of God. Similarly authoritarian ethics devoid of the ideal of self-realization has been responsible for the emergence of positive and emotive theories of ethics, which declare ethical judgements to be nonsensical and exclamatory respectively.

We have suggested in the Indian context that ethics is not autonomous without its metaphysical basis. It is this metaphysical theme that we pursued in this chapter. The conclusion of studies like the present one, on the nature of *dharma*, must be combined with an understanding of human agency and responsibility, *vis-à-vis*, values in order to constitute ethics, but that further task lies beyond the scope of this chapter. In general, we can say that the doctrine of *dharma* attempts to answer the normative significance of human conduct; it presupposes a world of contingent values affected by human conduct. It is because values can be augmented and diminished, created and destroyed, and individuals can be benefited and harmed, that our actions have ethical significance. Towards that end, the Indians have formulated *manavadharma* and *varanadharma.* It remains for a fuller exposition to explore, how divergent are the norms of a psychological valence that wired into our motivational springs of human actions generally and ethical behaviour in particular. Looked at in this way, *dharma* has both descriptive and prescriptive contents: descriptive, the way things are, and prescriptive, the way things ought to be. But both may be referred to as the nature of things particularly when it means the essential nature, not accidental properties, so that the distinction between nature and norm disappear. The above reflection suggests that Indian ethical theories are determined by the concept of *dharma,* which has metaphysical and ontological moorings. Value of an action is judged not only by the degree of personal sacrifice but also by the doctrine of *dharma*. An action is good and meritorious not only with renunciation on the doer's part but also in its conformity with *dharma*.

REFERENCES

Note : I have borrowed some of the passages from my book ***Casteism and Human Rights: Toward an Ontology of the Social Order*** published by Marshall Cavendish Academic, International, Singapore, A Member of Times Publishing House, 2005.

1. *Yada yada hi dharmasya glanirbhavati bharata.* (*Bhagavad Gita,* 4.7).
2. In the *Santi Parva* of the *Mahabharata,* we find the following objection rose against *dharma*: "*Sadacaro mato dharmah, Santas tvacara laksanah Sadhya-Sadhyam Katham Sakyam, Sadacaro hyalaksanah. dharma* is decided on the basis of the conduct of good men; and good men are said to be those who follow the *dharma.* Now what is to be proved by what? So, there cannot be fixed standard for *dharma.*
3. The candidate for *Vedanta* is supposed to be well disciplined as highly virtuous person. In the *Upadesa Sashastri of Sankara,* 16.72, it is stated thus "*Prasanta-cittaya jitendiyaya ca, prahina dosaya, yathokta – karine/Gunavitaya – nugataya Savada, Pradeyam etad Satatam mumuksave*".
4. The Greeks had a conception of the universe as an orderly whole—cosmos that is opposed to chaos.
5. *Ratam* (Sanskrit); *rhutmos,* (Greek), *Ordo, ritus* (Latin), rite, rhythm, order (English).
6. It is interesting to note here that the Vedic conception of the universe is depicted as the *Purusha* (Primary person, primeval person) and man too was conceived as *Purusha.* This bears a parallelism with the Greek view of the cosmos as the macro cosmos and man as the micro cosmos.
7. The *Dharma-Sastras* are based on the *Dharma-Sutras* that have embodied *dharma* or moral prescriptions. The important *Dharma-Sutras* are: (i) *Srauta-Sutra*; (ii) *Grihya-Sutra;* (iii) *Manava-Dharma-Sutras;* (iv) *Dharma-Sutras* of Vasistha and Gautama.
8. Creel, "*Dharma* as an ethical category". Philosophy East and West (Honolulu, April 1972).
9. Manu, 6.92; 10.63.
10. Zaehner, R.C. Hinduism, *op. cit.,* p. 142.
11. *Bhagavad Gita* 4.13 (The four-fold vernal (caste) is created by me on the basis of men's *gunas* (inherent qualities), *Karmas* (natural activities).

12 *Ṛg Veda*, 10.90.12
13. Bowes, Pratima, Hindu Intellectual Tradition, *op.cit.*, chapter 4.
14. Mahoney William K., *Dharma, The Encyclopaedia of Religion* (Ed.), Mircea Eliade, 1987, Vol. 4, p. 329.
15. *Mahabharata, Santi Parvam*, 188, 1-17.
16. Aurobindo, *The Foundations of Indian Culture*, p. 104.
17. Radhakrishnan, S., *Indian Philosophy*, Vol. I, Madras, pp. 505-506.
18. Radhakrishnan, S., *Religion and Society*, McMillan,1977, Bombay, p. 167.
19. Titus, H. *Ethics for Today*, Eurasia Publishing House, New Delhi, p.19.
20. *Manusmṛti*, Vol. VIII, pp. 335-336.
21. *Ibid.*, 335-336.
22. Bowes, Pratima, *Hindu Intellectual Tradition, op. cit.*, ch. 4.
23. *Satapata Brahmana*, XIV, 2.2.26
24. Bowes, *Pratima, Hindu Intellectual Tradition, op.cit.*, ch. 4.

Chapter – 19

Relation between *Dharma* and *Karma* in Vedic Ethics

A Philosophical Analysis

Shiva Bhanu Singh

Dharma is like a centripetal force in nature which keeps things to the centre; *dharma* is a centripetal force in man, society and the universe. *Dharma* is derived from the root *dhṛ* which literally means "to uphold", "to support", "to nourish". In the evolution of the concept, however, *dharma* came to mean as Dr. P.V. Kane says in the *History of Dharmasastra,* Vol. 1 : (i) the rights and duties of man as man; (ii) his duties and privileges as the member of the Aryan community; (iii) his special duties, rights and functions as a member of social group "caste", *varna-dharma*; and (iv) the rights and obligations of every man in the changing of stations of life as a student, householder, etc., *asrama-dharma*. *Dharma* has been used in the sense of virtue, justice, common law and conventions. *Dharma* is the counterpart in the moral sphere, the cosmic order or the law of the universe, which is unswervable and on account of which nature is uniform and well regulated. *Dharma* may be compared to the Jewish concept *TseDaka* which means law of nature as well as human charity and benevolence. The Greek word similar to *dharma*, means convention, religion and ethics. *Dharma* like the Jewish *mis chapat* (unwritten law) was always there;

scriptures only express it. *Dharma* is that which unifies and sustains the world. Roman word *Ius*, *Bonimores*, also have similar meanings.

The earliest idea of morals we find in the *Ṛg veda.* It talks of *'ṛta'* which stands for the whole cosmic order including the moral order and god *varuna* as its guardian. *Ṛta* here is considered as an intelligent metaphysical, and moral principle which regulates both the cosmos and the individual beings. It is the inexorable moral, law operating in the context of *karma* and its *phalas*.

In the Vedas morality is thought of as an expression of 'divine law'. *Ṛta* has its source in God's will; "Blessed shall be the mortal, O! Mitra, who serves thee according to thy law", "That is a good which the gods approve"[2]. In *Bṛhad-Aranyaka Upanisad dharma* has been defined in terms of *Satya.* It says, verily, that which is justice is truth. Therefore, they say of a man who speaks the truth, he speaks justice or a man who speaks justice that he speaks the truth. Verily, "both these are the same"[3]. It is to be noted here that *Satya* or 'truth' as used here is not a *propositional truth rather existential truth.* Here we are reminded of great phenomenologist Heidegger who regarded '*truth*', '*being*' and '*existence*' *as a single event. Upanishad* regards 'truth', 'being', 'existence' and 'good' as single event. The Hindu thinkers generally assume that *dharma* results in happiness here and here after. Only the virtuous deserve to be happy, they who defy *dharma* are unhappy.

Quite early in the history, Hindu thought developed a great belief in the principle of causality in the moral realm and in a strictly law-governed universe. It ascertains that virtuous actions result in happiness and immoral actions in unhappiness. In the support of this belief Hindu scholars established the theory of re-birth, the immortality of soul. It is believed that the soul has been making its entrances into and exists out of bodies from eternity, the process will come to a stop only when there is no more necessity for it to indwell in a body. This involves the belief that actions done by an embodied soul can in some way influence it, so that after death it enjoys or suffers in other worlds in proportion to the effects of its actions and by their momentum is also born again. Thus each new birth is an opportunity to enjoy and suffer in accordance with the residuary accumulated effects of past actions, and to seek out ways of escaping from further births or from further unhappy births, as one wants. The cycle of birth and death can be stopped by attaining liberation or salvation.

II

Concept of *karma* transforms the world into an intelligible ethical cosmos, and a more consistent theodicy does not seem to have been produced in any other culture. Both the theistic and atheistic systems of Hinduism adhere to this doctrine. It is to be mentioned, that great thinkers like Jaimini, Sabara, Kumarila, Kapil, Pancha Shikha and Ishwar Krishna were atheists but they strongly believed in the doctrine of *karma*. Generally Indian thinkers uphold that there is rational, ethical order in the universe and man is much more than matter and he is spiritual in his essential nature. However, there are some theistic scholars like Naiyayikas who have argued that actions produce their results under the control and the co-operation of God who is superviser of *karma* and renders its operation possible. They argue that a law requires a ruler, and a principle, an agent who will put them into operation. No unconscious thing can act by itself, so *karma* cannot be active by itself. God is, therefore, Karmadhyaksa, President of *karma*. Contrary to it, atheists like Mimamsakas maintain that it is unnecessary to postulate any person as superintendent of *karma*. Every act produces something which did not exist before. This may be an immediately perceptible effect or an invisible potential effect which when circumstances are congenial becomes actual and perceptible. Thus it is clear that every action produces an effect in the agent and this automatically gives him happiness or unhappiness either immediately or in due course of time. We have to presume the existence of actions producing *apurva*, an unprecedented potential factor in the agent which will in course of time in this or future lives makes him the subject of befitting experiences. This presumption, *Mimansa* says, is enough to make *karma* and moral injunctions intelligible. God is thus a superfluity for Hindu atheists. This doctrine makes one rationally understand why virtuous and evil acts sometimes do not produce perceptible desirable and undesirable effects immediately or even in one's life time.

III

Analysing the concept of *dharma*, Prof. K. Sachidanand Murti observes that it is imperceptible according to Hindu thinkers. It is not an existent thing but is something which has to be created *de novo* by our actions. It is neither empirically perceptible nor deductible through logic because we do not have a universally agreed major premise from which we can deduce the nature of *dharma*. Again, intuitions of different persons also differ. *Dharma* cannot be known by *yoga* because yogic practices can only heighten one's cognitive powers, it cannot make imperceptible as perceptible. Only an infallible authoritative source of knowledge can give us knowledge of *dharma*. *Vedas* are regarded as such infallible authoritative source. As far as *Vedas* are concerned it is accepted by some as eternal, others regard it as non-eternal. Some maintain that Vedas are the words of God. *Dharma* is conceived as the desirable type of action indicated by Vedic injunctions[4]. It results in happiness here and hereafter[5]. *Dharma* being what it is, there can be no propositions about it and no demonstrations of it for there can be propositions about facts and existent things only. There can be only injunctions, command sentences about *dharma* and this is what *Veda* contains.

Prof. Murti explains that in the Hindu scriptures like *Vedas*, *Upanishads* and *Gita*, morality expresses the divine law. If we want to please the gods, or attain union with the divine, we must be ethical. Such a course of action results in happiness for us here on earth and in the hereafter. In order to attain *summum bonum*, i.e., salvation, ethics is necessary because salvation consists in realizing the *atman* or attaining God, who is holy and free from all evils, and this goal is possible only for those who tread the moral path. Later on we find two trends : that which is true to the theistic impulse and makes ethics the foundation of religion, and another which frees ethics altogether from ideas of God and makes it autonomous.

Ethics is for our own sake, not to please God, it is for the sake of achieving the good life here and hereafter. Ethics is the means of obtaining happiness, and consists in following the imperatives found in the *Veda*. These imperatives are not commands of any person or society, but are eternal impersonal injunctions known by the wise from eternity to eternity, from one generation to another generation. Thus in these speculative systems, ethics become anthropocentric and non-religious as compared to earlier theistic systems theo-centric, and religious-morality. Nyaya represents the theistic system while *Mimansa* represents the atheistic systems. Here we can make a comparison between Hindu-concept of morality with confucianism and Taoism. Virtue is indispensable because it is natural and traditional, not to practise it would result in sundering oneself from the cosmic harmony, in alienating one self from the physical and social environment and to some extent in being responsible for wrecking society and so, the order of the universe. An ethics of this sort is humanistic, pragmatic, organicist and non-religious, if religion be defined as belief in God or at least a supreme absolute spirit.

IV

From the above observation, it becomes clear that the ethics of the Hindus is based on a three-fold scheme of the spiritual life comprising the stages of sociality, subjective morality and the life absolute and transcendental. The social ethics of the Hindus is represented in a scheme of *varanasramadharmas,* i.e., duties relative to one's *varna* or social class and one's asrama or specific stage and spiritual discipline. The duties of *varna* and *asrama* together constitute the code of relative duties, the duties of station in life, the duties obligatory on the individual in consequence of social status, temperament, specific powers and capacities. Traditional Hindu ethics believes that universe is rational and ethically determined. Man's birth, social and economic situation are determined by the actions of previous life. The unexhausted fruits of his actions in previous lives and his actions in his present life will determine the future life of an individual. Based on the doctrine of *karma*, Hindu morality conceived of an open society in which anyone belonging to any lower class can become anything, a high priest or a even God in future life, by negating the effects of past *karma* through his efforts and prayers. Again, the caste system supported by *karma* gave people an integrated metaphysically satisfying cosmology which gave each individual a sense of belonging to the social and cosmic orders, with clearly defined duties and responsibilities.

The above ethical cosmology posits that every human being has his own law of action (*svadharma*), which is dependent on one's authentic innate character (*svabhava*). *Svadharma* should thus be a movement which is evolved by an individual from within, in harmony with one's own being and its natural way of evolution. A man's life and work should express his own being, his *svabhava*, and should not be something imposed from outside as that will thwart him from reaching his full spiritual stature. According to Hindu scripture these are four types of functions and rules of life. If we know a man's *svabhava* his circle of duties and his social function can be deduced therefrom. If such a knowledge is available one ought to follow the rule of life and the law of action which are one's own even though it may appear that another rule of life and another rule of action are better or higher and though one could practice them better. When one's life and work do not express one's natural innate character, and are an alienation of one's own true being, they become spiritually dangerous to the soul.

Thus we see that *Dharma* makes no bifurcation between rights and obligations, for there are no rights without corresponding obligations. Leibnitz said that the monad 'mirrors' the universe from its own point of view, and F.H. Bradley said that we look at the absolute through an "aperture". It is the same with *Dharma*. In the, broad field of *Dharma*' everyone has his "station", everyone has his *svadharma* one's own *dharma*. *Svadharma* is like Plato's

'Justice', an ordering and regulating principle that orders the state or the community but varies from individual to individual, and enables everyone to do his 'business', and 'Justice', said Plato, is "doing one's own business". *Svadharma* is the principle of ordered social mobility which stands for the growth of social order that makes room for the growth of cultural and ethico-social diversities. It seems as if Indian social ethics attempted to reconcile the ideals of 'Liberty' and 'Equality' through the concept of *svadharma* and it seems that it succeeded in its attempt.

It seems that in the *Vedic* tradition, philosophy, religion, and morality are found overlapping and aiming at the same goal, ie., the realization of one's true identity as the identity of the individual soul (*atman*) and the universal soul (*Brahman*). This is taken as the *summum bonum* of one's life. In the empirical sphere this metaphysical doctrine of *atman* implies an ethical ideal. This metaphysical truth becomes a reason and justification for our love to the other, to the husband, wife, son or any other being sentient or insentient. Once we realize that this personal soul is *Brahman* and the whole universe is nothing but this *Brahman*, the extension of 'self to the other' in the realm of moral practices becomes complete. Therefore, our primary task is to see, hear and reflect upon this self because only by seeing, hearing and reflecting upon this self that we can know the above fact and behave accordingly. It is believed far sure, that once one realized this fact, one transcends selfishness and starts caring for others. Thus we see that in the *Vedic* tradition, especially in the *upanishads*, the metaphysical reality becomes the 'moral Truth', the source and foundation of morality. In general, the holy scriptures and the seers of truth claim to reveal the same truth and prescribe the ethical training and practices in obligatory tone. This is the most: striking fact about the *vedic* notion of morality which is mostly instructive, prescriptive and obligatory in nature and which turns out to be moral laws. Consequently, we find in the whole tradition various lists of 'what to do' and 'what not to do'. These moral laws are less rigid and more flexible in *Vedas* and the *Upanishads*, though later on became rigid in the *dharmasastras* and *Manusmriti*. The *vedic* and the *Upanisadic* prescriptions and advice, as a matter of fact, in practice, constitute the foundation of morality. In case of confusion, doubt, or ignorance in respect of moral laws, the *Taittiriya Upanishad* advises its students to imitate the Brahmans who are the realized souls and whose behaviour is the source of guidance[8] :

> . . . . . Ift there is in you any doubt regarding any deeds, any doubt regarding conduct, you should behave yourself in such matters, as the Brahmans there (who are) competent to judge, devoted (to good deeds), not led by others, not harsh, lovers of virtue would behave in such cases . . . . This is the command (*adesa*). This is the teaching (*upadesa*). This is the secret doctrine of the *Veda* (*Vedopanisat*). This is the instruction (*anusasana*).

Further, in case of doubt about the behaviour of a *Brahman* or a *Veda*-teacher himself, one should be the guide onto oneself as per the *dharma* prescribed in the *Vedas*, which are the laws of righteousness. Thus it can be concluded that Indian social-ethics is primarily dependent on *Vedic* ethics and *dharma* occupies the central place in the realm of morality as the guiding and regulating principle.

REFERENCES

1. Manusmriti VI, 92; *Bhagavada* XI. 17.21.
2. *Ṛg Veda*, 1.1.8; 1.2.8; 1.84.4; 1. 105.12; 11 23.15; IV 23.8. 10. 3. *Ṛg Veda*, 11.23.19.
4. *Bṛhad-Aranyaka*, 1.4.14.
5. *Mimansa Sutra*, 1.1.2.
6. *Vaisesika Sutra*, 1.1.2.
7. *Bṛhadaranyaka Upanisad*, 11.4.5
8. *Taittiriya Upanisad*, I.I.4.5.

Books Consulted

1. *The Indian Spirit,* K. Sachidananda Murti, Audhra University Press Waltair, 1965.
2. *The Ethics of the Hindus*, S.K. Maitra, University of Calcutta, 1963.

3. *Some Concepts of Indian Culture,* N.A. Nikam; Indian Institute of Advanced Study, 1967.
4. *History of Indian Ethics,* Dr. B.L. Artreya, Hindi Samiti, Information Deptt., Uttar Pradesh, Lucknow.
5. *Ancient and Hindu India,* J.T. Wheeler, Purthi Pustak, Calcutta, India 1961.
6. *An Outline of Indian Culture,* Annada Shankar Ray, Intellectual Book Corner, New Delhi.
7. *Ancient Indian Culture and Civilization,* K.C. Chakravarti, Vora & Co. Publishers Pvt. Ltd., Bombay.
8. *Ancient India*, B.G. Gokhale, Asia Publishing House, New Delhi.

Chapter – 20

Ethical Values in *Nyaya* Philosophy

R.I. Ingalalli

Introduction

The *Nyaya Philosophy* accepts the law of *karma* and believes in the persistence of the results of our actions. Some of the voluntary activities produce their results immediately while others take a longer time to yield fruits of actions. Normally, *Nyaya* thinkers do not clearly distinguish between willing and cognising or knowing; that is to say, all knowledge is purposive and knowable objects are either liked or disliked. Ethics as science of human conduct, deals with the practical side of human life which is concerned with voluntary activities. The aim of this chapter is to analyse the nature of voluntary acts which are morally evaluated as good or bad actions in a moral situation.

All voluntary acts have for their motive (*prayojana*) the desire to obtain pleasure (*sukhaprapti*) and avoid pain (*dukhaparihara*). According to Annambhatta and Visvanatha, the cause of happiness is moral virtue (*dharma*) and the cause of pain is moral vice (*adharma*). Accordingly, *dharma* (moral goodness) and *adharma* (moral badness) are the moral values.

In this article, the ethical views of Old Nyaya and New Nyaya Philosophy are considered and analysed. The concept of *kṛti* as voluntary action plays a cardinal role in Navya-Nyaya ethics, because, voluntary actions are morally evaluated. That is to say, that ethical discourse presupposes the concept of *kṛti* (voluntary action). For adequate understanding of the notion of *kṛti*, it is necessary to consider the questions (i) what is *kṛti*? (ii) What are the conditions of *kṛti* (voluntary action). The aim of this chapter is also to explicate the notion of *kṛti* as voluntary action in terms of contemporary ideas in moral discourse.

Every voluntary action is performed by the agent, or the man acts voluntarily if actions are generated in him. According to Annambhatta (1700 A.D.), "The agent is one who possesses three things, namely, intimate cognizance of the material cause, a will to act, and an effort". Accordingly the three attributes: *jnana* (knowledge), *iccha* (desire) and *prayatna* (effort) are causally related to each other. Consequently there cannot be an effort unless there is a will and a will to do can only arise if there is previously apprehended material cause on which the will is to function, *kṛti* being the final state, it necessarily presupposes knowledge and will pertaining to feasibility of action. To this effect Visvanath (Seventeenth century) thinks that just as cutting instruments such as an axe cannot produce any result without an agent, similarly the eyes and other instruments of knowledge cannot produce result without an agent. Thus an agent is inferred.

Normally an activity is that which brings into being an object to be produced so that whatever comes into being is also brought into being which is designated by the nominative case of the verb 'to be'. An activity of the agent towards the course of action terminates in a result. In case of imperatives the activity of an agent is conveyed by a verb, for instance we grasp the act of cooking etc., from the verb, 'cooks', etc. Consequently we made out the activity of an agent who is connected with the acts. The meaning of the verb 'cooks' implies one who does the act of cooking which becomes the object of the transitive verb 'does'. The action sentence *pakam karoti* is semantically equivalent to *pacati*. The word *paka* is derived from the root *pac* and it gets the second case-ending (*dvitiya vibhakti pratyaya*). Consequently this case ending points to the fact that *paka* is the object of *karoti*. Thus the verb *karoti* (does) designates the activity of an agent. Both the action sentences, 'Devadatta does cooking' and 'Devadatta cooks' are logically equivalent, for both answer the question 'what does devadatta do' in the same manner.

It is to be noted that generally *vibhakti-pratyaya*. Consequently this case ending points to the fact that *paka* is the object of *karoti*. Thus the verb *karoti* (does) designates the activity of an agent. Both the action sentences, 'Devadatta does cooking' and 'Devadatta cooks' are logically equivalent, both answer the question 'what does devadatta do' in the same manner.

It is to be noted that generally all transitive verbs having terminal inflexions refer to the activity of an agent. Of course actions can be individuated with reference to specific action terms. For instance 'he cooks', 'he reads', etc., reveal the specific nature of actions. Normally an agent chooses a relational course of action in pursuit of given ends. And in that case he must take into account relevant available information concerning particular circumstance in which the action is to be taken and the different means by which the given ends might be attained. Thus it is desirable to inquire into the necessary and the sufficient conditions of voluntary action.

In Navya-Nyaya especially in Visvanatha's *Bhasapariccheda* (V. 149) and Siddhanta Muktavali we find the following conditions of voluntary action.

D1 : an act a is voluntary if and only if (i) the agent of an act **a** desires to do **a**; (ii) he knows that he can do **a**; (iii) he also knows that an act **a** is conducive to him; and (iv) he also knows the instruments or the means of doing **a**. For adequate understanding of **D1** it is necessary to analyse the key notions like desire (*iccha*), intention (*cikirsa*), etc. Desire may be relating to the result of an act or it may be regarding to the means of actions. The result of an act is in the form of pleasure and absence of pain. However, prior knowledge of the result of an act is the cause of a desire for that result. Thus happiness can be the object of human pursuit for that which being known is desired as belonging to onself is the object of human life. This kind of characterization of the pursuit of human beings reminds us Mill's utilitarianism. But there are fundamental differences, because utilitarianism implies empirical happiness whereas *Nyaya* theory implies spiritual *summum bonum*. Normally the desire for the happiness arises from the prior knowledge of it.

Next the concept of *cikirsa* is quite relevant for the explication of action because only when an agent possesses a specific state of mind then only he will be inclined to do the desired act. Visvanatha defines *cikirsa* (as the desire to do) is that wish (for an action) in which feasibility through one's effort is feature. Accordingly, *cikirsa* is a desire (*iccha*), however, every form of desire need not be *cikirsa*, because *cikirsa* is a special type of action oriented desire in which there is a belief regarding the feasibility of an act through one's own effort. The notion of *cikirsa* may capture the sense of intention of an act. Intention of a voluntary act is a necessary condition prior to the execution of an act; it consists of propositional and non-propositional elements like belief, volition, etc., relevant for doing a particular act.

According to Visvanatha happiness is what is covetable to the whole world. It is produced by merit. [*sukhantu jagatayeva kamyam, dharmena jayate*; *Bhasa Parichede*] (Bh.P) : 141). Accordingly pleasure or happiness is the object of desire. There is a causal relationship between pleasure and merit. On the contrary pain is caused by demerit (*adharma*) and it is repugnant to all the sentient beings [*adharma janyam dukhama syat, pratikula Sacetasam*] Bh. (P. : 141). There is also a causal relation between pain and demerit so that by avoiding the cause namely demerit one can avoid pain also. Further Visvanatha makes it clear that the desire for painlessness and pleasure arises only from the knowledge of them. The desire is two fold, namely, that relating to the result and that relating to the means or the instrument. Normally the cause of the desire for certain result is the knowledge of that result. Thus pleasure and absence of pain can be the object of human pursuit (*purusartha*). Because there is the definition: That which being known is desired as belonging to oneself, is the object of human life; it is the object of one's desire independent of any other desire.

According to *Nyayasutras* (1.1.12 and1.1.17) and *Nyaya-*

bhasya, activity is that which makes the voice, mind and body begin their action (*pravṛttih vagbuddhi sarirarambha iti*). Actions are classified into : vocal, mental and bodily each of which is sub divided as good or bad action.

Following bodily actions are good : (1) giving (*dana*) (2) protecting, and (3) helping. Vocal actions such as speaking the truth, speaking what is useful. Speaking what is pleasant and also reading sacred books. Good mental actions are compassion, refraining from covetousness, and devotion to higher values. (*Sarirena danam, paritranam, paricaranam, ca, vaco eatyam, hitam, priyam, svadhyayanceti, manasa dayama spraham, sraddham ceti seyam dharmaya.*)

Above actions may also be considered as duties as they are obligatory actions.

Modern Analysis of Human Actions

Normally actions are classified into voluntary actions and involuntary actions. Only voluntary actions are considered as rational actions, because they are intentionally performed by the human beings as their agents. Voluntary actions are again sub-divided into moral actions and non-moral as (secular actions). Morally evaluated actions are good or a bad, right or wrong. Moral acts are obligatory, permissible or forbidden. According to utilitarianism an act a is considered as morally right if it has more agent's utility than any other alternative act. According to rule utilitarianism an act a is considered to be morally right if it is prescribed by a correct moral rule. According to *Nyaya* view empirical ethics has utilitation values.

REFERENCES

1. Annambhatta : *Tarka-samgraha and Tarka Dipika*, (Ed.TV) by Athalye Y.V. & M. R. Modas, B.O.R.I., Pune.
2. Gautama : Nyaya-Darsana (*Nyaya-Sutra with Nyaya-Bhasya*, edited

by Ganganath Jha and Dundiraja Sastri (1925). Chaukhamha Sanskrit Series. Varanasi.

3. Madhyavananda Swami: (1977). Bhasapariccheda with Siddhanta Muktavali, Advaita Ashram, Calcutta.
4. Matilal, B.K. (1985) : Logic, Language and Reality, M.L.B.H., New Delhi.
5. Visvanath : Bhasa pariccheda with Siddhanta Muktavali, ed. by Bhatta, V.M., Mysore.

Chapter – 21

Kierkegaard's Ontology of Faith

S.A. Shaida

In Kierkegaard's thoughts faith indeed is one of the most significant and crucial themes. It is on faith that the entire edifice of his religious thought is founded. Hence, with its tenability or untenability the most attractive and interesting aspect of his philosophy is at stake. His own rhetorical and ironical style of expressing his ideas often leads to misunderstanding of his thought and misconstruing of his intention. He has freely used words like 'madness', 'paradox' or 'passion' to characterise faith which may lead not so sympathetic readers to conclude that faith is not only unintelligible or meaningless but sheer absurdity in ordinary meaning of the term and not in the respectable existentialist sense.

In order to properly understand the concept of faith and its place in Kierkegaard's dialectics of religious experience or his dialectical theology we need to probe into his overall understanding of the nature of philosophical reflection. His conception of philosophy in general and religiosity in particular must be comprehended through proper interpretive understanding of religion, faith and other related issuse.

I propose to limit my discussion of Kierkegaard's concept of faith mainly in the light of his views elucidated in Fear and Trembling (*Fear and Trembling : The Sickness unto Death*, Doubleday Anchor Books, 1954, hereafter FT), which has been genearally accepted as his best work on religion and the *Concluding Unscientific Postscript* (tr. Swenson and Lowrie, Princeton University Press, 1968, hereafter *CUP*). The former is a phenomenological account of religious experience, woven around his concept of faith which, according to the translator, involves "the particularity of its relationship to God. . . the infinite resignation with respect to finite goods . . . the teleological suspension of the ethical as exemplified in Abraham (FT, p. 15). The latter's canvas which was intended to be a sequel to the Fragments is wide enough to include his version of Hegel's philosophy and his critique, his coneept of truth and subjectivity, the truth of Christianity, the conflict between faith and reason and the problem of becoming a Christian.

I

In an attempt to thematize the concept and our understanding of faith, it may be necessary to introduce his distinction between the objective and the subjective ways of thinking as well as the polarity of the universal and the individual which is manifest in his conceptions of the ethical and the religions. His best known identification of truth with subjectivity has not been discussed separately as it is the undercurrent in his entire gamut of philosophical reflection.

Kierkegaard formulates his understanding of philosophical thinking by categorising it as subjective and objective. The intellectual background against which his fundamental polemics concerning the nature of subjective and objective reflection are situated is Hegelian philosophy. In the latter objectivity and universality are the most important or rather, overarching theoretical constructs. It is interesting to note that almost in his entire bulk of writings he hardly speaks of 'reason', 'rational' or 'rationality' but of 'reflection', 'absolute thought' or 'pure thought'. His basic categories or frames of reference are those of objectivity and subjectivity and the universal and the individual (particular).

Kierkegaard's preoccupation with the subjective and the

individual is rooted in his elucidation of the Being of the individual existence which he shares with other existentialist thinkers, Sartre's emphasis on subjectivity and Heidegger's on Dasein are clearly anticipated by Kierkegaard though the former two have undertaken these formulations in wider conceptual spaces. Before clarifying what is subject or subjectivity as against what is object or objectivity, it may be stated that for Kierkegaard the rate of objective thought in logic (Non-Hegelian), mathematics or science is unquestionable but inconsequential for one whose main concern is to understand man's existence. What is important is his religiosity (for Kierkegaard, Christianity) and truth as it relates to the concrete individual in his existence which is inalienable from his subjectivity. Therefore, we scarcely find any discussion of formal *a priori* disciplines or of natural sciences which concerns merely material or physical phenomena. Of course, if we understand 'logic' in Hegelian sense (which is based on the metaphysical view of identity of thought and being), Kierkegaard displays, profound interest in it. As a matter of fact, Kierkegaard had first entitled his *CUP* as 'Logical Problems' ('logical' in the sense of conceptual or metaphysical, one is reminded here of the well known description of Hegel's logic as his metaphysics). But, lest anyone may feel tempted to think that Kierkegaard's *CUP* was anti-science, it may also be pointed out that the .... word 'unscientific' in the title of *CUP* was later mentioned replacing the word 'simple' which Kierkegaard himself had proposed as the correct (or nearest) translation of the original Danish word. Perhaps, he was thinking of it as non-scientific or non-technical since in this book his aim essentially was to problematize "what it is to be a Christian?" In the light of the above, should be clear as to what meaning or interpretation of truth he seeks to identify with subjectivity.

One may approach 'the heart of the matter' in Kierkegaardian 'discourse, which moves around a cluster of concepts, by starting with anyone of them since they all are interpenetrated and each one of them draws its significance and meaningfulness from the other. We, however, intend to explain and interpret his notion of 'subjective' or 'subjectivity' as our starting point. To this end, we may state what it is not and how it is contradistinguished from its opposite, i.e., 'objective' or 'objectivity'.

It may be instructive to see how Kierkegaard seeks to explain what objective reflection (i.e., Hegel's pure thought or Kant's pure reason) is in opposition to subjective reflection. In his own words,

> For an objective reflection the truth becomes an object, something objective, and thought must be pointed away from the subject. For a subjective reflection the truth becomes a matter of appropriation, of' inwardness, of subjectivity, and thought must probe more and more deeply into the subject and his subjectivity (*CUP*, p. 171).

For Kierkegaard, inwardness of the existing individual is subjectivity and, therefore, the existing individual is the subject which objective reflection turns into something merely "accidental and thereby transforms existence into something indifferent, and this indifference is precisely its objective validity". In other words, for Kierkegaard objective reflection which is adequate for formal logic, mathematics and historical knowledge, makes the existence or non-existence of the subject completely irrelevant. Kierkegaard takes a lot of care to differentiate his idea of existence and subjectivity from Hegel's concept of man which Kierkegaard considers to be a mere possibility of actual existence. Whenever a universal concept is applied to existing things it cannot go beyond possibilities or operational . . . . functional rules of meaning. In his own conceptual scheme, the living concrete individual or the living subject is rooted in his inwardness or subjectivity whose *sine qua non* is the necessity of commitment to particular mode of being. The human being exists as a 'passionate' individual-master of his own life and having the creativity of making his own values. His personal freedom with its consequent commitment and responsibility enables him to transcend his mere existence within his own subjectivity. This realization he always calls 'passionate' as it is the mode of Being within which he moves and breathes with the sincerity and authenticity of a 'lover'. It is this sort of inwardness with which he exists. Hence, as he says in *CUP*. "It is impossible to exist without passion". In this mode of existence the search and demand for objective validity or justification of our ultimate choices are as uncalled for as the demand of proof for Moore's intrinsic value (in *Principia Ethica*) or for Mill's questions of ultimate ends (in *Utilitarianism*). For Kierkegaard, absolute choices, specially in the spheres of morality and religion are paradoxical. They lack objective proof or justification because the categorical Either/Or is decided by a choice about a future-oriented project or action which is as uncertain as future itself. Despite the lack of objective certainty, there is subjective certainty based on the inwardness which alone can give rise to the only sort of justification which one can offer to oneself born out of self-understanding. Hence, 'inwardness' or 'subjectivity' in Kierkegaard's thought is the total mental framework or 'horizon' (in Gadamar's sense) which essentially is the manifestation of the 'form of life' one has adopted out of his free choice irrespective of the fact whether the choice is for the ethical or the religious life.

Now, let us briefly look at his views concerning the individual and the universal which he has expounded in the general context of his concept of truth as subjectivity, his notion of existence and in the specific context of the ethical way of life.

In *Fear and Trembling* while discussing the possibility of a 'teleological suspension of the ethical' he observes:

> The ethical as such is the universal, and as the universal it applies to everyone . . . conceived immediately as physical and psychical, the particular individual is the individual who has his telos in the universal, and his ethical task is to express himself constantly in it, to abolish his particularity in order to become the universal (*FT*, pp. 64-5, italics mine).

Here Kierkegaard introduces a conception of the individual which may appear to go against what has been said above about the notion of the individual in his mode of subjective existence. But this apparent inconsistency can be explained in the light of what he has said in the passage just quoted. Here he speaks of the particular 'conceived as physical and psychical'. This is not his concept of the 'true' or whole individual. In *Sickness unto Death* he talks of man as a totality of body, mind and spirit which is the subject or individual in the religious state. Thus, man within the religious sphere transcends all the limitations and boundaries which operate at the aesthetic and ethical levels of existence. At the aesthetic stage it is the body which is predominantly the locus of his experiences. At the ethical stage *WS* body and mind both are engaged in performance of duties prescribed by the ethical ideal he has chosen for himself. At this state he can transcend his self-love or his narrow conceptions of expediency but has to remain within some general and universal principles necessary for the ethical telos. It is not, therefore, surprising that in Guilty/Not Guilty or in Stages on Life's Way he almost concedes the objectively necessary duties or moral laws which by definition are universal. He seeks to combine the Socratic dictum 'know thyself" with Kantian prescription to do one's duty for the sake of duty. Once one has chosen the ethical and as long as one decides to remain within it, one cannot but continue to subscribe to its rules. To violate this requirement would be self-betrayal. But he can be ethical if at all it is needed from a higher, i.e., religious, point of view. It is here that the dynamics of faith comes into full play and gains the prominence it deserves in Kierkegaardian conception of religiosity and spirituality. We will return to this point later. Within the ethical the particular is subservient to the universal (laws/principles) and the individual, as far as she finds her telos in it, would not give in to the temptation of violating it. In this respect, Kierkegaard's conception of the ethical as discussed in the second part of Either/Or comes closer to the Hegelian notion of the relation between the universal and the particular despite of the persistent polemic that for Hegel the ethical marks the objective necessity in the dialectical movement of history. For Kierkegaard the other hand, it comes about as an act of the individual's free decision, guided by subjective choice, in the language of Kant — an act of autonomous will. Hegel, Kierkegaard would say, in fact does not properly understand the nature of the ethical "by denying the individual the inwardness of her choice as a concrete individual — living on her own terms. Kierkegaard indirectly admits the relatively narrower or wider realms of the ethical universals and there is always a possibility of movement from one to the other though the desirable movement is from the narrower to the higher. The ethical individual can thus accept a choice of the higher domain of 'ethicality' by transcending the narrower domain, but all the time remaining within the ethical mode of existence without ever marginalising her individuality. This happens in cases of conflicts between what Ross calls the *prima facie* duties. His own allusion to the decision of Brutus to kill Caeser is a case in point. It was chosen by Brutus in order to save his country though Caesar was his mentor and a friend. This too may be understood in the context of the subjectivity and inwardness involved in such a choice. At the ethical stage the individual and the universal both are real in a certain relation of the self to itself. But even here Kierkegaard would not admit the possibility of mediation between the two as all choices for him are in the mode of either/or — whether it concerns choices within the telos of the ethical or it is a choice between the ethical and the religious.

There is an interesting dimension of the problematic of relation between the subjective and the objective or between the individual and the universal. This comes out in his understanding of the nature of communication which is scattered in a few pages of *CUP*. In section 1 of Chapter II, he says:

> While objective thought is indifferent to the thinking subject and his existence, the subjective thinker is as an existing individual essentially interested in his own thinking, existing as he does in his thought. His thinking has, therefore, a different type of reflection, namely the reflection of inwardness, of possession, by virtue of which it belongs to the thinking subject and to no one else. While objective thought translates everything into results . . . subjective thought puts everything in process and emits the result . . . as an existing individual he is

> constantly in the process of coming to be, which holds true of every human being who has not permitted himself to be deceived into becoming objective . . . (*CUP*, pp. 67-8).

The significant point here is concerning the reflection of inwardness in subjective thought. He further observes :

> The reflection of inwardness gives to the subjective thinker double reflection. In thinking, he thinks the universal; but as existing in this thought and as assimilating in his inwardness, he becomes more and more subjectively isolated . . . The difference between subjective and objective must express itself also in the form of communication suitable to each (CUP, p. 68).

In a footnote to the last lines of the preceding passage Kierkegaard seeks to clarify his notion of communication with the help of what he means by double reflection. For Kierkegaard, it is "implicit in the very idea of communication" in which the existing subject is in isolation of his inwardness, expressing the life of eternity *sans* sociality and thus making communication unthinkable. But the subject may still seek to communicate with others. He further explains it :

> Ordinary communication between man and man is wholly immediate, because men in general exist immediately. When one man sets forth something and another acknowledges the same, word for word, it is taken for granted that they are in agreement and that they have understood one another. Precisely because the speaker has not noticed the reduplication requisite to a thinking mode of existence, he also remains unaware of the double reflection involved in the process of communication. Hence, he does not suspect that an agreement of this nature may be the grossest kind of misunderstanding (*CUP*, p. 69).

Thus for Kierkegaard understanding which is assumed in any proper act of communication can be arrived at only when the elements embedded therein are gone into over again in order to arrive at proper meaning and significance of what is communicated. It implies that the subjective initially is posited against the objective and the subjective is first expressed through objective meanings but after understanding it objectively one has to refer back to the subjective meaning which is couched in objectively meaningful words or expressions. Even the terms 'objective' and 'subjective' are so correlated that both have to be understood in relation to each other. The dominant tenor of Kierkegaard's s espousal rests on arguing how objectivity distorts the subject and his subjectivity. It is only after one understands the objective approach that the real significance and meaning of subjectivity comes to the fore. Hence, a circularity, which appears non-vicious, is involved in the understanding of subjectivity. This movement of reflection comes close to the view of understanding developed by Heidegger and Gadamar in and through their emphasis on the 'hermeneutic circle'. In one of its formulations it involves a method of interpretation which considers a whole in relation to its parts and parts in relation to a whole. We will adopt this minimal and simple version of 'hermeneutic circle' while interpreting the significance of faith in Kierkegaard.

II

Having said something about 'subject', 'subjectivity' and 'individual', it may be appropriate to locate 'faith' in Kierkegaard conceptual space.

Apropos what we have said earlier about the particular and the universal and in the idiom of what has been called hermeneutic circle, Kierkegaard thus tries to formulate his view of faith :

> Faith is thus paradox, that the particular is higher than the universal — yer in such a way. . . that the movement repeats itself, and that consequently the individual, after

> having been in the universal, now as the particular isolates himself as higher than the universal (*FT*, p. 65).

What Kierkegaard wants to assert is that first the individual is subsumed under the universal but when she recognises the consequence of this subsumption, e.g., the loss of her individuality and subjectivity she reverts to the reaffirmation of subjectivity with the authentic understanding of her spirituality and accepting her relation to God which is anchored on faith. The return of understanding to the subjective as a result of second reflection can be said to be the self-understanding of understanding itself. In *Being and Time* (Oxford, 1962, hereafter *BT*) Heidegger talks of understanding as a mode of Being of Dasein itself and interpretation is grounded existentially in understanding (*BT*, p. 188). We will soon have occasion to see how faith for Kierkegaard is a mode of Being like Heidegger's understanding which attains the reflexivity of self-understanding within 'hermeneutic circle'. Faith is something surrounded by objective uncertainty, unprovability, highest subjectivity, inwardness or individuality which Kierkegaard calls it paradoxicality:

> . . . faith is normally expressed in him whose life is not merely the most paradoxical that can be thought but so paradoxical that it cannot be thought at all. He acts by the virtue of the absurd, for it is precisely absurd that he as the particular is higher than the universal (*FT*, p.67).

Illustrating his understanding of faith which prompted Abraham's will to sacrifice Isaac by teleologically suspending the ethical, he holds that Abraham's action is purely private and individual where objective proof or reason pales into absolute insignificance as it is irrelevant. However, Kierkegaard talks of suspending the telos of the ethical, not of its rejection. Nevertheless, the higher telos relegates the lower to a position of relative insignificance which is true of Kierkegaard's all the three stages, an life's way the aesthetic, the ethical and the religious. Each has its own telos and based on it we can talk of various framewords or forms of life or, to use Kuhn's term, paradigms. It may be more instructive to use Kuhn's terminology (in *The Structure of Scientific Revolution*, Chicago 1962, second ed. 1970) and suggest that for Kierkegaard the movement from one sphere to another is like 'paradigm shift' with the added qualification that there is incommensurability among them. Similarly the paradigms of the subjective and the objective, the individual and the universal, the instrumental rationality and 'heart's reasons' (Balzac) represent different and incompatible universes of discourse with their own 'logics'. In Abraham's case, he accepts his relation to God as absolute, irrevocable and final. God asks for the proof of his faith and Abraham immediately accepts to give it without any mediation of the ethical which for him is important but not as important as to overcome his religiosity whose only ground is faith. As Kierkegaard holds, the ethical becomes the temptation and his supreme duty is to abide by the expression of God's will. At the same time it may be noted that at the level of inwardness, subjectivity and faith the intersubjective awareness of the dynamics of faith can be effected only in the light of one's decisions, choices and actions which are located within the bounds of one's subjectivity though in faith ultimately he stands in complete isolation. Kierkegaard feels that it is extremely difficult though not impossible to have some sort of communication with others. As he says :

> The knight of faith is obliged to rely upon himself alone, he feels the pain of not being able to make himself intelligible to others . . . The pain is his assurance that he is in the right way (*FT*, p. 90).

Abraham's faith and his acceptance of the supremacy of his commitment and relation to God brings about a tension free unity of God's will and his own. Here again emerges the paradox that an individual puts himself in an absolute relation to the absolute despite being finite. As opposed to any objective justification, he has only a justification as a particular individual. This is indeed absurd but, as Kierkegaard says, "by virtue of the absurd faith enters upon the scene" (FT. p. 79), or "the absurd is the object of faith, and the only object that can be believed" (*CUP*, p. 189).

In order to understand the true nature and place of faith in Kierkegaard's philosophy we should also note that faith is not an attribute or a mere disposition or an attitude of the individual. The man in his religiosity is an individual whose primordial mode of Being is faith. In scholastic (or even Kantian) terminology, faith is both the ratio essendi and ratio cognoscendi of man's engagement with God. Faith, primarily, is not the regulative but the constitutive principle of man as Dasein-Being-in- the world (-of-religiosity). Kierkegaard once said that we may begin possessing faith but we end up being possessed by faith. It appears that Kierkegaard ontologises faith as a religious man's mode of Being. For Kierkegaard the individual man's essence lies in his inwardness or subjectivity which is identical with his ontic reality. It thus has the ontological dimension. Since faith is identified with passion and inwardness, it also becomes, a mode of Being of the spiritual subjective man. For him "faith is the highest passion in the sphere of human subjectivity" (*CUP*, p. 118). One should not call such a being a man of faith. Rather, he is a man in faith (i.e., faith-ful). Faith is essentially ontical (not mere ontological) as the essential dimension of an individual's existence at the religious stage. Inwardness, subjectivity, despair, dread, passion, individuality, commitment to God, surrender or resignation are all collateral characteristics of faith. Kierkegaard points out that faith is to be seen as a paradox, not a temptation which detracts a man in faith from his ethical duty. The characteristics I have just referred to can be called criteria (of application) not the meaning of faith. This view possibly can be seen in what Kierkegaard intends to say in the following:

> . . . those who possess faith should take care to set up certain criteria so that one might distinguish the paradox from a temptation (*FT*, p. 67).

To conclude, our attempted interpretation of Kierkegaard's faith bends towards the ontological hermeneutic but it may also be admitted that within traditional hermeneutics Kierkegaard's position is on the side of the subjective which has been fiercely criticised by social philosophers like Betti or Dilthey. Nevertheless, if Heidegger's (and even Gadamar's) concept of understanding, as admitted by Gadamar in Truth and Method, 'carries an ontological weight', faith has possibly stronger shoulders to carry it on.

Chapter – 22

The Ethical Virtue and Virtues in the *Bhagavad Gita*

Nityanand Mishra

In this brief chapter I shall give a brief account of the ethical, that is, the moral virtues as propounded in the Hindu scripture of Srimadbhagwad-*Gita*. This scripture has a very special importance in the Hindu culture as it is one of the *Prasthana-Traya* which means a collection of three authoritative treatises. The other two are the *Upanishads* and the *Brahma-Sutra*. Be it noted here that if the *Gita* is regarded as an excellent religious work, it is no less excellent as an ethical one. In this chapter, I am concerned with *Gita*'s ethical side and that, too, in respect of virtues. Well, virtue is a topic which has a very special importance insofar as morality is concerned.

But then, what after all is a virtue? Well, it is a proclivity, a tendency, an inclination or, if you like, a disposition of a person. That is, it is a trait of a human being. One may recall here what the great Oxonian philosopher Gilbert Ryle said. His distinction between 'disposition' and 'occurrence' is indeed very famous. Well, if disposition is just a tendency, occurrence is actual happening. When you say that *X* is honest, it is not at all necessary that at the time of your saying so *X* must have to be doing some honest work. Mahatma Gandhi is no longer alive, but even then we say that he was an honest man. Similarly even when an Englishman is sleeping, one can very well say that he knows English. Mark that 'knows' is a present tense verb. And the sleeping Englishman was not speaking then. This implies that the Englishman at that time was not undergoing any conscious mental occurrence. True, he might have been dreaming at that time. But then, how do you know that when he was dreaming, he was speaking in English. So his knowing English while he sleeps is just a tendency or disposition and is not an occurrence.

Now, anybody's knowledge neither in its dispositional state nor in its occurrence state is a virtue, because the latter is a moral concept, whereas knowledge is an amoral one. The distinction between 'moral' and 'amoral' is very important one. When the wind blows, you neither praise nor blame the wind. Blowing of wind is not within the domain of morality, and whatever is not within the domain of morality is 'a-moral'.

Virtue, however, is a moral concept. But this 'moral' as the anti-thesis of 'a-moral' has two applications – (1) positive, and (2) negative. When negative, it is 'immoral and when positive, it is just 'moral'. This 'moral' is 'moral' in the restricted sense because it excludes 'immoral'. The concept of virtue is positively moral and its opposite is 'Vice'. Vice is immoral yet it is moral in the wide sense, but it is never 'a-moral'.

We thus find that a virtue is a disposition which under suitable conditions propels a person to do morally good actions. What then is 'moral goodness'? Well, the criterion of moral goodness is the promotion of the well-being of all existences what the *Gita* calls '*sarvabhutahita*'. And all existences include human, animal, vegetative and also inanimate ones. And well-being implies preservation and amelioration of those eixstences. Obviously it is only the human existents who can promote such preservation and amelioration. So moral agency belongs only to persons, though all existences even the persons are objects of moral action.

We can gather from the above that a person in his or her role of a moral agent must acquire virtues so that he or she can be able to perform morally good actions. In other words, a person must acquire moral character in order to be able to undertake moral behaviour. Being and doing are two very essential aspects of a human personality. And these two aspects are interdependent. One without the other is not possible.

Now, even though the *Gita* is predominantly a religious treatise and it does not treat religious and moral virtues in clearly distinct way, it does deal with moral virtues all the same. In order to illustrate a religious virtue as of the *Gita*, I shall draw the attention of my readers to the very famous *Gita* verse XVIII-65 which says "Fix thy mind on me; be devoted to me; sacrifice to me, prostrate thyself before me". One's mind being 'fixed' or 'being devoted' denotes a religious virtue. In the present case, the virtue is 'God-oriented' one. And this, therefore, is a religious virtue. And this religious virtue is causative of the action of prostrating before God. But 'equal-mindedness' is (samadṛstitva) is a moral virtue par excellence. The *Gita*-verse V-18 says, "Sages see with an equal eye a learned and humble, a Brahmin or a cow or an elephant or even a dog or an outcaste".

Now, moral virtues do not have any fixed number; they are numberless. I will just mention here some of them as delineated in the *Gita*. In its 13th Chapter Verses 7 and 9 the following virtues are named: humility, integrity, steadfastness, self-control, non-attachment, absence of clinging to son, wife, home and the like and equal-mindedness. This list is not at all exhaustive and there may arise doubt in the case of them as to whether they are moral virtues at all. The list is not exhaustive, because it does not include courage, which obviously can be regarded as a virtue and can even be a moral virtue. But then, courage can be instrumental in two opposite ways. If in some context it is a moral virtue, in some other it is a downright vice. Courage on the part of the challengers of terrorism is surely a moral virtue, but in the context of terrorists themselves it is a moral vice. In the *Gita* itself Lord Kṛṣṇa fosters courage in war. Arjuna who had given up his arms. And He by different sorts of manoeuverings and tricks had made him to fight at last. But even then, it can *very well be debated on moral grounds* whether the courage which the Lord fostered in Arjuna was in fact moral. Was the war of *Mahabharata* actually a war fought unavoidably? Could Mahatma Gandhi have given 'a good' certificate to the *Mahabharata War*? If in the onward process of this war the Lord was justified in His use of miracles well, even in the avoidance of the above violent war, He could have very well used His miracles.

And again in the above list of virtues we find mentioned the virtue of 'absence of clinging to son, wife, home and the like'. This appears obnoxiously very strange. If the very basis of morality is the well-being of the whole world which includes the entire humanity, a clear-cut mandate not to cling to one's son or wife or home is definitely immoral. Such a trait ought to have been listed surely as a vice. But then, the point is how you interpret the word '*clinging*'. There is a charge against the late Mahatma Gandhi that he neglected his sons and dedicated his life solely towards the upliftment of humanity at large. And today the whole world realizes very well the importance of what Mahatma Gandhi preached. The twin principle of truth and non-violence is what Mahatma Gandhi preached. True, h. would allow a woman to use violent means to thwart any attempt for her being raped.

It would appear then that no moral virtue is a virtue *per se*. There are no 'absolute' virtues. And the *Gita* does recognise this. We can exemplify this by citing the *Gita* itself. The *Gita* in VIII/5 says "Acts of sacrifice, gift and penance are not to be relinquished but should be performed". This implies that the proclivities to such actions are moral virtues. But then all such virtues are context-laden. Let us see what the *Gita* says in respect of *prima facie* gift-making trait of gift or *dana* (*dansalata*) seems to be a moral virtue. But then we shall do well to look at the *Gita* verses 20, 21 and 22 of which the English versions are:

> The gift, which is made to one from whom no return is expected, with the feeling that it is one's duty to give and which is given in proper place and time and to a worthy person, that gift is held to be "good". (20)
>
> But that gift which is made with the hope of a return or with the expectation of future gain or when it hurts to give, is held to be "passionate" (21)

> And that gift which is made at a wrong place or time or to an unworthy person, without proper ceremony or with contempt, that is declared to be "dull". (22)

Obviously then a 'moral' gift is one which is neither 'passionate' nor 'dull' but is 'good' as described in Verse 22 alone.

Now, I shall take up one verse of the *Gita* which is very relevant here and then finish my article. The *Gita* verse III-25 says "As the unlearned act from attachment to their work, so should the learned also act, O Bharata (Arjuna), but without attachment, with the desire to maintain the world-order". So we find that here both non-attachment and attachment go hand in hand, as it were. But, whereas non-attachment is implicative of unselfishness attachment that of maintenance of the world-order (*lokasangraha*). And what after all the morality is concerned with, if not with *lokasangraha* or for that matter *lokakalyana*. Accordingly, *asakti* of the alone verse is very much a positive moral virtue. According to me in this very verse the *Gita* very clearly mandates what a person ought to be and what he ought to do. He should be *asakta* in the above sense and he ought to be doing actions promoting *lokakalyana*. I would here dare to say that this verse of the *Gita* epitomises the very kernel of all morality.

Chapter – 23

Ethical Thought in the *Gita*

Niskama Karma Context

Shiva Nath Prasad

The Indian *Sastras* say "*Na hi satyat paro dharmah*" and "*ahimsa parmodharmah*", that God takes *avatar* when *dharma* starts to wane. The *Gita* is a part of the *Mahabharat* and the same *granth* also lays down-

Ahimsa Sarvabhutanametat Kṛtyatamam matam,
Etat padamanudvignam Varishtham dharmalakshanam.

(Aswaparv, 50-2-3)

(अहिंसा सर्वभूतानामेतत् कृत्यतमं मतम्।
एतत् पदमनुद्विग्नं वरिष्ठं धर्मलक्षणम्।।)

which means, that *ahimsa* is the highest duty, this amounts to the highest *dharma*. The same text (Aswparv. 50.4) says, that those who take resort to *himsa* fall into hell, owing to the effect of or influence of *lobha* and *moha*, and such people are *nastikas*.

Hiṃsaparascha ye kechit ye ca nastika vṛtayah.
Lobhmoha samayuktaste vai nirayagaminah.

(हिंसापराश्च ये केचिद् ये च नास्तिक वृतयः।
लोभमोहसमायुक्तास्ते वै निरयगामिनः।।)

In the *Gita* itself, Lord Kṛṣṇa emphasises on *ahimsa*, which we can know from the texts of the *Gita,* I shall refer to chapter X, Verse 5, whereby the Lord says that diverse good traits, like *ahimsa*, etc., emanate from Him alone.

अहिंसा समतातुष्टितपो दानं यथोऽयशः।
भवन्ति भावा भूतानां मत्त एव पृथविधाः ।।

In chapter XIII, *sloka* 7, Lord Kṛṣṇa speaking in the context of *Kshetra* and *Kshetrajna*, emphasises on *ahimsa*. In chapter XVI-2, He speaks about *ahimsa* as *daivi sampada*. In chapter XVII-14, Lord speaks about *ahimsa* as a very good quality equivalent to penance. In the same chapter XVIII, verse 25 and 27, He has decried *himsa* as being *Tamasic*. But strangely enough, the Lord is time and again insisting Arjun to fight. We may refer to some of the places in the *Gita* where He is found to be forcing Arjun to fight. In chapter II, while speaking about the soul's immortality, in verse 37, he says "*yuddhaya kṛtanischayah*" (युद्धयकृत निश्चय:), in verse 38, he utters *naiva papabhavapyasi* (युद्धाय युजस्व नैव पापभवाप्यसि), i.e., fight, you will not incur sin in fighting, i.e., even by killing soldiers in the war. It is not only in this context of soul's immortality, but throughout the text of the *Gita*, Lord Kṛṣṇa is reminding Arjun to fight, as if, Arjun is unaware, that he is standing in the battle field only for the purpose of fighting, not for discussing with the Lord. We see in chapter III-30, He says to fight free from hope and feeling of meum and cured of mental fever, *nirasirnirmamo bhutva yuddhasva vigatajvarah* "निराशीर्निर्ममो भूत्वा युद्धयस्व विजतज्वर:" He says that fighting is the duty of a *kshatriya*, it is their *swadharma* and in performing *svadharma*, Arjun will not incur sin. In chapter IV-42, He is insisting Arjun to fight. In chapter VIII-7, He says, all the time remember Me and fight. In chapter XI-33, 34 the Lord insists on fighting and to gain the kingdom, He also says that your foes are already slain. While Arjuna in chapter-I, verse 31, begs the Lord, that he does not want to become a '*means*' of war or killing, but in chapter-XI, the Lord says to Arjuna, only to become a *means*, *nimitta*, the rest be left to Him. In chapter XVIII-59, 60, He insists Arjuna to fight, realising that even if he does not want to fight, his own nature, *swadharma* would force him to fight. In the above background, how is God benevolent? Can His divine qualities be reconciled with the Lord's advice for fighting, which is not a sign of kindness and sympathy? This question requires an answer to which we shall return later.

The *Puranas* also stress on *ahimsa*, *satya* speaking of truth, non-thieving, etc., "*na himsyat sarvabhutani nanṛtani va vadet kvachit.*" The *Gita* also in chapter XVI-2, gives the ingredients of *daivi sampatti*, He decries killing, but why is it that it is said that "*Vaidiki himsa himsa na bhaviit*", i.e., killing during the performance of *vaidik yajnas* does not amount to sin? Why is it then that Lord Kṛṣṇa who is the highest deity, the Purusottama, Sri Vasudev, Sri Visnu Himself "*Kṛṣṇastu Bhagavanasvayam*", the Prime Divinity, the close friend, *sakha* as well as close relative, also *guru*, rather the world's *guru* "*Jagat Guru*" as He is called, forces upon his *sisya* who is in His grips "*prapannam*", presses Arjuna to take resort to the dastardly act of war, one of the world war (The *Mahabharata War*), the first world war being the *Ramayana War* and engage Arjuna to the causing of mass-slaughter, wild genocide, mass murder? Does this mass-murder, slaughter not amount to *himsa* which is a great sin, declared by all the great Indian *Sastras* and Manu, the Law maker? The *Gita* also amplifies the forceful arguments of Arjuna, who refuses to enter into this dastardly and vilest war on solid grounds, which Arjuna puts before Lord Kṛṣṇa, accusing Him, by saying as to why, you are forcing me to this ghastly act "*Tatkim karmani ghore mam niyojayasi kesawa*" (तत्किं कर्मणि घोरे मां नियोजयसि केशव). Kṛṣṇa starts speaking about several things of metaphysical concerns, which Arjuna feels, are out of context and Arjuna feels dazed and puzzled and he bursts forth, accusing the Lord by saying, "*Vyamisreneva vakyena buddhim mohayasiva me*" (व्यामिश्रेणेव वाक्येन बुद्धिं मोहयसीव मे). Arjuna admits that he is feeling deluded, he says that he is His disciple, *sisya*, he has surrendered to Him "*Sisyaste' ham sadhi mam prapannam* (शिष्यस्तेऽहं शाधि मां प्रपन्नम्-II-7) He open-heartly speaks to the Lord (II-6) that he is unable to decide what course has to be taken, as the best course available to him, either to fight or not to fight, he is also unable to conceive in his mind about the actual outcome of the war, as to who will win or who will lose, न चेतद्विम्नः कतरन्नो गरीयो यद्वा जयेम यदि वा नो जयेयु (*Na chetadvimnah kataranno gariyo yadva jayema yadi va no jayeyu-II-6*), he also does not understand what would he get by killing his elders, his *gurus* and how can he enjoy blood-stained victory (II-5), he also accepts that he is on the horns of dilemma and he wants to come out of such state of affairs; he uses the word "*dharma-sammurshcheta* (धर्मसम्मूढ़चेता i.e., puzzled) for himself, so he wants a very decisive advice of action and he uses the word '*nischitam bruhi*' (निश्चितं ब्रूहि-II-7) as he has already surrendered before the Lord. Arjuna uses the word '*nischita*' several times, by way of knowing the final answer to his one question, whether to engage in war or desist from war, as he does not see any good on his own grounds in engaging in war, he does not know how to get away from the grips of grief "*na hi pasyami*". Here Arjuna is placed into a very grave existential situation of choosing between "*either-or*", which leads him to stoop before the Lord, to show the way out in a surrendering mood, Arjuna is not an incorrigible man, so he wants a rational solution suited to his best interests, without causing any dislocation, inconvenience to any side. Had he been an incorrigible irrationalist like Duryodhana for whom He uses the words *durbuddhe, dustah* (I-23) "*atatayinah*" he would not have thought in this way of recklessness.

In chapter I, out of a total of 47 verses, Dhritrashtra utters only *one verse* by way of a query, addressed to Sanjay, who was also blessed with divine eyes and he has depicted what happened in the battle field as per Dhritrashtra's query "what did my children and the Pandavas do", Sanjay has uttered verses from 2 to 20½ at one stretch and again from 24 to 27, and the last verse of this chapter, i.e., verse no.47, i.e., a total of 24½ verses and the rest 21½ verses are spoken by Arjuna, while Lord Kṛṣṇa has not uttered a single verse in this chapter. The first verse which Dhritrashtra utters, shows his anxiety over the happenings in the battle, which *smack of his guilty conscience* since he was quite aware that his son's claim was not righteous and a guilty mind is always suspicious. Lord Kṛṣṇa who is merely a charioter, a *sarathi* of Arjuna's chariot was with Arjun, while huge *Sena* (army) of His, was with the Kaurvas. Arjuna starts with one request to Kṛṣṇa to place his chariot in the middle of the battle-field so that he may see with wide eyes, with whom he has to fight. After looking at the opposite side, who have stood upright to fight with Arjuna or the Pandavas, his own dears and nears, the elders, the respected and venerated persons, *gurus* etc., shakes his whole physique and psyche and whatever he has spoken are the fallout of the spectacle of the array of soldiers standing on heels and ready to fight, without a realisation in the heart of their hearts, that they are standing for fight for an unrighteous, as well as, unethical cause, that they are ready to fight for an unethical claim of the Duryodhana, at whose behest they have assembled to fight, without the least sense of desisting from war, though there are the elders like *Bhisma Pitamah*, the venerated *gurus,* but all blinded with moral sense, having no call of conscience, no ethical consideration in their mind. Arjuna's ethical sense is aroused from his inner sense, at the sight of the opposed party ready to start to fight for an immoral cause, thus forcing the party with righteous claims, to bear atrocity without any rhyme or reason. Arjuna is shocked at this unjust war forced on him. Dhritrashtra starts with the two words '*dharmakshetre*', '*Kurukshetra*'. Taking literally, *Kurukshetra* is the place of war, a specific territory of war, but it is not known why Dhritrashtra uses the word '*dharmakshetre*', when he is fully aware that his cause is unrighteous, he himself has made '*kurukshetra*', the vitiated territory, by making it a place of disaster and massacre, a vitiated and defiled place due to his *putramoha*, ill-control over his son, given to riotous defilements and allurements. Arjuna's curious uttering with begging for an advice from the Lord Kṛṣṇa is a *serious ethical question* which find *deep consideration in the Gita throughout*, it is a question of the *ethics of war*, the futility of war, *lack of ethics for unrighteous* war, *unjust war*. Arjuna feels, why do not end war, scrap war, and let a one party claim be asserted, rather than engage the innocent soldiers/ warriors to lay their lives for their no personal interest, an unholy and unjustified, forced war, like a same side goal, in a football match, leave the *Kauravas* to do as they like.

Arjuna pleads for the futility of war, a serious ethical problem, which no sane man would fail to realise. His pleas for ending an unjust aggression, on the righteous claimants, ranges from several counts, e.g., his *personal causes*, the *social causes*, *psychological, existential,* etc. Arjuna is in despair, he is in the state of *existential crisis*, the *psychological* crisis and *physical disability*. He analyses the situations very deeply, his pleas range from metaethical to normative, *virtue*, *value considerations*, he describes the situations and wants a *prescriptive response* from the Lord. Arjuna gains the sentimental support of any man and every man, due to this. Arjuna has spoken about several *dharmas* in place of one utterance of Dhritrashtra of *'dharmakshetre'*, he has raised the question of several *dharmas*, the *kuladharma* (43), *varnadharma, Jatidharma* (I-43), *varna-sanskar,* etc. In the *Gita* I-41, he uses the word '*adharma*' to be forced on the widowed women, owing to the killing of their husbands. He raises the fundamental question of the concept of the different debts, the ṛṇas (I-42), the ṛṇas of the dead ancestors, the paying off the debts to the ancestors by giving *pinda* in the *Sraddha Karmas*, leaving the ancestors devoid of their share of food or drink from their sons, since it is the *putras* who relieve the dead ancestors from *pung narak* by non-performance of *sradaha karmas* etc., there would occur a serious religious breakdown, this amounts to *adharmic act*. He raises the questions of values, of *narak, papa*. He speaks of this war as a great *papa*, great sin, merely for the sake of *rajya* and *rajya sukha* (I-45). In order to rid from the sin of killing the elders, brothers, etc., *on his personal score*, he says "it is better if the son of Dhṛtrashtra kills me unarmed and unresisting", a highest type of self-sacrifice, which he is ready to do. (46) Since it is most undeserving and unwelcome to kill so many soldiers, merely for the greed of wealth or territory(45). He says that he does not see any good in killing kinsman or *svajana* (*sloka* 31). He uses the word '*sreya*', which is reminiscent of *upanisadic sreya* and *preya marg*. He also says that he does not want victory, kingdom, nor luxuries (32), he says that victory is dear to everyone, if the same is enjoyed in the company of all the dears and nears, the kiths and kins, but if there is no one left to accompany in the joys, such lone joys cannot be joyful or enjoyable. Further blood-stained enjoyment, after killing all relatives would be merely remorse, sorrow and grief rather than joy (34). That he does not want to kill, even though the other party slay him, nor even for the *Lordship of the three worlds*, such act of killing cannot be dear to him; the life of the kith and kin are more precious than the kingdom of the three worlds (35). He would better like to *live on alms* rather than engage in war. I shall take up the verse 32 and 35 again while giving Lord Kṛṣṇa's reply. In this chapter, Lord Kṛṣṇa has not uttered a single verse, I shall explain how these two verses are important for Lord Kṛṣṇa.

On the social counts, as it has been hinted above, that if Arjuna is killed and war is stopped, it would amount to a lesser harm, a lesser sin, than killing of warriors in a mass scale genocide. Such mass scale massacre and slaying would result into women being widowed for no fault of theirs, merely for his (Arjun's) lust or *lobh (lobhapahatchetasah-38)* for wealth and territory, it would amount to *mitra-dosa patak* (sin), the widowed women would resort to sexual crimes, it would destroy not only the healthy families, but also family traditions, (*kuladharma* or *kulakshaya dosa*) it will destroy all *dharmas*, the *achara* would be vitiated, virtue would be lost, vice would reign the entire race, *varna sankars* would be born, the *varna sankars* born out of corrupt women, will result into intermixture of castes, the dead ancestors would become devoid of their *pindas, sraddha* and *Tarpanas,* etc., the loss of family traditions would not only degrade them, but also throw them into hell alongwith their ancestors. We see that in this chapter Arjuna is the prime speaker. Here, we find that Arjuna is "humanised and seen as a representative of man, so that his predicament is seen existentially as the predicament of any man face-to-face with a limit situation in which the ego script breaks down, churning confusion and depression from deep within."[1]

"In chapter II, Lord Kṛṣṇa behaves more as an specialist *deep psychologist*, a *Saṃkhyan psychologist, guna psychologist*, an analyst *psychologist*, an *action psychologist*, stressing on *categorical imperative*, an *existential theory* of the existential situation which transcends the *dichotomy between* oneself and the other, the *subject and the world*".[2] His suggestions are based not on the action performed by the ego but by the *gunas*. Kṛṣṇa's *existentialism* is quite *unlike Sartre's* whole ethics which is bordering on unethics through his speech "the other is hell", while Kṛṣṇa's ethics is far more sound based on '*sarvabhuta hite ratah*'.

In chapter II, there are altogether 72 verses, out of which Sanjay speaks 3 (verse 1, 9, 10). Arjuna speaks a total of 6 verses from 4 to 8, and 34 and the rest 72-9=63 verses are spoken by Lord Kṛṣṇa. In this chapter, Kṛṣṇa is the *major orator* to reply or rebut Arjuna's contentions of convictions, to cure the existential crisis, arisen all on a sudden in the battle field with the very sight of the persons with whom Arjuna has to fight. Arjuna's questions are begging for an *action ethics*, he wants the advice and prescriptions of the Lord, so that his action is not vitiated by his personal considerations disastrous to the occasion, and Kṛṣṇa has tried to give his prescriptions, the do's and don'ts in much details, but in the end. He does not force Arjuna to go by the Lord's orders, but to act according to his best sense suited to him, and he says "*yat ichchasi tatha kuru*", i.e., do as you please, so Lord has always left open option for an independent decision, as such Kṛṣṇa's advices are only *advices,* not *commandments*, not a predetermined choice, but free choice, so that he cannot blame the Lord for his deeds or misdeeds, Lord has kept the door of ethics always open. Lord gives his own mega-doses of metaphysical recipes, evading the direct and decisive advice for a single point of action, which to an ordinary reader appears to be out of context, Kṛṣṇa hammers Arjuna to fight on His own grounds, which falls into the ears of an ordinary man, as something of conundrum, rather than proper line of action or proper dose suited to the disease. Arjuna is suffering at that particular moment, of sudden paralysis, the symptoms of which he expresses in his own words before the Lord. The Lord himself is all through watching Arjuna. In I-29 and 30 Arjuna speaks about his symptoms of the disease, born of infirmity, at the very sight of the great many elders with whom he has been forced to fight. That his *Gandiva Dhanusa* is slipping, which is a great ominous and portentous, unhealthy symptom, being a great warrior his limbs *giving* are almost failing his mouth is parching, his body is shivering, he cannot stand erect and these are strange occurrences for Arjuna. Arjuna explains his view-points for avoiding war on ethical grounds, his individual ethics and social ethics, and Lord Kṛṣṇa also tries not only to give single reply but many pronged reply. Arjuna is a warrior of the top order, an unmatched warrior, so the body symptom arisen in him, is not due to outer or physical causes, but his psychological *crisis of depression*, and Arjuna as a warrior is not adept to that, an extrovert man as he is. Lord Kṛṣṇa is a deep psychologist.[3] He attempts His psycho-therapy rather than prescribing any therapeutic treatment, his ethical doses are far mixed with metaphysical elements, which arouses a sense of something as unrequired interruptions, as it would seem to an ordinary man as quite uncontextual.

At this moment one thing must have to be always kept in mind that Arjuna claims himself as a *sisya* and take Lord Kṛṣṇa as a *guru*. The *guru* has an extraordinary role to play. Literally, the word '*guru*' means one who dispels the darkness of ignorance, and since ignorance is the cause of worldly bondage, so once bondage is removed, man can attain highest bliss, attain *moksa*. As a '*guru*', Lord Kṛṣṇa has to dispel Arjuna's darkness of ignorance and ignite his self or soul. Kṛṣṇa first of all tries to pick up the shortfalls of Arjuna. There is a principle that "crime always leaves a tail behind"., and Lord Kṛṣṇa picks up the tail as a starting point for tutoring Arjuna. Kṛṣṇa is not an *education instructor but a real guru*, strictly as per the Indian terminology. This point has allusion to Arjuna's speech, chapter I, verses 31 and 35. In verse 31, Arjuna uses the word "*nimittani*". This word may be interpreted in the sense that Arjuna does not want to become a *'means' of war* by himself. The claim of Arjuna as becoming a *'means'* of war is an *extravagant* claim, since when Lord Kṛṣṇa, the Supreme Deity is also there, who is he to have such a big boastful claim? Arjuna is a mere ordinary man, not a Divinity. This echoes an ego-sense, (Arjuna) and in a sense *ahankara*, and *ahankara* is a phenomenon of lower ego-sense, a vain pride. Further in the *sloka* 35, Arjuna says, "*etanna hantu-michhami ghnato pi madhusudana*", which literally means that "I do not want to kill them". This sentence also echoes Arjuna's self sense, for Kṛṣṇa this means that Arjuna is still in the lower states of ego sense, so Kṛṣṇa takes upon Him as an essential task to cure Arjuna's ego-sense and give such spiritual metaphysical doses, by which as a '*guru*', his self-sense is far too sublimated, and the simple Arjuna, a warrior, is lifted to the highest state of consciousness, to attain eternal existence, eternal blessedness, so that his ego may attain the status of a Divinity, an *amṛtasya putrah*, attaining *amaratva*. It would be very good to point out, that it is only on the sacrifice of ego that higher consciousness or divine consciousness or cosmic consciousness can awake. Its parallel can also be laid down with *Jungian psychology*. So placing the metaphysical layering the outer covers with deep ethics hidden inside, becomes essential for the Lord. So the Lord starts with metaphysical concepts and dictums and these metaphysical dictums are really metaphysics of ethics or ethics of metaphysics. In the *Gita*, we find plethora of such concepts of the ethics of action being discussed throughout, till the end of this treatise.

As a *guru*, Lord Kṛṣṇa speaks pragmatically and metaphysically, "In metaphysics, He is ontological and cosmological."[4] He illustrates matters with examples as ordinary teachers do with the child. Lord gives not only example of others but his own example, so that concreteness of His teachings cage into Arjuna's heart. Lord Kṛṣṇa is turned into a major metaphysician, ontologist and *yogi* all rolled into one and thus make a "*complete gestalt* "Kṛṣṇa adopts two methods, instruction and relating. This two way approach turns Arjuna curious and he is hooked.[5]

One fact has to be taken in mind that the *Gita* is '*Kṛṣṇa-Arjuna samvad*'. The word '*samvada*' is translated into English as, '*dialogue*'. In any dialogue or discussion, there is one side, the positive side, call it a thesis, then there is the opposite side, who says against the motion, i.e., the negative side, call it this opposite side, the anti-thesis. And after considering both sides, one comes to a conclusion, which may be called 'synthesis' as per the Marxian dictum of thesis, anti-thesis and synthesis. All the three can be known as *vada, vivada* and *samvada.* Lord Kṛṣṇa in chapter X-verse 32, says that He is right type of reasoning "*Vadah pravadamaham*", i.e., He is the thesis side, but really speaking, like the Marxian thesis, anti-thesis and synthesis, the *vada vivada* and *samvada* are not in the present context rewarding interpretation, since there is no *vada* or *vivada* between Lord Kṛṣṇa and Arjuna, the two are only discoursing, conversing. Both are very close friends, and when Arjuna himself says that he is the disciple of the Lord, hence, it will not be justified to interpret it in the Marxian way. The '*samvada*' also means 'a *message*' and the Lord Kṛṣṇa is giving a message to Arjuna and through Arjuna, to any man of the world. Arjuna's questions are really common man's question, it is every man's question and Lord's message is every man's message, a universal message who is confronted with life. The *Gita* presents a message in the battle-field, it is a message for any man, facing a Complex problem in his life.

One more thing which apparently comes to mind for an adequate answer is, on Lord Kṛṣṇa's words of wonder and amazement at Arjuna. Kṛṣṇa says in II-verse 2 and 3, "How has this infatuation overtaken you at this odd (in the battle field) hour as it is shunned by noble souls, which will neither bring heaven nor fame to you (Arjuna)". He says in verse 3, "yield not to unmanliness, ill does it become you, shaking off this paltry faint-heartedness, stand up O scorcher of enemies". Now, *one may ask Kṛṣṇa*, He is also keeping with Arjuna as a *sarathi* of Arjuna's chariot and rebuking him not to be shaky in the battle field. The words "कुतस्त्वा कश्मलभिदं विषमें समुपस्थितम्" at this odd hour, this means that Arjuna *should not have been shaky at this specially odd place* (*visama sthiti*) as if, the Lord Himself is forgetting, that He is also with Arjuna in the battle field. If for Arjuna's shakiness Lord rebukes him, *is He not aware* that He is going to utter a full book of 700 verses in the battle-field, does it sound natural and proper in the very battle-field (where both Arjuna and Lord are standing), is it not odd for Lord Kṛṣṇa to utter such a long text, and also, is it possible for any soldier placed in the battle field, to have the patience to hear so much mindfully, amidst the cries and clamours, the trumpet, drums soundings of the war and come to a conclusion for adopting one course of action, rather the other? It is as much odd for Arjuna, to be so feverish and panic of war and also for Lord Kṛṣṇa, to have *selected this odd hour to utter the whole book in the battle field.* Arjuna had long been a victim of Kaurava's tortures and he was knowing full well, that this war has been occasioned by ill-adventured Duryodhana, who is not under the proper guardianship of his father, his father also so feeble before the strong-headedness of his son that he all through remains a silent spectator, blinded *physically*, *mentally*, *psychologically* and under the *sway* of his *son's whims* and *compulsions*, Kṛṣṇa is also fully aware of the fact, that this war had been forced by reckless Duryodhana. Lord Kṛṣṇa had also tried to resolve this dispute as a mediator, conciliator, but failed his mission. So there was nothing new either for Arjuna or for Kṛṣṇa, and if this (the war) was all known much before, why did Lord not instruct Arjuna all about the trickery traits of war from before, rather than select such an occasion for His long and strange utterings of metaphysical concepts? Does it not all sound unnatural? If, it may not be so natural for the Indian spiritualists, who revere the Lord, but how can the materialists like the Charvakas/Lokayatas, as well as, the Western materialists, would keep mum to all this and not waive a raising finger, symbolising accusation.

Be it noted, that Kṛṣṇa and Arjuna were very close friends and what the Lord says in chapter X. 37, "वृष्णीनां वासुदेवोऽस्मि पांडवानां धनंजयः", i.e., "I am Kṛṣṇa among this Vṛsnis and Arjuna (Dhananjay) among the sons of Pandu", means that Kṛṣṇa and Arjuna are one and the same, two bodies but one soul. We may also refer to some more verses from the *Mahabharata* which dwells upon the affinity between the two. The *Mahabharata Sabha Parva*, says —

आत्मा हि कृष्णाः पार्थस्य कृष्णास्यात्मा धनंजयः
यदं् बूयाद्दर्जुनः कृष्णां सर्वं कुर्यादसंशयम्
कृष्णो धनंजयास्यार्थे स्वर्गलोकयपित्यजेत।

This means that Arjuna is the very soul of Kṛṣṇa, and Kṛṣṇa is the soul of Arjuna. What Kṛṣṇa would say, Arjuna would definitely do, Kṛṣṇa can kick off even the supreme abode, and Arjuna can risk his life for Kṛṣṇa. This shows Kṛṣṇa's unfathomable love for Arjuna. Kṛṣṇa further says (*vide Vana Parv* 12/45-47)

ममैव त्वं तवैवाहं ये मदीया स्तवैवते।
यस्त्वांएष्टि समांद्वेष्टियस्त्वामनु स मामनु।
नरस्त्वमसि दुर्धर्ष हरिनरियणो ह्वय्
काले लोकमिमं प्राप्तो नरनारयणावृष्ठो।
अनन्य पार्थ मतस्त्वं त्वत्तश्रचाहं तथैव च
नावयोरन्तरं शक्यंवेहितुं भरतर्षभ।

i.e., Krsna is Arjuna's, and Arjuna is Krṣṇa's, whatever is of Arjuna is of Krṣna and *vice versa*, whoever hates and opposes Arjuna, Krṣna hates him. *Arjuna* is *Nara* and Krṣṇa is *Narayana*, the two cannot be differentiated. Krṣna further says, no one e.g., wife, relation, friend is more loving than Arjuna. He cannot see the world without Arjuna, as we see from *Drone Parv*, 79-26-28

न हि दारान भियाणि ज्ञातयो न च बान्धवाः
कश्चिनन्यः प्रियतरः कुन्तीपुत्रान्मयार्जुनात्
अनर्जुनमिमं लोकं मुहूर्तमपि दारूकः।

(Krṣna says this to Daruka)

Again in *Drona Parv* 79/33-34, if a man who is enemy of Arjuna is mine enemy too. One who is friend of Arjuna, is also my friend, Arjuna is half of my body.

यस्तिं दृष्टि समाद्वेष्टि यस्तं चानु स मामनु
इति संकल्प्यतां बुद्धया शरीरार्ध ममर्जुनः

In *Adi Parv* 233-13, states that when Indra asked Arjuna and Krṣṇa to ask for most precious boon for the *mṛtaloka* (this decaying world) He asked for His increasing love for Arjuna.

वासुदेवोऽपि प्रीतिं पार्थेन शाश्वतीम्
ददौ सुरपतिश्चैव वरं कृष्णाय धीमते।

Such being Krṣṇa's relation with Arjuna, it is impossible that Krṣṇa was not knowing what went in Arjuna's mind, nor Arjuna was unknown of Krṣṇa's mind. Krṣṇa always utters this word, *sakha* and Arjuna also uses the word '*sakha*' for Krṣna and the word has been uttered several times in the course of the *Gita*. If they were one soul, two bodies, why did not Krṣṇa give all the instructions for this work before hand, rather than choose such an occasion and such a place. Both Krṣṇa's and Arjuna's deep love for each other, can be heard in the different names by which Kṛṣṇa addresses Arjuna, as well as the different names by which Arjuna addresses Kṛṣṇa. Some such names can be read in the *Gita's* text.

Besides this, Lord Kṛṣṇa to says Arjuna "that you are exceptionally dear to me" (XVIII-65). He also says you are my disciple (*sisyosi*-XVIII-65). Such being the background of the two, how can one think that Kṛṣṇa had no prior occasion to instruct Arjuna for the way to fight, for gaining victory of which Lord was very sure. No one will feel convinced, that such utterances of the instructions for the war, could not have come from beforehand, rather than in the midst of the battle-field alone. Both Arjuna and Kṛṣṇa were very close friends and the apparent closeness can be heard in the various verses of the *Gita,* whereby. Arjuna calls Kṛṣṇa by various names and Kṛṣṇa also calls Arjuna by various names out of deep love for each other. Not to say of some intimate and lovely names, in chapter XVIII-65, the Lord very expressly says, that you are exceptionally dear to me, you are my disciple and in the face of all these, it seems quite unnatural to open up a huge metaphysical discussion in the battle-field. Scholars are led to conjecture in two ways. Firstly, the *Gita* portion of the *Mahabharata,* either the whole of it, or partly it, is an interpolation or addition, by the *ṛsi* Vyas himself or any other, or addition, after the original text had been completed; *secondly,* it may be that, originally some verses might have been uttered to influence upon Arjuna to fight, rather than flee from war, and later on more verses were added, to make the work more impressive and by so doing, make it very important.

One more thing may be noted here. That Arjuna accepts himself to be disciple of Kṛṣṇa and Kṛṣṇa also addressed Arjuna at some places, as *'sisyosi'*, we may refer to what is done by *guru* to a *sisya,* in order to initiate in the *guru-sisya* tradition. Was it a fact that the Lord Kṛṣṇa was initiating Arjuna in the battle-field? The usual way of initiating a *sisya,* is uttering, really whispering, a few words in the ears of the disciple and ask the *sisya* to map the same in his heart, as we see in the case of *Brahma Sutra,* which opens up *'athato Brahma-jijnāsa'* or in the *Mimansa-sutra, 'athato dharma jijnāsa*', and since Kṛṣṇa was to teach Arjuna the whole philosophy of duty or *karma*, if the *Gita* were in the form of *sutra*, Lord Kṛṣṇa would have spoken in Arjuna's ear '*athato karma vyakhyamah*'. Kṛṣṇa was the *sarthi* or charioter of Arjuna's *rath* and was in the close range of Arjuna, He could have whispered something like the above, and Arjuna might have done the rest. As it is said, the *Gita* is the crux of *Vedas*, *Upanisad*, the *Brahma sutra*, could all these be condensed in a few slokas or verses? Lord Kṛṣṇa is the *avatar* of Viṣṇu and He is creator, sustainer and destroyer and His duty as a *avatar* is to maintain righteousness and whenever unrighteousness starts reigning and righteousness starts waning, He takes *avatar* to bring righteousness (Chapter IV). By saying that Arjuna is the dearest of all, He had not only blessed Arjuna for a victory, but had already spoken, as if most emotionally, that all his enemies are already slain by Him. We may refer to the *Gita* chapter XI-verses 32, 33, 34, whereby the Lord says: "I am the inflamed *kala*, the destroyer of the worlds. I am out to exterminate these people. Even without you all those warriors arrayed in the enemies camp must die. Further in other verse He says "do you arise and win glory, conquering the foes, enjoy the affluent kingdom. These warriors stand *already slain by Me*, be only an *instrument*." We may be reminded that in the very beginning of the *Gita*, Arjuna says that he does not want to become a *nimitta* or *means of killing*, but Lord now tells Arjuna to become a *means*, a *nimitta* and leave the rest on Him. He says that all the Elders, like Bhisma, Drona are killed by Him—

द्रोणं च भीष्मं च जयद्रथं च कर्णं च तथान्यानपि योर्धकणन्।
मया हतांस्त्वं जहिमा व्यथिष्ठा युद्धयस्वजेतासिरणे सपत्नान।।

Meaning, "Do you kill Drona, Bhisma and Jayadratha and Karna and even other warriors, who *stand already killed* by Me; fear not *you will surely conquer* the enemies in the war, therefore, fight". Arjuna gets ready to *fight not due to moral reasons advocated by* Kṛṣṇa, but by *His personal influence after showing His Bibhuti*, His prior to war utterance that He has *already killed his enemies*. Hence, not to fear. What does all these mean to an ordinary man? Does it *not mean everything pre-determined*? And if *everything* is predetermined by the Lord, *where is the 'freedom of will'* though, formally the Lord says, at the end "*yad icchasi tatha kuru*". Does it not *amount to near formality*, rather a *duty on the part of Arjuna* to fight. Whether Arjuna could fight or not, the *result was already ordained*, the end of the *unrighteousness adopted by the enemies* of Arjuna. There is no question of duty, *karma*, *swadharma*, or *kshatriya dharma* or anything. It is only the Lord, who is the player of all, He knows all, He does all, all else are only means. Then what *does all the do's and don'ts of the Gita mean* or why all these lots to be said or done? Whether Arjuna fights or not, if God wills to destroy anyone, who can save? Does it not show jugglary of words, the entire story itself?

II

Arjuna's objection to war is common man's approach, to desist from war which results in killing, killing is a sin, a *papa*, a disvalue, unvirtuous, *adharma*. The normativity of his pleas lie in his thought that gaining a crown or kingdom is a selfish act, directed to self-gratification, and self-interest is far less important than mass murder. He is right in this matter, not that Arjuna was afraid of war, not that Arjuna was a coward, not that he was not knowing that he came of kshatriya class, not that it was the first occasion for him to fight, he had already faced many ordeals. He raised the question of *dharma* as "*dharma-sammurhcheta*". The Lord replies in His own way to make Arjuna to concede by all means, 'fair or foul' as it is sometimes called. He applies all head and tail method. He applies all the arts of politics, *sama*, *dam*, *danda* and *bheda*. He applies all his logics, all metaphysics, all ethics. He shows his *virat rupa*, by which Arjuna is frightened. He applies dilemmas and all several methods to puzzle Arjuna, so that he becomes ready to fight. As a creator Lord has to serve His own purpose, to bring order out of unrighteousness by defeating the devilish persons or evil forces. He has His own axe to grind. So He applies all means.

Prof. Rajendra Prasad has tried to peep into all these in his own logical and ethical incisive style. In the post-modernism, the dictum is the end of meta-narrative, there is also the dictum "*trust the tale not the teller*". But in the case of Mahabharat, the reverse is the case "*trust the teller' not the tale, since post-modernism has respect for "process"*, not the *finished* product, the tale is always in process and so long as a reader is reading the tale, the conclusion is still in flux, while the teller is in full know of the first and last events of narration, for him, everything is fixed in his own mind. Here in this case, the narrator has to be trusted at all costs, since the narrator is Vyās *ṛṣi* or a *maharṣi*, and it is about God himself, hence, there cannot be a question of distrust on the ṛṣi Vyās or God. Even the topmost commentator, knowing full well wherein lies the malady cannot question the 'trust' of such elevated *ṛṣi.* This Prof. Rajendra Prasad calls this "*ṛṣi bias*" which is a great hinderance in impartial study of any of the Indian traditional texts and for this reason no logical or truly normative study of such text becomes possible.

Dr. R. Prasad has explained the arguments of Arjuna who is faced with a problem in the dilemmatic way of presentation, which have been presented in the following logical form :

On Arjuna's Side

On the basis of the *Gita* I-26, ..., 31, 34, 36, 37 :

(A) To fight the battle is to fight to kill relatives (*svajanam*) (arrayed on Duryodhana side— The relatives (arrayed on Duryodhana side are no doubt wicked people (*atatayinah*). But to fight to kill relatives, even if wicked, is morally wrong. Therefore, to fight the battle is morally wrong.

(B) Basing the text I-38, 39, 45 —To fight the battle is to fight to kill relatives. I (Arjuna) know(s) that to fight to kill the relatives is morally wrong but Duryodhana does not know it. To do what one knows to be morally wrong is morally wrong. Therefore, for me (Arjuna) to fight the battle is morally wrong.

(C) Basing II-4, 5 — To fight the battle is to fight to kill adorable elders like grand-father Bhisma and the teacher Drona. It is morally better to live on alms than to kill the adorable elders, and even after killing them, I (Arjuna) would get only blood-soaked material goods to enjoy (which again is morally wrong).Therefore, to fight the battle is morally wrong.

(D) On I-40-4 — To fight the battle is to cause the destruction of the Kaurava ethos (*kuldharma*) (as there would be none left to perform the Kaurav family rites and duties). To cause the destruction of *kuladharma* is morally wrong. Therefore, to fight the battle is morally wrong.[6]

Now, on Kṛṣṇa side dilemmatic presentation has been put in the following "logically and psychologically coercive way" with the conclusion to fight (ought to fight). On Lord's side, Dr. Prasad says :

(E) "You would choose either to fight or not to fight. If you choose not to fight, then you would get infamy of running away from the battle field, which would be worse than death for a respectable valiant, *kshatriya* as you are.

(F) If you choose to fight either you would lose or win. If you lose, i.e., get killed in the battle field, you will go straight to heaven. If you win, you would be ruling over the world as –conquerer. Therefore, you ought to choose to fight. (II-31-33)[7].

This is a very clever presentation of an open-ended dilemma, both the alternatives plead for war, it is begging the question. Prof. Rajendra Prasad says that the whole consideration of Arjuna is based on *sāmānya dharma* or general morality, which supersedes caste-ethics. Kṛṣṇa instead of answering Arjuna's point of concern, rather He tries to make "all of Arjuna's argument otiose, or ineffective, in one sweep"[8] and speak about the *chaturvarna, kshatriya dharma, swadharma, sthitiprajnata, niskama karma*, the soul's immortality, of *Prakṛti* and its modifications, etc., making the situation confusion worst confounded. Arjuna says that he does not want to kill, so commit sin, but Kṛṣṇa impresses upon him, how killing in this war would not be sin, *firstly*, because the soul is immortal, that death is inevitable to all, that it is body which decays at death, that since soul is immortal, no one can kill it nor can it be killed at death, only the soul changes its garment of the body. All these arguments show that every act of Arjuna is predetermined, death is fixed, even if Arjuna kills, it is only the body that is killed, the soul is still there. If this logic is adhered to, then every killing would be non-killing, the very concept of sin or *papa* in doing *himsa* would be obliterated. This does not seem to be a good logic as put forward by Lord Kṛṣṇa.

Niskama Karma

By way of another attempt at convincing rather pressing upon Arjuna is that, in desireless action or *niskama karma*, even in killing no sin is committed. But such an assertion may be open to objections. Firstly, there cannot be action without a desire. To think to do any action without desire is itself a desire. The highest *purushartha* is of *moksa* and the attaining of *moksa*, a kind of *purushartha* is itself a great desire. The word *'mumuksa'* means desire, and this *mumuksa* for liberation is a very great desire as Acharya Shamkara says. There can be no action without desire. Lord says that one should do action without desire, and that one has the right to do duty, without the anticipation of fruit of action. This reminds of Christian dictum "By its fruits you shall know it." which is the reverse of Lord's dictum of "without desire for fruit of action". Anticipation for fruit only compels one to act, desire is the spring of action. No desire, no action.

What Lord Kṛṣṇa speaks is not only of 'desirelessness' but also of giving up all attachment of senses or sense—object contacts and emotions, since attachment (*moha*) leads to desires, hankerings, and when desires and hankering are not satisfied, it causes anger, (*krodh*) anger causes delusion, delusion causes loss of memory, leads to loss of understanding, and this leads to perfect ruination.

(*Gita* II-61-64).This type of unattachment is far more elevated act, rather pragmatic or realistic only, it leads to withdrawal of man from all external objects and be satisfied in his own self, a state of perfect *'dhirata'*, *'sthitahdhi'* or *'atmanye atmatusthati'*, this itself amounts to a great desire for perfection, rather than plain satisfaction.

Lord also pleads Arjuna not for complete cessation of action, but become active for the welfare of the world *'lokasangrah'*, as some great men like Janak or even the Lord, is always active though He has no need to do anything. He is *'aptakama'*, i.e., above desires. The word *'lokasangrah'* means doing good to the general public, the welfare of all. Though works for *lokasangrah* is altruistic, even doing anything for the good of others, not of the self, cannot be exempt from desire to do good. To intend is essential for doing any good act, good act is not any reflex act or instinctive act. One has to will for doing any good act, and this is the result of a desire to do good. The rider in this case is not *only self intended act*, *lokasangrah* is *other-oriented*, and intended for others, rather than 'ones' own. This is *altruistic desire*, though of *course a desire.*

Prof. Rajendra Prasad contends that the very concept of *'niskamkarma'* is "unidirectional" since as he says, *niskama* is "*directed towards the agent rather than towards the action he does.* '*Niskama*' is an adjective of the doer. Only the doer can be desireless not any action. It qualifies the motivation of the doer, the motivation with which he does it, and not the action which he does . . . . if the doer is desireless in doing it, it would not have any bondage causing effect" (p. 55). Prof Prasad further says that "desirelessness cannot be a test of morality of an action or that of a person" (p. 55) and adds that the *Gita* does not give satisfactory answer as to why doing good to others does not amount to a desire, though altruistic desire. The desires are said to be bondage causing, but Prof Prasad says, "it is not moral reaction", in fact it may be *non-moral.* Call it spiritual if you like" (p. 56). If a man does not believe in rebirth, all such explanation for bondage causing or bondage, even *varnadharma* for further birth would be having no effect. Prof Prasad further stressfully says that, "*niskama* theory is not a moral theory because an actions being desireless is neither a necessary nor a sufficient condition of its being morally right . . . . because a benevolent action is not desireless but morally right . . . . because one may do a wrong action in desireless manner. Rather, the latter's being desireless would make it not just wrong but wicked." (p. 56) Even doing a duty without desire would not improve the situation and Prof. Prasad says "that if as per Kṛṣṇa's advice desireless fighting the battle and killing or causing injury by way of *varnashram dharma* follow up is not binding act or cause bondage, how should Arjuna's plea for living on alms without the desire to the kingdom be causing bondage. Desireless action is recommended for liberation, this liberation is a big desire. Prof. Prasad says, if desirelessness is taken to be means to *moksa*", it degrades duty, since the emphasis is not on duty but on desirelessness, it either downgrades even the notion of duty or it gives to it a lower status than to desirelessness" (p. 59)

Prof. Prasad further says that there is insuperable difficulty in deciding which act is done by anyone without desire. *Niskama karma* has to be technological or consequentialist (for the purpose of *moksa*, it is a "prescription about how and about the manner in which a duty is, any action should be done". It is not possible to get rid of the doctrine of consequentialism, i.e., "to give a deontological reason for doing a duty desirelessly" (p. 67). To avoid the "consequentialist route is to commit the fallacy of infinite regress". But Indian tradition allows such argument placements, otherwise it seems paradoxical to an ordinary person.

According to Dr. Y. Masih, *'Lokasangrah'* simply means the conservation of Hindu society on the basis of established caste system, which according to Dr. Ambedkar is the root cause of inequality and untouchability. According to Prem Nath Bajaj, *niskama karma*[9] is the philosophy of upper class meant to be utilized . . . . as a weapon for maintaining frustrated society in some sort of stability and equilibrium by inculcating ideas of patience and contentment in disinterested, exploited and downtrodden millions.[10] Lakshman Sastri Joshi agrees with above view by holding "To keep the *sudras* in slavery, to retain the dimension of the three *varnas* and the have for the priestly class a dominating voice appear to be threefold principles underlying the social order described in them".[11] And Prof. Masih adds, "True, caste-system might have been a conservative force in Indian History, but now its further continuance cannot but stand as an obstacle in the way of progress, and, this is clear in relation to the doctrine of 'Lokasangrah'.[12] There is a seeming contradiction with regard to *Gita* IX-32, which opens the door for the *sudras* and the *Gita* XVIII-45 makes caste-duties as compulsory. How can the two contradictory claims be decided? This can be reconciled in *Bhaktiyoga*, whereby there is no caste in *bhakti*. In *bhakti*, all are equal. According to Prof. Radhakrishnan, there is nothing absolute about caste. Dr. Masih opines, that in view of our present equalitarian society, *lokasangrah* based on caste is unacceptable as well as obsolete.[13] According to S.T. Telang, caste was not firmly established while the *Gita* was composed.[14] Y. Masih feels a touch of conservatism in the *Gita* doctrine of *lokasangrah*, because one has to go beyond caste and *ashram* duties. This concept is comparable to F.H. Bradley's concept of "Station and its duties". But his view suffers "imperialism and conservatism", yet unable to attain the ideal of absolute goodness[15] and he does not give any rationale of one's station of life. Prof. Masih compares the *Gita's niskama karma* with Kant's "*goodwill*" as well as with '*duty for duty's sake*'. According to Mill, it is not necessary for an act to have actually produced good consequence as a constitute of moral goodness, for instance, a doctor may perform an operation with all good intention, with all his capacity, yet he may fail to recover the patient, and yet this action may be called moral. Kant holds, "A goodwill is good, not because of the consequences . . . . A good will is good in itself, and shines like a jewel shines in its own light." Here Kant's '*good will*' is directed out of regard for moral law, which must be universal exceptionless and without any feeling. Masih says, that the *Gita's niskama karma* is more in the tradition of Kant than any of other western ethicist, though there are some glaring differences between the two. *Firstly*, Kant's morality is wholly autonomous and independent of theology and religion. Some other writers have regarded Kant's theory of morals purely formalistic. *Secondly*, "a *good will*" includes intended consequences. *Thirdly*, it is rational and bereft of emotional charges. *Fourthly*, for Kant, a moral action is also at the same time a social act, because one has to act towards, others, in return as one would like to be done by others in return. But contrary to this, morality of the *Gita* is God-centred, and consequences whatever it may are left to the "divine dispensation". According to the moral teachings of the *Gita* consequences are for maintaining the welfare of society, *sarva-bhuta-hite-ratah* or for *loka sangrah* or welfare of society. The *Gita* goes beyond Kant's duty for duty's sake as F.H. Bradley terms it and also gives his own theory of "Station and its duties" by way of an improvement on Kant. *Gita* gave such ideas thousands of years before Bradley was born. Bradley's theory lacks clearness as to "station and one's duties". Prof Masih sums up the *Gita's* view saying that an action is moral – if (1) there is performance of one's duties in relation to one's caste and station of life. (2) The motive of the act includes (a) conservation of *Loka sangrah* or the maintenance of society, through caste principles (*varna vicara*); and where (b) all consequences are offered as sacrifice to the Lord. So *niskama karma* is not desireless act but proceeds from sanctified motive and desires, bereft of individual gains (positive or negative) for attaining release from the chain of rebirths and God-realisation. Here *Karma Yoga* is opposed to *Karma Sannyasa*. All *karmas* are performed by *Prakṛti*, the *jiva* falsely takes all acts as a doer and enjoyer, this is illusory identification of *jiva* as doer and enjoyer and so remains in bondage (as the *Gita* says, III-28).

Gandhi finds in the *Gita*, something higher and sublimer than *Koran* or '*The Sermon on the Mount*', (*The Bible*) and calls the *Gita*, the mother. He, in place of using the word *Karma-yoga* or *niskama karma*, uses *karma 'anasakti'*, as the highest ideal, which is unattachment to the fruits of action as well unattachment of the senses, *phalasakti*, or *visayasakti*. His entire philosophy whether religious, social, ethical, economic and political are all based on this '*anasakti*' *yoga*, as he terms it. The use of the word '*dharmakshetre*' '*kurukshetre*' implies, that the latter is the realm of actual life situation in which man is engaged in fighting the battle for *dharma*. Virtue does not lie in mere recognition of good and evil but in practice, this practice is the real word of practice and it is comparable to Feurbach's VIII thesis that "social life is essentially practical. "The deep emphasis on practice (for *dharma*) implies that life is real struggle for some achievement by praxis, it offers the reality of the world and that those who deny the world are deprived soul (*nastatma*) oligophrenics (*alpabuddhayah*) hypocrites (*dambhamanamadanvitah*) and only the *asuras* or devilish persons can say that the world is unreal and without a basis (*asatyam apratistham,* i.e., *jagadahur anisvaram*). The world denial is mental perversity. The *Gita* at the very outset lays stress that no moral ideal can be realised by world-negation or renunciation, but man has to seek self realisation through praxis as Arjuna does. This *anasakti* leads to the crushing of egoism and personal possessive spirit, which hankers for more and more and which leads to dehumanisation. Gandhi says that all man face despair in life, but he has to try for regeneration. Arjuna's problem is a universal problem, Arjuna's *visada* is "a dramatization of the recurring predicament of man and Prof. Radhakrishnan says "Man, on the threshold of higher life feels disappointed with the glamour of the world and yet illusions cling to him and he cherishes them". This sort of existential anxiety and moral despair is considered to be a prerequisite of moral regeneration. "The modern existentialism" says Sartre, "also confronts man with a possibility of choice". Such a crisis also appears as Prof Tucker points out in moral theory of Kant, in the form of inner conflict or 'natural dialect' of duty *versus* inclination. We hear such things from life and utterings of great moral teachers, like Buddha, Marx, Socrates, etc. It has been pointed out that Arjuna's state of '*lobhopahatcetasah*' is state of *self alienation*, Arjuna is confronted with evil forces and the lustful tendencies "which have taken humanity to ransom". Prof Radhakrishnan says that Arjuna's depression is like a stranger thrown into self alienation or self estrangement" as threatening chaos. This really is like Hegelian Philosophy. This is also Arjuna's alienation of social obligation as some scholars opine. Such scholars hold that when Arjuna says, what pleasure can there be in slaying these sons of Dhritarastra, Arjuna is hinting towards material comforts and discomforts. When Arjuna says "Here I would not kill not even for the kingship of the three worlds", his thinking is polluted by hedonistic consideration, his own personal hedonism. Here Arjuna is alienated from "socialised self", he is in a state of 'atomised thinking' of self, separated from the social responsibility and obligations. This amounts to *asakti*, "the desire for measuring his worth in material terms that made him forgetful of his obligations to the society and generated despair in him. He was feeling himself alone, isolated and atomised, as if his soul was circumscribed into an awful singleness. This was symptomatological of alienation". The remedy to this lies in the *anasakti* of the *Gita. Gita*'s maxim of morality lays down that *anasakti* leads to liberation from the snares of materiality, egoity, possessiveness, lust for senses, greed for more and more. Sidgwick shares with the *Gita's* view in so far as he holds that "a certain degree of disinterestedness seems to be necessary in order to obtain full enjoyment". *(Manual of Ethics,* pp. 56-57). Real enjoyment cannot come out with purely Epicurean mood, whereby the chase of pleasure really misses to have a full-view pleasure, as we have "the paradox of Hedonism". Rashdall has also held that the existence of "disinterested affection" is not a myth but a psychological fact. He says "Reasonable man, contemplating the world as an impartial spectator, uninfluenced by private desires or passions, would necessarily recognise benevolence as that affection, which ought to be gratified in preference to merely self-regarding desires." So, scepticism about the practicability of non-attached action is unwarranted. *Gita's* action of *loksangrah* are also unattached actions as acts of moral excellence which countered the charge of blind scepticism on the one and also of mechanical performance of one's duty. Sacrifice for sacrifice is not the tone of the *Gita* as Rashdall has held. "Self-sacrifice for its own sake is always irrational and immoral. It is the object for which the sacrifice is made that gives it moral value". By sacrificing one's personal interests for some social good, the sacrifice becomes valuable. It is, thus, welfare of humanity gives moral value to an action and not more Kantian formalism. Bradley also seems to defend the *Gita's* theory of *anasakti* from his own point of view, since hedonistic pleasures are momentary and their pursuit is wastage of moral endeavours, because in this endless pursuit, as Bradley says, "we have not found ourselves and we are not satisfied." So there is no use pursuing them in context of sense or *indriyanigrah* is essential for the realisation of loftier ends of human life.

The Lord Kṛṣṇa saying "action is thy province not the fruit", He gives the key-principle which puts embargo on the level of human ambitions and aspirations. The importance of this assertion is that man cannot change the laws of nature according to his own convenience. Even God cannot change the natural laws at His discretion, *Gita* specifically points out that the Lord creates neither the agency nor action for the world; neither does he connect action with fruits. It is nature which is at work...... *physico-chemical* and *bio-physiological* laws of nature will not care for the wishful thinking of individual". So man has to be careful in adopting right choices not the wrong choices, wrong choices would waylay man, right choices liberate man. Lewis also holds that "half of the world's avoidable troubles are created by those who do not know what they want, and pursue what would not satisfy them, if they had it". Social laws cannot be subjected to individual whims and idiosyncrasies. Therefore, the individual should adjust the domain of his legitimate freedom upto the exercise of his own choice, without worrying for the problem of causal determinism or indeterminism in the events of nature. Sidgwick has taken pains to show that "the question of determinism is much less important to ethics than it has been thought to be." So we may agree with the *Gita*, as we sow, so we reap. The choice is in sowing the good seed, selecting a good soul and for this individual is free. The *Gita* says that from "*fried seed, no plant can grow*".

According to R.N. Srinivaschari, *niskama karma* is a "unique concept" and is a perfect synthesis of the opposing aspects of moral life which though comparable to Kant's categorical impoerative is far superior for it, as it is based on a "synthetic view of human nature and harmonises its contradictions; it does not suppress the senses and their activities, but sublimates them to spiritual purposes. The senses are spiritualised, and *karma* is transformed into '*kainkarya*'. In the Kantian thought, there is antithesis between ethics and metaphysics. *Gita's* ethics is grounded on metaphysical attitude and it means to secure religious attainment. The *Gita's* ethics of *niskama karma* is based on view of life characteristic of rational metaphysics and paves the way for divine life closer to itself, until he becomes full of it and ultimately one with it". (p. 57)

Niskama karma is based on the fundamental fact of the universality of *karma*. There are two types of minds, according to the psychologists, the *active* and *ascetic*. Accordingly, the former attitude of "*Voluntoristic ethics*", as the above, another says, "addresses itself to the dynamic ordering of nature as illustrated in flux of phenomena and it furnishes the apparatus of moral achievement. Every thought, act or word is an effect of *karma* whether it is sensory-motor or ideo-motor. Morality implies activity, which is at once the birth right and inescapable duty of man" (p. 51) opposed to this, the ascetic or *sannyas* or renunciation recommends complete cessation of work, since all activity involves worry, if it is not crowned with success of achievement. The contemplative ideal insist on attainment of peace or *Shanti* which is incompatible with the 'fever and fret of life' associated with *karma*. The ascetic insists an introversion and extinction of desire as *sine qua non* of securing eternal life (*amṛtatvam*). The *Gita* offers a compromise between the two, the active as well as ascetic ideal by giving their concept of *niskama karma* what is needed is only *change of attitude.*

The *Gita* insists on moral discipline of the intellect known as *samkhya buddhi* and *Vyavasayatmika buddhi*. One has to realise that *Purusa* and *Prakṛti* are different, *kshetra* and *kshetrajña*, *deha* or *dehi* are different, soul is *aparinami*, the body is aggregate of elements, *bhuta sanghato* and owing to *parinama svabhava*, the body goes through a flux of cyclic transformations and is subject to birth, youth, manhood, age decay and death, known as the six fold changes (*sadbhava vikaras*) (II.22). A *sthiprajna* or *sthitahdhi* realises this. As reason and will are one, *samkhya buddhi* develops into *Vyayasātmika buddhi* without which no spiritual endeavour is possible. "*Vyayasātmika buddhi* consists in non-attachment to sensuous objects, in the stability of reason and concentration of will", the mind becomes stilled, *visaya karma* or material pleasures yields to *atmakam*, he becomes satisfied in his own being, *atmano tustah,* his *karmas* are freed from moral particularism and base it on a rational comprehensiveness, thereby moral fixity arises, and this being endowed *niskama karma* is practised easily. By *niskama karma* the *Gita* establishes a harmony between *karma* and *akarma* by dissolving the dilemma of ethics of 'is' and 'ought', *jnāna* and *karma*, etc. In this context, the author says "There is violent warfare in the moral life between the "is" of sensibility and the "ought to be" of reason is reconciled by the concept of *niskama karma.* In the history of this conflict, the "is" at first ousts the "ought" and the sensualist follows the propulsions of the sensitive self as a matter of course and enjoys sense-gratification. But the appetitive self thrives on desire and grows by what it feeds on . . . . . In the second stage there is a reaction on the side of ascetic suppression in which passion is sought to be eliminated by reason. The moral law excludes all sensible springs. But excessive impulsion. In the third stage, a reconciliation is effected between sensibility and reason by the formula of *niskama karma.* "*Karma* is the dynamic power of duty exalted by inner detachment" (p. 67).

"*Niskama karma* is not *karma* but of *kama* (desire) not of *karma* but of doer-mentality aid of deed (iv-19) it is not *kama-tyaga* but *karmaphala tyaga. Niskama karma* does not consist in mere conformity to a dogma which is fixed on formal. It is not simply right action but righteous action regulated by reason and *śradhā.* Mere *karma* without *jnāna* all blind and mechanical, like a human body without head, mere *jnāna* without the dynamic power of *karma* is emptied of content, a head without a trunk. *Sankhya-yoga* are theory and practice. "*Jnāna* is not abstract thought devoid of content, but is immanent in volitional activity and illumines its nature. *Karma* is the dynamic side of moral law". (p. 66)

The *Gita* insists on the performance of *yajna* as *niskama karma* (XII-11, 12, 13). The author says, "*yajna* is only a grateful offering mode by the *jiva* as the moral self to the universe for what it has received from it in its psycho physical make up" in the form of *matr, pitr, deva, bhuta, brahma-yajna*. The *Gita* speaks of three kinds of *yajna, sattvic, tamasic* and *rajasic*. It speaks of three kinds of *dana*, three kinds of *tapa* these three distinctions are psychological.

The *niskama karma* of the *Gita* resolves the differences and offer a reconciliation between the contradictory approach adopted either by a pacifist or militarist. Arjuna faces a moral dilemma between *ahimsa* and warfare. "The pacifist is shocked by the disastrous consequences of war, righteous or unrighteous, points to the paralysing and demoralising effect and hopes for the millennium when *ahimsa* will be the order of the day. The militarist takes his stand on the pugnacious or warring instinct of man which makes for self preservation and, contending that might alone preserves right, advocates war as the solvent of all disputes. Both pacifism and militarism are extreme theories. The first is desirable, but not possible; the second is possible but not desirable". (p. 72)

Ethics, however, may or may not localise war, but in no case can totalise war. There are three types of warrior also. Only a *tamasic* warrior can totalise war, like Duryodhana but not Arjuna who is born noble as Lord Kṛṣṇa says. A *tamasic* warrior can kill indiscriminately but not a *sattvic* Arjuna. The *Gita* does not speak of totalising war, adopt militarist attitude. He speaks of adopting of rationalistic approach of particularised cases of war by adopting attitude of rational approach of *samkhya buddhi* but "without any sophistry or casuistic dialectic. It insists of the inner worth of action emptied of the subjective inclination of *karma* or *raga* and the objective ideas of utility and love of honour. The *dualism* between pleasure and pain success and failure, does not enter into the content of the moral imperative. The mind is thus disciplined and well-balanced and acquires an attitude of *samatva* or equipoise which is consummation of all moral endeavour. The moral self is no longer slave of sensibility (*kama, krodha, raga, dvesa*) but has attained self-sovereignty, or moral autonomy (*jitatma*). This view of duty avoids the perils of hedonism and intellectualism and effectively bridges the gulf between the two *mimansas kayena mimansa buddhya kevalair indriyair api/yoginah karm kurvanti sangam tyaktatvatma suddhaye* (V.11).

The *Gita* has been interpreted in various ways to suit one's own whims and choices. There are traditionalists views, there is modern views. Prof. Rajendra Prasad does not like to adopt the traditionalist views since their views are based on *ṛsi* bias. He has tried to look into *Gita* through his incisive logic, metaethics, etc. He is right in his own way and his approach is a rich research oriented approach worth the name. While the views of R.N. Srinivaschari's approach (His work 'Ethics in *Gītā*') is traditionist and befitting the religious temper which adopts that whenever *dharma* wanes, God takes *avatar*. The *Gita* itself or even the *upanisads* speak that *tarka* or *logic* is no proper tool to know the Almighty, and it all depends upon the type of person to interpret it in *sattvic* mode, *rajasic* or *tamasic* mode, in terms of *jnana* as did Acharya Shankara, as *karma sastra* as did *Tilak,* or *bhakti* as Ramanuja etc. did. But there is no denial of the fact, that *Gita* offers a practical approach to life's vicissitudes, which led the despaired Arjuna, to adopt a way of activity, rather than go away from his duty, obligation, ridden with personal gain or loss, love or hate, joy or sorrow, the *samatva yoga,* attitude, which though is difficult to achieve. The Gita adopts a synoptic and synthetic approach, it reconciles *jnana*, *bhakti*, *karma* at one stretch and in the same vein, taken in the context of the present volume, of which this chapter forms a part; the *Gita* speaks of reconciliation of all moral activities, it reconciles and contains what may be said, to form a part of metaethics, normative ethics, virtue ethics of great ethical values as well as applied or practical ethics, as a present trend of ethics. It is not the place to elaborate all these in this chapter, but we shall in other have occasion to discess more and more volumes to come, discuss in detail, as to its metaethics, to applied ethics in separate chapters which would be rewarding.

REFERENCES

1. *New Sights into Gita,* S.P. Ranchan, Ajanta Publications.
2. *Ibid.*
3. *New Sights into Gita* – S.P. Ranchan.
4. *Ibid.*
5. *Ibid.*
6. Prof. R. Prasad *Varna Dharma, Niskama Karma and Practical Morality*. pp. 39, 42.
7. *Ibid.*
8. *Ibid.*
9. *Hindu Religious Thought,* Y. Masih, Motilal, p. 228.
10. *Ibid.,* Quoted p. 229.
11. *A Critique of Hinduism*, Lakshman Sastri, Popular Prakashan, Mumbai, 84, 107, 109.
12. *Hindu Religious Thought,* Y. Masih, p. 224.
13. *The Bhagwat Gita,* S. Radhakrishnan, pp. 160-161.
14. *The Hindu Religious Thought,* p. 243.
15. *The Bhagwat Gita,* S.T. Telang, Introduction.

Index